Teilhard's Proposition for Peace

Teilhard's Proposition for Peace:

Rediscovering the Fire

By

Jean Maalouf

> "The day will come when, after harnessing the ether, the winds, the tides, gravitation, we shall harness for God the energies of love. And, on that day, for the second time in the history of the world, man will have discovered fire."
> (Teilhard de Chardin)

Cambridge Scholars Publishing

Teilhard's Proposition for Peace: Rediscovering the Fire

By Jean Maalouf

This book first published 2018

Cambridge Scholars Publishing

Lady Stephenson Library, Newcastle upon Tyne, NE6 2PA, UK

British Library Cataloguing in Publication Data
A catalogue record for this book is available from the British Library

Copyright © 2018 by Jean Maalouf

All rights for this book reserved. No part of this book may be reproduced, stored in a retrieval system, or transmitted, in any form or by any means, electronic, mechanical, photocopying, recording or otherwise, without the prior permission of the author.

Unless otherwise indicated, the Scripture quotations contained herein are from the New Revised Standard Version Bible, copyright © 1989, by the Division of Christian Education of the National Council of Churches in the U.S.A., and are used by permission. All rights reserved.

ISBN (10): 1-5275-1819-1
ISBN (13): 978-1-5275-1819-3

I dedicate this book
    to my beloved companions on the path to peace,
    to those whose eyes perceive the inter-connection of all things in the one earth, one universe, and one God,
    to those who are or will be engaged in reconciling what seems irreconcilable, in bringing love where hatred seems to predominate, and in making peace prevail where violence seems to have the upper hand,
and to those who are the peace they want to see around them.

With love, faith, and hope.

A new way of seeing, combined with a new way of acting – that is what we need.
— Teilhard de Chardin (AE, p. 295 -- VII, p. 308)

If we are to be able to love one another must we not first effect a change of plane?
—Teilhard de Chardin (AE, p. 74 -- VII, p. 81)

Indeed, at the rate that consciousness and its ambitions are increasing, the world will explode if it does not learn to love.
—Teilhard de Chardin (VP, p. 214 -- III, p. 300)

We are standing, at the present moment, not only at a change of century and civilization, but a change of epoch.
—Teilhard de Chardin (VP, p. 75 -- III, p. 107)

The age of nations has passed. Now, unless we wish to perish we must shake off our old prejudices and build the earth.
—Teilhard de Chardin (HE, p. 37 -- VI, p. 46)

We now have to accept it as proven that mankind has just entered into what is probably the most extensive period of transformation it has known since its birth. The seat of the evil we are suffering from is to be found in the very foundations of thought on earth. Something in the general structure of Spirit: it is a new type of life that is beginning.
—Teilhard de Chardin (SC, pp. 128-9 -- IX, p. 169-70)

And then, struck at its source, the conflict will die of its own accord, never to break out again.
—Teilhard de Chardin (AE, p. 20 -- VII, p. 26)

It will not be long before the human mass closes in upon itself and groups all its members in a definitively realized unity.
—Teilhard de Chardin (HM, p. 184 -- XII, p. 267)

To see or to perish.
—Teilhard de Chardin (PM, p. 31 -- I, p. 25)

Mankind is not only capable of living in peace but by its very structure cannot fail eventually to achieve peace.
—Teilhard de Chardin (FM, p. 157 -- V, p. 194)

The day will come when, after harnessing the ether, the winds, the tides, gravitation, we shall harness for God the energies of love. And, on that day, for the second time in the history of the world, man will have discovered fire.
—Teilhard de Chardin (TF, pp. 86-7 -- XI, p. 92)

If the doors of perception were cleansed, then everything would appear as it actually is, infinite.
—William Blake.

What you are is God's gift to you, what you become is your gift to God.
—Hans Urs von Balthasar

Love is the only future God offers
—Victor Hugo

Table of Contents

List of Abbreviations x

Introduction: Who Is Secure? 1

Part 1: Is Peace Possible?

Chapter One 9
Is Peace Possible?

Chapter Two 14
Impediments to Peace

Chapter Three 22
What Peace Is Not

Chapter Four 30
The Battlefield

Part II: The Revolution of the Incarnation

Chapter Five 41
The Revolution of the Incarnation

Chapter Six 49
The Cosmic Importance of the Incarnation

Chapter Seven 63
The Divine Milieu: Our Home

Chapter Eight 73
The Third Way

Part III: The Birth of a New Consciousness

Chapter Nine 85
A Transformed Consciousness

Chapter Ten 93
The Unitive Consciousness

Chapter Eleven 102
"Union Differentiates"

Chapter Twelve 109
The Cyberpeace Way

Part IV: The Future Has a Goal

Chapter Thirteen 121
The Future Has a Goal

Chapter Fourteen 129
The Project of Personalization

Chapter Fifteen 138
On Human Rights

Chapter Sixteen 147
Hope: The Ultimate Reality

Part V: Call to Action

Chapter Seventeen 159
"To See or to Perish"

Chapter Eighteen 167
Rediscovering the "Fire"

Chapter Nineteen 176
Call to Action

Chapter Twenty 184
Process Peace

Part 6: On the March

Chapter Twenty-One 195
Toward a Curriculum for Peace

Chapter Twenty-Two.. 203
Toward a New Religious Order

Chapter Twenty-Three.. 214
Toward a Theological and Teleological Ecology

Chapter Twenty-Four 223
Toward a New Type of Life

Conclusion: The Peace Revolution... 232

Chronology of Pierre Teilhard de Chardin's Life..................... 238

Bibliography.. 241
    I. Works by Pierre Teilhard de Chardin
        Oeuvres de Pierre Teilhard de Chardin, Editions du Seuil, Paris
        Letters
        Other Works and Selected Writings
        Chronology of Teilhard de Chardin's Works
        Index of Writings
    II. Works on the Thought of Pierre Teilhard de Chardin
    III. For Further Reading

Acknowledgments 278

Index.. 281

About the Author 286

Also by Dr. Jean Maalouf.. 288

LIST OF ABBREVIATIONS

AE	*Activation of Energy*. Trans. by René Hague. New York: Harvest Book, Harcourt Brace Jovanovich, 1963 – *L'Activation de l'Energie*. Paris: Seuil, 1963. (VII)
AM	*The Appearance of Man*. Trans. by J.M. Cohen. New York: Harper & Row, 1965 – *L'Apparition de l'Homme*. Paris: Seuil, 1956. (II)
CE	*Christianity and Evolution*. Trans. by René Hague. New York: Harvest Book, Harcourt Brace Jovanovich, 1971 -- *Comment Je Crois. Paris:* Seuil, 1969. (X)
DM	*The Divine Milieu*. Trans. by unidentified. New York: Harper Torchbooks, Harper & Row, 1960 – *Le Milieu Divin*. Paris: Seuil, 1957. (IV)
FM	*The Future of Man*. Trans. by Norman Denny. New York: Harper & Row, 1964 – *L'avenir de l'Homme*. Paris: Seuil, 1959. (V)
HE	*Human Energy*. Trans. By J.M. Cohen. New York: Harvest Book, Harcourt Brace Jovanovich, 1969 – *L'Energie Humaine*. Paris: Seuil, 1962. (VI)
HM	*The Heart of Matter*. Trans. by René Hague. New York: A Harvest/HBJ Book, Helen & Kurt Wolff Book, Harcourt Brace Jovanovich, 1979 – *Le Coeur de la Matière*. Paris: Seuil, 1976. (XIII), and 5 essays first appeared in the French edition of *Ecrits du Temps de la Guerre*. Paris: Editions du Seuil, 1976, and Editions Bernard Grasset, 1965.
HU	*Hymn of the Universe*. Trans. Gerald Vann. New York: Colophon Books, Harper & Row, 1965 – *L'Hymne de l'Univers*. Paris: Seuil, 1961.
LF	*Lettres Familières de Pierre Teilhard de Chardin Mon Ami (1948-1955)*, presentées par Pierre Leroy. France: Le Centurion, 1976.
LI	*Lettres Inédites : Lettres à l'Abbé Gaudefroy et à l'Abbé Breuil*. France : Le Rocher, 1988.
LIV	*Lettres Intimes à Auguste Valensin, Bruno de Solages, Henri de Lubac, André Ravier (1919-1955)*. Paris: Aubier-Montaigne, 1974.
LM	*Lettres à Jeanne Mortier*. Paris: Seuil, 1984.

LT	*Letters from a Traveller*. Trans. by William Collins Sons & Co., Ltd. New York: Harper Torchbooks, Harper & Row, 1962 – *Lettres de Voyage (1923-1955)*. Paris: Bernard Grasset, 1956.
LTF	*Letters to Two Friends (1926-1952)*. New York: The New American Library, 1967 – *Accomplir l'Homme: Lettres Inédites (1926-1952)*. Paris: Editions Bernard Grasset, 1968.
LZ	*Letters to Léontine Zanta*. Trans. by Bernard Wall. New York: Harper & Row, 1969 – *Lettres à Léontine Zanta*. Bruges, Belgique: Desclée de Brouwer, 1965.
MM	*The Making of a Mind: Letters from a Soldier-Priest (1914-1919)*. Trans. by René Hague. New York: Harper & Row, 1965 – *Genèse d'une Pensée: Lettres (1914-1919)*. Paris: Bernard Grasset Editeur, 1961.
MPN	*Man's Place in Nature*. Trans. by René Hague. New York: Harper & Row, 1966 – *Le Groupe Zoologique Humain*. Paris: Albin Michel, 1956 – and *La Place de l'Homme dans la Nature: Le Groupe Zoologique Humain*. Paris: Seuil, 1977. (VIII)
PM	*The Phenomenon of Man*. Trans. by Bernard Wall. New York: Harper Torchbooks. Harper & Row, 1959, 1965 – *Le Phénomène Humain*. Paris: Seuil, 1955. (I)
SC	*Science and Christ*. Trans. by René Hague. New York: Harper & Row, 1968 – *Science et Christ*. Paris: Seuil, 1965. (IX)
TF	*Towards the Future*. Trans. by René Hague. New York: A Helen & Kurt Wolff Book, Harcourt Brace Jovanovich, 1975 – *Les Directions de l'Avenir*. Paris: Seuil, 1973. (XI)
VP	*The Vision of the Past*. Trans. by J.M. Cohen. New York: Harper & Row, 1966 – *La Vision du Passé*. Paris: Seuil, 1957. (III)
WTW	*Writings in time of War*. Trans. by René Hague. New York: Harper & Row, 1968 – *Ecrits du Temps de la Guerre*. Paris: Bernard Grasset Editeur, 1965. Paris: Seuil, 1976. (XII)

Introduction

Who Is Secure?

Are there individuals so powerful that they feel totally safe and secure in any circumstances and at any time? Do the super-power nations, with all the most sophisticated weapons they possess, feel so safe and secure that no one can bring them any harm? Does militarism and massive might bring peace to the world? Why does war, temporary by its nature, seem not to ever end? Why do we need enemies in the first place? Why is war an easier choice than peace? What makes us afraid of peace? Can one uproot fear and distrust by a gun ready to shoot? Does a life lived in a deep underground bunker make us immune to attacks and terrorism? Then, and if this is the case, why is it that the safest city in the world is the one that does not need police officers in the street?

Like the other false gods, the illusion of a "militarism" mentality does not bring peace to an individual or to a nation, and much less to the world. The reality is that violence begets violence. No matter how much we would like to see it otherwise, the war on terror, for example, remains violence versus violence. Both sides invoke God, morality, justice, and peace, and both sides accuse the other of crimes against humanity. Yet, the end result remains the same: no peace.

What is wrong with this picture?

What is wrong is that the fight is taking place on the wrong battlefield; we are just fighting the symptoms. The real battlefield is far beyond. It is in the very depths of the human minds and hearts. That is why no matter how powerful we think we are with our muscles, wealth, positions, and weapons, we remain very vulnerable to any adversity, and our security remains a myth. The truth is that we are at war, declared or undeclared, at all times and on all fronts.

Indeed, we have wars of religions and ideologies, and wars of races, languages, and classes. We have economic wars, commercial wars, and technological wars. We have cultural wars, demographic wars, and generational wars. We have family wars, gender wars, and personal wars. We have legal and illegal wars, social and human rights wars, and partisan and prejudicial wars. We have nuclear wars, north-south wars, and world wars. We have wars of necessity and wars of choice. We have wars for the control of energy sources and raw material and for power and domination. We have terrorism wars and wars on terrorism, wars for property, drugs, alcohol, and sex, and wars of values, priorities, and references. We have frictions, divisions, partitions, dysfunctions, and destabilizations – individual and collective. Nothing seems stable, definite, or definitive.

Think of the "forever" Middle East fights. Think of the millions of refugees in any country and continent. Think of the violence that strikes our biggest American and European cities. Think of the huge number of those who commit violent crimes for a reason or for no reason at all. Think of the dictators who are always ready to kill anyone who does not seem loyal enough. Think of the abusers. Think of "us" versus "others" mentality. Think of those who die simply because they happened to be in the wrong place at the wrong time.

The world is on fire.

In such a context, doesn't it look naive and childish to speak of peace? Yet, we all speak about peace and we prepare for war. We all preach peace and we make sure that the fighters have the necessary weapons to continue the fight. We sign peace treaties with each other and we hurry to break them at the surge of other interests. We form alliances to minimize the risk of an enemy attack and we find ways not to comply with our promises. We create international agencies to help create an atmosphere of reconciliation and understanding among all the peoples of the earth and we find ways to neutralize these agencies and make them ineffective. We urge others to work for reforms, transparency, and free elections, and we often fail to do what we urge others to do. We condemn the barbaric acts we see elsewhere and we forget that our history was not immune to these same acts.

Is this a hopeless situation for which there is no solution?

Paleontologist Pierre Teilhard de Chardin (1881-1955) who also was a philosopher, theologian, poet, and mystic, did not believe that. He declared the final war – a war against all wars. He wanted the energy that was used for wars to be used for peace instead. Wars cannot be solved at the sociological and political levels; a discussion and agreement at these levels did not achieve much. Wars have their solutions at the philosophical, theological, and mystical levels. Wars begin in the mind and heart and they will end where they started. "… struck at its source," Teilhard wrote, "the conflict will die of its own accord, never to break out again." [1] Therefore a change of mind and heart will bring reconciliation to divided

---

[1] AE, p.20 -- VII, p. 26.

families, cities, nations, races, and civilizations, and will make bombs unnecessary, outmoded, and obsolete. When we change our way of thinking and we aim to a higher consciousness, the walls that separate us from our true selves and from each other will inevitably collapse of their own accord. Teilhard indicated clearly where the real battlefield was. He wrote in 1940: "I am more and more convinced that the real battlefield, today, is not in Dover, Egypt, or Rumania," (he would have certainly added 'or in the Middle East, or in Africa, or in any corner of the earth,' if he was writing this day), "but in Man's mind and soul."[2]

Humans seem bored because they don't have a purpose to justify what they are doing. They need to know why they are doing what they are doing, but they don't, and that is a big problem. In his book *The Search for Meaning*, Alfred Stern insightfully wrote:

> In principle an individual life becomes meaningful when it is based on a *life project*, for then it has a *purpose*, the execution of which is its *justification*. Antoine de Saint-Exupéry wrote the famous sentence: "Celui qui donne un coup de pioche veut connaître un sens à son coup de pioche » -- he who gives a blow of the pickax, wants to ascribe a meaning to the blow of his pickax. He can do it, by integrating this blow into the totality of a life project. Within this project, every blow of his pickax could grain a meaning. The great crisis of the search for meaning we are undergoing now comes from the fact that in spite of all the progress of science and technology, modern life does not seem to offer enough stimulating projects which would make it meaningful. One of the first modern men who became aware of this crisis was probably Friedrich Nietzsche. He called it nihilism. "What does nihilism mean?" he asked, and his answer was: "That the supreme values are depreciated.... The goal is lacking, the answer to the question: "What for?"[3]

André Malraux also thought that our civilization did not know the answer to the question: what are people doing on earth?

Teilhard disagreed. For him, "Man will never consent to labour like a Sisyphus."[4] He knew why we were here for; he called for the formation of "a human front"[5] to "build the earth"[6] transforming it into "Super-

---

[2] LTF, p. 149 -- *Accomplir l'homme*, p. 179.
[3] Alfred Stern, Ph.D., *The Search for Meaning: Philosophical Vistas* (Memphis: Memphis State University Press, 1971), p. 12.
[4] VP, p. 231 -- III, p. 323.
[5] SC, p. 145 -- IX, p. 187.
[6] HE, p. 37 -- VI, p. 46.

Humanity, Super-Christ, Super-Charity."[7] A radical transformation should take place at the deepest level of our being, first. From within, we will learn how to see. "*Seeing*," wrote Teilhard, "We might say that the whole of life lies in that verb – if not ultimately, at least essentially.... *To see or to perish* is the very condition laid upon everything that makes up the universe, by reason of the mysterious gift of existence."[8]

To build the earth or to destroy it; what are we going to decide? Humanity is at a crossroads and we have to choose. We must believe in the world, in life, in progress, in human beings. We must find ways to be more creative in order to reach our common goal. There is an exit to despair. There is an answer to our problems. There is a meaning, a sparkle of light, a twinkle of hope to our life. We should believe in that, as a first step. Teilhard offered the following striking comparison:

> Imagine a party of miners, cut off when their roof collapses, and trying to regain the surface through a rescue tunnel. It is obvious that they will not continue to make their way towards the top unless they have reason to believe from some indication (a glimmer of light, a draft of air from above) that the passage is not blocked ahead of them. Similarly (though not sufficient attention is given to this) man would have no heart, no reason, to exert himself in causing mankind to advance beyond itself through unification, if the only effect of this fine effort were one day to bring it sharp, with added force and impetus, against an impossible wall.[9]

In fact, at the present time, we are like such prisoners living with all kinds of obstacles that block our roads and blind our views. If we don't believe that it is possible to get out, there will be no exit. There will instead be despair and loss of taste for living and working.

We need to choose to build the earth. By faith, confidence, work, progress, personalization, socialization, and unification, we need to build the earth. Then, peace becomes not only possible, but also inevitable.

It is amazing how Teilhard, the prophet of this age, as he was called, the mystic of today, and the "pilgrim of the future,"[10] seems so optimistic,

---

[7] See SC, pp. 151-173 -- IX, pp. 193-217. With regard to the "Super-Christ" that could bring doubt and confusion, Teilhard was quick to clarify by saying: "By Super-Christ, I most certainly do not mean *another* Christ, a second Christ different from and greater than the first. I mean *the same* Christ, the Christ of all time, revealing himself to us in a form and in dimensions, with an urgency and area of contact, that are enlarged and given new force" (SC, p. 164 -- IX, p. 208).
[8] PM, p. 31 -- I, p. 25.
[9] AE, pp. 173-74 -- VII, p. 180. See also X, p. 239 and II, p. 361.
[10] LT, p.101 -- *Lettres de voyage*, p. 61.

so sure of his vision, and so certain that something transformative is about to happen to the human race. He must have had grave and earnest reasons for believing in it that strongly. Let us see how he sees things. Let us see why his vision, in spite of obvious lacunae, is so attractive that it stirs every mind. Let us see how he builds by destroying, by letting go, by pushing beyond walls and frontiers, and by being creative. Let us see how he conceives the universal civilization by being more ethnic. Let us see how to unite with the whole by being more *one* and more *personal*. Let us see how to become citizens of the world by working to be more nationalistic. Let us see how love, the most difficult thing in the world, does not consist in clinging but rather in being *detached*. Let us see how he can conclude: "everything that formerly made for war now makes for peace."[11] Let us see who we really are and where we are going.

No doubt, a shift – an about-turn – has to occur. We must change direction because "if you don't change direction," says a Chinese proverb, "you are most likely to end up where you are going" – an apocalyptic disaster. We must change. Peace cannot come as we are. We still glorify the most criminal and blood thirsty people the earth has ever seen in our history books, schools, and the mass media. We still spend most of our time on secondary things at the expense of the essential. We may prune here and there, change branches, location, culture, and society, and wear another mask, but nothing will really happen. What is needed is a deep transformation, another state of consciousness, and another way of seeing things. This deep transformation should take place especially at this time in human history where we are facing an "axial age," as Karl Jaspers called it, a new state of evolution, and a "change of epoch,"[12] as Teilhard liked to say.

Does humanity have a future? Does God have a future? Do you have a future? Do I have a future? This is what this book is directly or indirectly trying to answer. It is a conversion to peace. It is a new awareness. It is a searching for a state of being where one feels at home. It is a new light on old truths and also new truths about old lights.

However, this book is not a package book by any means. Nor it is a prescription book. It is more than that. It describes a way of thinking. It portrays a life-style. It calls for a change in attitudes. It could provoke a kind of "nuisance," "disturbance," "confusion," or "mess" situation. This is what a profound purification process does, especially when the process targets the aim of freeing oneself from all biases. If this "war" happens,

---

[11] FM, p. 156 -- V, p. 193.
[12] VP, p. 75 -- III, p. 107.

then this book will have achieved what it has been written for. It was intended to be "The Book of Peace,"[13] indeed. Peace is a simple by-product of this "war." It is the authentic "zest for living,"[14] the "discovered fire"[15] of love, and the true fullness of life.

---

[13] MM, p. 143 -- *Genèse d'une pensée*, p. 184.
[14] AE, p. 229 -- VII, p. 237.
[15] TF, p. 87 -- XI, p. 92.

PART I

IS PEACE POSSIBLE?

CHAPTER ONE

IS PEACE POSSIBLE?

From the point of view of history, times of war were by far more numerous than times of peace. Even these three or four hundred years of peace during the entire history of humankind, as some historians would like to say, were just years of relative peace or maybe years of preparation for new wars. Our modern history is even worse. "The most obvious characteristic of our age," as Thomas Merton observed, "is its destructiveness."[1]

But is this a reason that forces us to conclude that peace must be impossible and we will never see it realized? Some people came to such a conclusion. Teilhard de Chardin was not one of them. For Teilhard, peace is not only possible, but it is also certain, inevitable, whole, and cosmic.

Peace is possible

Teilhard clearly states: "In the first place I maintain that peace – I mean, some form of universal and stable peace – is *possible* in human terms."[2] More than that, he even goes on to condemn "the affected resignation and false realism with which in these days a great number of people, hunching their shoulders and drawing in their heads, predict (and in so doing tend to provoke) a further catastrophe in the near future."[3] If war was a conceivable event, this was when humanity was in the period of expanding on the planet and when war was a means of solving a problem in a more decisive way. But, in a humanity that is of "converging branches,"[4] war does not solve problems for the simple reason that it works from the outside when the real problem and the solutions are not from the outside. The real battlefield is elsewhere.

---

[1] See *The Literary Essays of Thomas Merton,* edited by Brother Patrick Hart (New York: New Direction Publishing Corporation, 1981), p. 355.
[2] FM, p. 155 -- V, p. 192.
[3] FM, p. 154 -- V, p. 191.
[4] FM, p. 154 -- V, p. 193.

Peace is certain

We keep trying and trying to find an appropriate way to achieve a state of a highly desired peace, and we keep failing every time. Then we conclude that a lasting peace is out of reach and never certain. But this is not what Teilhard thinks.

Teilhard tells us that peace is not only possible but it is also assured. He wrote: "Do you not see that the peace which you no longer dare to hope for ... is possible and indeed certain, provided you will grasp what the word 'peace' means and what it requires from you?"[5] He also wrote: "Peace therefore is certain: it is only a matter of time. Inevitable, with an inevitability which is nothing but the supreme expression of liberty, we are moving laboriously and self-critically toward it."[6] This certainty is based on the sequence of crises the universe has lived and experienced from the beginning. At each stage, when any impasse would have blocked any development, new solutions have emerged and a new push has occurred to enable the earth to organize itself, and humanity to develop and grow. Teilhard wrote in 1942:

> Taken as a whole, the phenomenon of the present war (precisely because it can be seen to be total and universal) bears a positive mathematical sign. Whatever you may say, then – whatever appearances may suggest to me – whatever may happen – there remains a *fact* of a higher order than all other facts, in virtue of which I can only answer: after five hundred million years of mankind the earth is still developing its organicity: its psychic temperature is rising. Therefore it is still advancing.[7]

It is curious and fascinating at the same time to see an architect of the future, as Teilhard was considered by many, taking undeniable events from the past to consolidate his vision of a greater expansion of life for centuries to come. It is no less curious and fascinating to see an architect of peace using the war event as a possible way for a future peace. Such an approach, unless one puts it in the context of the big picture of Teilhard's gigantic vision, remains for the short-sighted person shocking and completely "politically incorrect." Indeed, if taken out of context, it might be so.

---

[5] FM, p. 154 -- V, pp. 191-92.
[6] FM, p. 158 -- V, p. 195.
[7] AE, p. 91 -- VII, pp. 97-8.

Peace is inevitable

An attitude of total optimism and confidence in the future can be justified by a great vision. Teilhard had this vision. Completely convinced of it, he did not hesitate to write: "It is hard to escape the conclusion... that despite all appearances to the contrary Mankind is not only capable of living in peace but by its very structure *cannot eventually fail to achieve peace.*"[8] Therefore, one should think that it is not war that is inevitable but peace.

In spite of the historical evidence against the possibility of peace – each generation having had its wars and all kinds of conflicts that give the impression that evil is rather increasing with the growth of civilization – humanity is nonetheless heading towards peace. That is because the human species shows a convergence into races, peoples, nations, and universalism. If, at a lower level, success comes through the elimination of opposition, the real success, at the human level, is the outcome of a *"union* [that] *differentiates,"*[9] as Teilhard calls it. Then, he goes even further. While admitting, of course, that we are free and that everyone, individually, could say "No," collectively, we cannot say, "No" because we cannot escape the tide of life.[10] Teilhard is so adamant about that that he affirms without hesitation:

> ... the earth is more likely to stop turning than is Mankind, as a whole, likely to stop organizing and unifying itself. For if this interior movement were to stop, it is the Universe itself embodied in Man, that would fail to curve inwards and achieve totalisation. And nothing, as it seems, can prevent the universe from succeeding – nothing, not even our human liberties, whose essential tendency to union may fail in detail cannot (without 'cosmic' contradiction) err *statistically*.[11]

---

[8] FM, p. 157 -- V, p. 194.
[9] PM, p. 262 -- I, p. 291; also VI, pp. 80-81, 129, 179,; VII, p. 122; X, p. 200.
[10] Beatrice Bruteau observed that Teilhard "has renewed hope by projecting a vision of the future in which our dreams of unity, peace, and full development come true through an almost inevitable evolution. He has not, of course, delivered us from all insecurity, because the evolution is not absolutely inevitable, but depends upon our own actions. Man's freedom constitutes the very path along which the forces of evolution now must pass – or in which they can be blocked. Teilhard admits that the issue may fall either way." (Beatrice Bruteau, *Evolution Toward Divinity: Teilhard de Chardin and the Hindu Traditions* (Wheaton, Ill: The Theosophical Publishing House, 1974), p. 8.
[11] FM, pp. 157-58 -- V, pp. 194-95.

Peace is, therefore, inevitable – inevitable by structure. It is a structural peace. It is coming. "It is only a matter of time,"[12] as Teilhard clearly indicated.

Peace is indivisible

Coherence, harmony, suitability, congruity, unison, consonance, euphony are among the many names for peace. To live in peace is to live undivided as societies and as individuals at any level – physically, emotionally, intellectually, and spiritually. A shattered and fragmented mind shatters and fragments reality. The earth, as it is the case for the individual, will survive only if it keeps its integrity as a single organic reality. The elements of nature and the nations of the earth are important for the whole, as the body, mind, and soul are important for the human being. The earth is for every nation, and every nation is an indispensable and unique part of the earth. No nation can possess the air on earth, or the waters, or the light, or the temperatures…. Those things must circulate everywhere. They sustain the very life of the whole as well as every part of it. Partial air entails death. So it is for peace. Peace in pieces entails death, too. Air must circulate everywhere. Peace, too, must circulate everywhere. A divided peace, like a divided nation, a divided body, a divided mind, a divided heart… is no peace. Peace is *"the awareness of Unity,"*[13] wrote Teilhard. In fact, we are on the march towards this unity, and soon we will be "one solid block." This is how Teilhard put it:

> It will not be long before the human mass closes in upon itself and groups all its members in a definitively realized unity. Respect for one and the same law, one and the same orientation, one and the same spirit, are tending to overlay the permanent diversity of individuals and nations. Wait but a little longer, and we shall form but one solid block. The cement is *setting*.[14]

Peace is dynamic

"The unity of the world," wrote Teilhard, "rests on constructive work – work directed towards concentration and not release of tension."[15] In a converging effort, tension remains but changes direction. The energy that

---

[12] FM, p. 158 -- V, p. 195.
[13] WTW, p. 110 -- XII, p. 148.
[14] HM, pp. 184-85 -- XII, p. 267.
[15] TF, p. 49 -- XI, p. 55.

was previously spent in war is channeled now toward unification, transformation, and progress. Teilhard says: "Everything that formerly made for war now makes for peace.... In short, true peace, the only kind that is biologically possible, betokens neither the ending nor the reverse of warfare, but war in a naturally sublimated form."[16] He sometimes sees in wars "a crisis of growth,"[17] and says that "Peace cannot mean anything but a *higher process of conquest.*"[18] In this sense, wars, especially when they are not frontier conflicts, or interest conflicts, can be for more universalization and more liberation, at least in their consequences. Peace, therefore, is a dynamic process not a static state; a stirring awareness not a passive calmness; and a transforming human convergence not an idle standstill.

Peace is cosmic

The cosmic dimension of peace adds a very important note to the dynamic condition of peace. That is because the human being is not only a social being, but also a cosmic being. Teilhard explained: "This, then is *the word that gives freedom*: it is not enough for man to throw off his self-love and *live as a social being. He needs to live* with his whole heart, in union with the totality of the world that carries him along, *cosmically.*"[19] He also said: "Indeed, we are called by the music of the universe to reply, each with his own pure and incommunicable harmonic."[20] This is how we prove practically that we are aware of our "cosmic sense" and that we are collaborating with the universe, and actively participating in it. Such an awareness of our "oneness" with the "all" must have a direct effect on reducing our fear or repulsion of others. This also puts us on the right path toward a realized peace.

If peace is possible, certain, inevitable, indivisible, dynamic, and cosmic, it is not by any means an easy matter to achieve in an overnight setting. Hard work is to be expected. Many obstacles, that are found in our backyards before other places, need to be removed. Our prejudices, our learning, our interpretations of the facts, and especially our biases, need to be carefully reconsidered, reexamined, and reevaluated.

---

[16] FM, pp. 156 and 159 -- V, pp. 193 and 196.
[17] WTW, p. 281 -- XII, p. 421 ; AE, p. 14 -- VII, p. 20.
[18] LTF, p. 146 -- *Accomplir l'homme*, p. 176.
[19] WTW, p. 27 -- XII, p. 33.
[20] HE, p. 150 -- VI, p. 186.

Chapter Two

Impediments to Peace

Is there any secure place on earth? Where is it? Could it be a prison?

Paradoxically, a prison is supposed to be the most secure place on earth. In fact, it is much more difficult to murder a prisoner – at least in principle – than to murder a leader of a country. A prisoner must feel safer than a leader does.

A prison is a safe and secure place; in the "peace" of a prison, there is no danger. But who wants to live there? The reality is that safety and security can cohabitate with the lack of freedom, but not as much with freedom. In the open space of freedom, there are "risks," "adventures," "dangers," and "insecurity." But there is also deep faith and great hope.

No wonder we somehow create our own prisons, and we also are eager to escape from them.

We create our own protection tools and places with our minds; we build bunkers; we erect walls; we establish frontiers; we invent systems, categories, institutions, and laws; we fabricate refuges, masks, and covers; we manufacture armors, guns, and bombs; we rely on lies, deceptions, and hypocritical lifestyles; we escape through drugs, alcohol, and "spiritual fantasies." We do all these things and much more because we are afraid – afraid of our reality. We looked for peace in these measures of protection but we found only another prison waiting for us, and we also found ourselves wanting to scream: "… we cannot breathe. We must have air."[1]

These things, in Teilhard de Chardin's world, have particular names and they all are impediments to peace. They are: slavery to "words," the "demon of immobilism," "nostalgia for the snows of yesteryear," "religion," "loss of true values," "fear and enclosure," "boredom-impasse." Teilhard thought that these were against life and they impeded the way to a real peace. How so?

---

[1] SC, p. 144 -- IX, 185.

Slavery to "words"[2]

"Words, words, words,"[3] says Hamlet. We seem to live in a world of words. They are basic structures in our minds and in our culture. But do the same words mean the same things to everyone who uses them? Of course not. That is why a literal interpretation, as well as a literal way of thinking, and a literal mentality, should be rejected. This is what Teilhard did. The examples of his position are numerous in his writings. Look at this:

> *Liberty, Equality, Fraternity.* It was in 1789 that this famous slogan electrified the western world: but as events have shown, its meaning was far from clear to the minds of those it inspired. Liberty – to do *anything*? Equality -- in *all* respects? Fraternity -- based on *what* common bonds? ... Even today the magical words are much more felt than understood.[4]

Then Teilhard goes on developing what meaning to give to "Liberty, Equality, Fraternity" which are "no longer indeterminate, amorphous and inert, but directed, guided, dynamised by the growth of a fundamental impulse which underlies and sustains them."[5] He also wrote: "I think I cried ... when I read the famous slogan, 'Work, family, country!' .... Where are our fathers of '89!"[6] Elsewhere, he went on to consider that the "old ideologies (democracy, communism, fascism) no longer have meaning"[7] and that they cover growths that are completely heterogeneous.

When pushed to their extreme, liberalism and legalism become diseases that invade especially religions, traditions, politics, ways of thinking and living, and consequently rule our minds and behaviors. Words become a means of control and a way to power, prestige, and business. Human beings give their lives for words, for mere words. They

---

[2] MM, p. 201 -- *Genèse d'une pensée,* p. 261.

[3] Shakespeare, *Hamlet*, Act II, Scene 2. In response to an annoying question from Polonius: "What do you read, my lord?" Hamlet says "Words, words, words."

[4] FM, pp. 250-51 -- V, p. 312.

[5] FM, p. 251 -- V, pp. 312-13.

[6] LTF, p. 100 -- *Accomplir l'homme*, p. 122.

[7] In a letter to l'Abbé Gaudefroy dated on 11 October 1936, Teilhard wrote: "Il me semble que toutes les vieilles catégories (démocraties, communisme, fascisme) ne signifient plus rien et couvrent des poussées absolument hétérogènes. Je conçois un nouveau mouvement ... qui opèrerait le ralliement sur les 3 mots suivants : non plus liberté, égalité, fraternité, mais universalisme, futurisme, personnalisme... » (LI, p. 114).

can kill for a mere word. A single word can provoke a profound disturbance and, sometimes, it can cause a war.

Literal thinking is stereotyped thinking. Literalism creates prejudices. It does not bring peace; it kills.

The demon of immobilism"[8]

People of our time and perhaps of all times are, according to Teilhard, divided into two categories. Some are very optimistic, perhaps too naïve, and think that humanity, in spite of its many contradictions and evils, is heading toward a radiant future. The others, on the contrary, are pessimistic, too pessimistic, and think that nothing changes, and the best is already behind. Thus, they think that the best thing to do would be to maintain the present order or make it conform to what was in the past. Since their model is in the past, progress for them has not only a real content, but it can be even dangerous. What there is, they may think, is at least known and experienced, and the new is a risk. The universe is closed. Period. Teilhard observes that "For the sake of human tranquility, in the name of Fact, and in defense of the sacred Established Order, the immobilists forbid the earth to move. Nothing changes they say, or can change."[9] Therefore, "immobilism" would be the ideal.

Such an attitude might be a fertile ground for certain hardliners, nationalists, sectarians, racists, integrists, chauvinists, or any kind of religious fanatics. However, being a person of principle is one thing, and being completely closed to the other and the universal is another thing. Paradoxically, if we keep the window open to the universal, the universal in return will make us more nationalist, more conservative, more sectarian; for unity is neither conformity, nor abolition of diversity. On the contrary, "*union differentiates*,"[10] as Teilhard likes to say. So, keeping our door closed does not help world peace, and it does not help to win the theoreticians' argument of these pessimistic attitudes.

Teilhard did not only dislike the immobilist attitudes, but he saw in them a cause for war. He wrote in 1941, for example: "I am convinced that the present war is, at bottom, a conflict between 'mobilists' and 'immobilists', and that it will stop the minute the mobilists, in each camp, will recognize each other and drop the political and religious immobilists."[11]

---

[8] FM, p. 159 -- V, p. 196.
[9] FM, p. 12 -- V, p. 24.
[10] PM, p. 262 -- I, p. 196.
[11] LTF, p. 156 -- *Accomplir l'homme*, p. 189.

A few years later, he thought that if there was no agreement yet, that was because "the demon of immobilism"[12] was still there.

"Nostalgia for the snows of yesteryear"[13]

The so-called original harmony and stability of the past is like a dream – a fairy tale dream in which the heroes find themselves in peace ever after. This is a creation of the mind. Peace cannot be built on something that does not exist anymore. No wonder Teilhard says, "The past is left behind…. Our nostalgia for the snows of yesteryear is morbid. What has been has now no intrinsic interest."[14]

Why is the past "morbid" when we can learn so much from the past and from history? Teilhard did not mean that we learn nothing from the past when he, himself, was a paleontologist who by definition deals with, and learns from, life forms from the past, especially prehistoric life forms. Teilhard wanted to draw attention to the present and the future because living in the past can never bring peace. We live in different times.

A single ideal model for anything no longer exists in our world today. We no longer have a well-defined reference center. We now think differently, live differently, and act differently. The individual no longer finds his or her identity through one simple belonging (family, village, church, company, organization), but through many belongings which intersect or lie parallel (ideology, conservatism, liberalism, intellectual pursuit, clubs, leisure places, electronic connections, etc.). More and more the social body is becoming so huge and differentiated that no one can pretend to have the last word on things. Everything seems to be becoming temporary and ephemeral. Pope Francis denounced many times this kind of what he called "the culture of the provisional." He said, for example: "Contemporary society and its prevailing cultural models – the 'culture of the provisional' – do not provide a climate conducive to the formation of stable life choices with solid bonds, built on the rock of love and responsibility rather than on the sand of emotion."[15]

In such a given context, no real peace can be based on principles received from the past that are already formed and finished products. On the contrary, peace must be developed through new reactions to continually moving structures caused rather by visions from the future.

---

[12] FM, p. 159 -- V, p. 196.
[13] VP, p. 188 -- III, p. 265.
[14] VP, pp. 187-88 -- III, p. 265.
[15] See https://zenit.org/articles/on-overcoming-the-culture-of-the-provisional/

Teilhard seems to be saying that the interest of the past lies in seeing the evolution of things. So, learn from the past, but don't let the past lead and rule you.

Moreover, since the past is never objective because we usually perceive it as we wish to perceive it, there is a good chance, almost a certainty, one could argue, that the past creates prejudices. Prejudices and peace do not get along. The past, even if it is a source of beauty, honor, and dignity, can also be a colossal enemy as well. Triumphalism and "nationalisms" that are by-products of a glorious past are not really ways for peace. Teilhard would disgrace them with blunt terms. He does not hesitate to say that he hates nationalisms and "their apparent regressions toward the past,"[16] while retaining the human part of it, "What is no more than national may well disappear, but what is human cannot be lost."[17]

Religion

Believe it or not, believing in God can be the most serious and, in a sense, most efficient, obstacle to peace. This is what would happen when we create our own god or gods, our own commandments, and our own codes of ethics and practices. Religion was not meant to be this way at all. It was meant to be for growth and not for destruction.

Strangely enough, God has probably become item number one in our technological and materialistic culture. Take a tour in bookstores. Listen to people in the street. Turn on the television. Browse web sites. There are always people talking about God. So, God has not died, even though one would have wished that this "god" we have created to fit our greed and desires would have died. We conduct holy wars in God's name. When we kill in God's name, we do it in many different ways, and not only with weapons. We can kill with words, oppressions, imposed systems, attitudes, sarcasms, and all kinds of intolerances. "Religion," when it allows us to create our own god, can be the most sophisticated weapon for killing people. It would be a great contribution to world peace if this kind of religion just vanishes. After all, the number one enemy of real religion is not heresy, or schism, or skepticism, or even atheism. Its real enemy is the "dogma" itself, when the dogma becomes an ideology, a dead idea, a conventional arrangement, and especially a political means for power. Then it becomes simply a tool for killing both humanity and truth.

---

[16] In a letter to Père Valensin dated on 28 December 1933, Teilhard wrote: "Je hais les nationalismes, et leurs apparentes régressions vers le passé" (LIV, p. 261).
[17] SC, p. 131 -- IX, p. 172.

Furthermore, religion cannot be considered as a tranquilizer, a drug, or an "opium"[18] that can help for a consolation and a feeling that everything is perfectly well. Teilhard warned: "Religion can become an opium. It is too often understood as a simple soothing of our woes. *Its true function is to sustain and spur on the progress of life.*"[19] God must draw us forward:

> Ever since Aristotle there have been almost continual attempts to construct "models" of God on the lines of an outside Prime Mover, acting *a retro*. Since the emergence in our consciousness of the "sense of evolution" it has become physically impossible for us to conceive or worship anything but an organic Prime Mover God, *ab ante*.[20]

Loss of true values

Our culture exalts human usefulness and it measures the worth of human beings by their titles, powers, positions, incomes, or assets. Plus, we live in a world of technology and machinery in which only little chances are left for true relationships. What is offered in the first place is a world that prizes consumer products; consequently any sense of commitment, fidelity, or sacrifice tends to be exceptional, if not bizarre, at least in some cases. In the eyes of the world, what makes money makes sense and what does not make money does not make sense.

Seeing the world through materialistic eyes only can be a real impediment for world peace because someone can justify killing others by the many benefits that can be collected as a result of a war. If one comes to separate the material world from the spiritual one, he or she runs the risk of putting the values upside down. Teilhard keeps reminding us that "… the two aspects, spiritual and material, of the real necessarily and complementarily call for one another, like two sides of one and the same objects."[21] He also wrote: "Matter and Spirit are not opposed as two separate things, as two natures, but as two directions of evolution within the world."[22] Thus, no solution for peace is possible if it does not spring from the depths of our hearts and souls in the first place.

---

[18] "Religion is the opium of the people" is probably one of the most best-known quotations by Karl Marx, the German economist and Communist political philosopher.
[19] HE, p. 44 -- VI, p. 53.
[20] CE, p. 240 -- X, pp. 288-89.
[21] AE, pp. 124-25 -- VII, p. 131.
[22] SC, p. 51 -- IX, p. 79.

Fear and enclosure

Fear does not inspire peace. It is rather the absence of love and peace. Even if we consciously think we want peace, if we hold onto fear, the other part of our mind will be unwilling to accept it. The fearful ego believes that a justified attack is more valuable than peace of mind. The ego wants to destroy and murder. The ego knows peace only by subduing and destroying.

Fear comes under different forms and modalities. None of them is the fruit of peace.

Teilhard sees many kinds of fear. There is "the fear of being lost in a world so great and so full of indifferent or hostile beings that humanity seems positively to have no more importance in it... the fear of being henceforth and for ever *reduced to immobility*... the fear of being *shut in*, imprisoned within an irremediably closed world... [the] fear of no longer being able to move... [the] fear of not being able to get out...."[23] He also talks about: "Cosmic" fear,[24] "existential fear,"[25] "Fear in confrontation with Matter,"[26] "Fear in confrontation with the Human."[27]

No wonder such fears provoke a feeling of enclosure. Teilhard wrote: "To be cosmically shut up, all together, in the universe; to be shut up, as individual atoms, each on his own, each inside himself: must we accept that such is the tragedy of man's conditions?"[28]

Fear is certainly a serious impediment to peace, especially when hate is added to it. Teilhard observed that "Another Man is... another World, a rival World.... It is really the other, the rival, whom we fear and hate in Man; and this aversion ceases as soon as we find a way to bring this other back into our unity."[29]

Boredom-impasse

Boredom is one of the greatest maladies of our time. Teilhard tells us: "The great enemy of the modern world, 'Public Enemy No. 1,' is Boredom."[30] Boredom invades our lives when everything seems closed

---

[23] AM, pp. 208-09 – II, pp. 295-96.
[24] CE, p. 199: note -- X, p. 234.
[25] AE, p. 184 -- VII, p. 190.
[26] AE, p. 185 -- VII, p. 191.
[27] AE, p. 188 -- VII, p. 195.
[28] AE, p. 190 -- VII, p. 196.
[29] LTF, p. 63 – *Accomplir l'homme*, pp. 79-80.
[30] FM, p. 150 -- V, p. 184.

ahead of us and when we no longer know where we are going. Also, it invades our lives when we no longer know what to do with ourselves, when there is no longer meaning for our actions, and when we ask ourselves if life is worth living. Teilhard wrote:

> Despite all appearances, Mankind is bored. Perhaps this is the underlying cause of all our troubles. We no longer know what to do with ourselves. Hence in social terms the disorderly turmoil of individuals pursuing conflicting and egoistical aims; and, on the national scale, the chaos of armed conflict in which, for want of a better object, the excess of accumulated energy is destructively released... "Idleness, mother of all vices."[31]

Violence accompanies boredom. So does the feeling of being trapped in the web of "space-time" without knowing why. So does the feeling of the uselessness and the meaninglessness of life. So does the feeling of being in a closed space – being at an impasse.

There is nothing more explosive than being at an impasse.

---

[31] FM, p. 151 -- V, p. 185.

Chapter Three

What Peace Is Not

Peace! Peace! Peace! We all talk about peace. We all want peace. We all need peace. But, instead, what we have is war – a war that knows no end, as it appears.

Since we seem to constantly be at war, we must not have been talking about the same reality when we utter the word "peace."

Indeed, the word "peace" means different things to different people and in different contexts and circumstances. Look at some of the ways we use this term. We hear, for example, people talking about "world peace," "peace time," "peace at any price." Other people talk about "inner peace," "peace of mind," "being at peace." Others talk about "peace treaty," "keeping the peace," "peacemaker." Others talk about "the Prince of peace," and about "making peace with God, with others, and with oneself." Still others use the greeting, "peace be with you," or they say, "I wish they'd leave in peace." In addition to that, in the name of "peace," injustices have been committed, people have been oppressed, and wars have been declared. Under the pretext of "peace," some powerful nations subdued other nations in order to rule them and exploit their resources. In such a case, as well as in many other circumstances, the term "peace" is rather used as a pretext for starting a war. Wasn't this the purpose anyway?

The word "peace," therefore, is used in a wide variety of ways, driven by diverse assumptions, perceptions, situations, desires, and practices. The result is clear and the same: "'Peace, peace,' when there is no peace."[1]

Teilhard de Chardin has his own understanding of "peace" as well. He had a different approach because he had a different explanation of the universe. In order to fully understand what he meant by "peace," we need to understand what peace is not, in the first place.

---

[1] Jeremiah 6 :14.

"Peace is not the opposite of war"[2]

Peace is not a synonym of no-war and no-violence. It is not defined by its opposite: strife, conflict, bondage. It is not the unconditional surrender that is usually imposed on the enemy after victory. It is not simply a state or condition of quietness, rest, and tranquility. Peace does not *exist* this way because a *static* peace is impossible. Teilhard wrote:

> In short, true peace, the only kind that is biologically possible, betokens neither the ending nor the reverse of warfare, but war in a naturally sublimated form. It reflects and corresponds to the normal state of Mankind become at last alive to the possibilities and demands of its evolution.[3]

Peace is not the counterbalance of terror

The common sense wisdom that many people believe in is the use of fear. If your neighbors, they argue, have a lot of guns and they are threatening you, go and find guns that are more advanced and sophisticated, and they will be afraid of using their guns against you. Likewise, if a nation has nuclear bombs and threatens another country, the common sense wisdom would be to let the threatened country have its nuclear bombs, too, so that the other country will not dare to throw the bomb first. We have to admit that the weapons dissuasion has a direct influence on the decisions of those who intend to shoot. But does this counterbalance create peace? Yes and No.

Yes, a counterbalance of terror may have a certain power of preventing a disaster. No, because a counterbalance does not eliminate fear. The dissuasion that is based on fear and terror would transfer war and violence to other human fields such as economic wars, technological wars, energy wars, demographical wars, consumerism, sexism, racism, militarism.... Simply put, the whole atmosphere is poisoned. Teilhard summarized it this way: "More than all the remnants of hatred lingering between nations, this terror of inevitable war, which sees no cure for warfare except in even greater terror, is responsible for poisoning the air we breathe."[4]

By the way, when Teilhard paradoxically welcomed the birth of the atomic bomb, he just wanted to express his recognition for the human

---

[2] LT, p. 267 -- *Lettres de voyage*, p. 260.
[3] FM, p. 159 -- V, p. 196.
[4] FM, p. 154 -- V, p. 191.

power of creating and improving in science. He was not, as some people thought,[5] bringing his support—how can he!—to the catastrophic consequences that the bomb left behind, and he was not trying to find, as some others thought, a kind of counterbalance,[6] or find a way to convey the message that a generalized war was impossible from now on.[7] Although we seem to have reached a certain kind of unification due to such a planetary danger, but this unification can only be ephemeral because it is coming from outside and it does not touch minds and hearts. Teilhard wrote:

> The great fear aroused by an imminent planetary danger might be enough, of course, to galvanise and momentarily unite all the egoisms and nationalisms of the earth. But this provisional unification of interests *by an*

---

[5] Thomas Merton wrote: "At this point, it must be admitted that one of the most serious criticisms of Teilhard bears precisely on this point: an optimism which tends to look at existential evil and suffering through the small end of the telescope. It is unfortunately true that Teilhard, like many other Christians, regarded the dead and wounded of Hiroshima with a certain equanimity as inevitable by-products of scientific and evolutionary progress. He was much more impressed with the magnificent scientific achievement of the atomic physicists than he was with the consequences of dropping the bomb. It must be added immediately that the physicists themselves did not all see things exactly as he did." (*The Literary Essays of Thomas Merton*, edited by Brother Patrick Hart (New York: New Directions Publishing Corporation, 1981), p. 216.)

[6] Mary Lukas and Ellen Lukas wrote that Teilhard argued that "Once human consciousness appeared [...] there was no longer any biological necessity for animal species to keep on replacing one another in evolution's rush to self-awareness. The murderous instincts of the cave could not, of course, be expected to have vanished overnight. But now that man had at his fingertips the power to destroy himself as well as the very planet that he stood on, it was plain he had reached the point where he must weigh the advantages of using force against the disadvantages." (Mary Lukas and Ellen Lukas, *Teilhard: The Man, The Priest, The Scientist* (Garden City, NY: Doubleday and Company, Inc., 1977), pp. 236-237.

[7] Cf. FM, pp. 145-53 – V, pp. 177-87. Benjamin T. Hourani observed that there are many who "insist, however, that since World War II we have had other wars, the population explosion, the energy and ecological crises and point out that the Atomic Bombs which Teilhard thought might have the effect of eliminating all wars are still with us and now we have more than 50.000 nuclear bombs. Some of these bombs have one million times the destructive power of the first two bombs." (Benjamin T. Hourani, "Teilhard's Political Ecumene: Empire or Commonwealth" in *The Desire to Be Human*, "International Teilhard Compendium" Centenary volume edited by Leo Zonneveld and Robert Muller (Netherlands: Mirananda Publishers b.v. Wassenaar, 1983), pp. 209-210.)

external agency would certainly lack the stability and heat required to produce a real and fertile union of wills and hearts.[8]

Peace is not pacifism or a manifestation of non-violence

Non-violence in itself lacks dynamism, and peace manifestations, even though well justified and necessary, are usually rooted in fearfulness or in some utopian ideal. No doubt they may have a real ambition for peace. However, they often lack the necessary profound analysis of the true causes of war. They also lack an attractive vision for the peace that would have the dynamics to realize a human wholeness. Therefore, they don't possess the right tools to prevent or stop a war.

While recognizing such official "statements" of words and actions, Teilhard prefers to turn to the institutions and associations where "a new spirit is silently taking shape around us – the soul of Mankind resolved at all costs to achieve, in its total integrity, the uttermost fulfillment of its powers and its destiny."[9]

Peace is not only a survival issue

Survival deals more with temporary situations than with permanent ones because it lacks the *élan* that is required for durability in an open end. For Teilhard, survival wouldn't be enough for peace because human beings will not continue to strive for life if they know they have a closed future. Even if survival is and should be desirable, it cannot be a goal which gives energy to humanity. Survival can never be a leitmotif.[10]

Peace is not the stillness of repose, immobility, boredom, or comfortable laziness

Teilhard rejects the "bourgeois" world, its activities, its values, its individualism, and its fear. He wrote: "A perfectly-ordered society with everyone living in effortless ease within a fixed framework, a world in a state of tranquil repose, all this has nothing to do with our advancing

---

[8] AM, p. 261 -- II, p. 358.
[9] FM, p. 160 – V, p. 197.
[10] Ct. PM, Book Three, Chap. III; Book Four, Chap. I; AE, "The Zest for Living"; FM, "The Human Rebound of Evolution and its Consequences" -- I, pp. 263, 237; VII, pp. 242, 426, 48; V, p. 271; IX, p.179; X, pp. 238, 136, 135.

universe."[11] True peace does not come out of weakness, but out of energy because our universe is on a growing convergence and concentration path. Therefore, there is no room for "tranquil repose" and laziness. We do have a common goal to reach, and a common goal does not allow stillness. "Peace cannot be the consequence of a general lassitude: it requires a passionate union of men with respect to common objectives."[12]

Teilhard had this kind of conviction all his life, it seems. Even at the beginning of his career as a writer, he was sarcastic about the kind of peace that followed World War I. He wrote:

> - And was peace, then, no more than this?
> - The peace that all through these long years was the brilliant mirage always before our eyes.
> The peace that gave us the courage to hold fast and to go into the attack because we thought we were fighting for a new world.
> The peace that we hardly dared to hope might be ours, so lovely it seemed....
> And this is all that peace had in store for us![13]

Teilhard certainly did not intend to praise the war as such.[14] He just wanted to draw attention to the fact that there is no solution for a lasting peace when this peace is the peace of tranquility, or the peace that comes from a formula such as "To fight simply from inertia; to fight in order to be left in peace; to fight so that we may be 'let be.'"[15]

Peace is not just a theoretical concept for a treaty

Peace is not an intellectual exercise, but a practical reality. It cannot be built on a certain logical utopian system, but on a constructive vision of the totality of things by the way of a comprehensive approach. What is the point of having the best treaties in the world if the signatories are not willing to implement the contents of these treaties? That is why a peace based on treaties is not a real peace. What is utopian is not the aspiration for reconciliation and harmony between people, but the illusion that the treaties are by themselves enough to prevent a catastrophic war. It was

---

[11] FM, p. 158 -- V, pp.195-6.
[12] LTF, p. 9 -- *Accomplir l'homme*, p. 14 (quotation in Prologue by René d'Ouince).
[13] WTW, p. 278 -- XII, p. 417.
[14] See Jean Maalouf, *Le mystère du mal dans l'œuvre de Teilhard de Chardin*, « Thèses/Cerf », Les Editions du Cerf, 1986, pp. 22-32.
[15] AE, p. 16 -- VII, p. 22.

clear to Teilhard that treaties were but a temporary palliative and not the solution. Analytic discussions are always good, but a practical synthesis that leads to action is what is needed.

Humanity has extensively recorded war times, but it did not do the same in regard to peace times. It has recorded how to reduce the tension of wars through legal means and the balance of power. Laws are supposed to be rational. Rationality is only possible in reference to a goal. But who sets the goals? Is our world a closed space? Where are our references? Here people can argue indefinitely. For Teilhard, our references cannot be only in the past. We should understand the past, he would say, by looking to the future, and especially the far future. This is to say that rationality and treaties are only one way – a temporary way – for peace. They are not a sufficient answer, and consequently not the right answer. Millions of books and articles are written. Millions of readers read books and articles every day. No danger. A book and an article in themselves are not a fire. Mental truths become real truths only when they are lived truths. Only existential truths are truths. Teilhard confides in a letter written in 1941: "And I have no confidence in reforms, however timely, that are built upon a foundation of cowardice. I think I cried a year ago when I read the famous slogan, 'work, family, country!' It is not with prudence that you make people move, but with a little passion. Where are our fathers of '89?"[16]

Knowledge is power, we usually say. But life requires more than knowledge. Somehow we are becoming a kind of storage, a bank, or a computer that can provide the required answer for our questions. No matter how powerful our memories are, peace remains beyond studies, statistics, conclusions, and adjustments. We will never achieve peace by just studying the "just" war theories, for example, or by reading about the consequences of nuclear conflagration, or even by adjusting frontiers and building walls. Although such things are helpful, they are not enough. Teilhard wrote:

> In order to avoid disturbing our habits we seek in vain to settle international disputes by adjustments of frontiers -- or we treat as "leisure" (to be whiled away) the activities at the disposal of mankind. As things are now going it will not be long before we run full tilt into one another. Something will explode if we persist in trying to squeeze into our old tumble-down huts the material and spiritual forces that are henceforth on the scale of the world.

---

[16] LTF, p. 100 -- *Accomplir l'homme*, p. 122.

A new domain of psychical expansion -- that is what we lack. And it is staring us in the face if we would only raise our heads to look at it.[17]

Peace is not even justice

Justice is certainly a very important factor for peace. But how does one defines justice, in the first place, when all depends on who is using this word, when, where, and why? That is why justice, from a practical point of view, has never given peace to the world, and that is because of the continuously evolving human reality. If there were only one way for humans to interact, it would have been easy to clearly define human rights. But the evolving world is lived through dialogues, differences, and dialectical forces. When Teilhard speaks about anthropogenesis, he speaks about justice, but he does not linger long on it because everything is in the ongoing process of evolution.[18] He does not believe either, that "simple justice, with its cool economy"[19] is able to bring a solution for human relationships, and that is because it lacks energy. He was concerned with "How to give back to Humanity its fullness of spiritual energy," as he confided, in 1936, to Henri de Lubac, and added that "It seems to me that what is moral is that which uses and promotes growth."[20]

In spite of the fact that he recognized the importance of these concepts for peace, Teilhard considered them as unsatisfactory. He, instead, made

---

[17] PM, p. 253 – III, p. 281.
[18] Cf. HE, pp. 178-79 -- VI, p. 221; IX, p. 201; X, p.170 ff.
[19] VP, p. 138 -- III, p. 192.
[20] In a letter dated on 22 November 1936, Teilhard wrote to Henri de Lubac: "La science pratique de l'Homme (Morale, Economie, Politique, etc.) semble avoir été surtout conçue jusqu'ici comme un problème d'équilibre : donner à chacun son droit, son pain, son territoire, etc. Or visiblement il s'agit maintenant de reconnaître là un problème d'*énergies*. Comment faire rendre à l'Humanité son plein d'énergies spirituelles ? J'imagine que là se trouvera de plus en pus la règle utilisée par l'avenir pour apprécier ce qui est le Bien.

Est moral, il me semble, ce qui utilise et fait fructifier la grandeur qu'il s'agit de moraliser. Donc l'usage de l'argent ne doit pas être dominé par la justice distributive (principe des vases communicants) mais par l'utilisation de la force vive de l'argent. Idem pour l'usage des puissances du cœur et de la liberté. (*Lettres intimes de Teilhard de Chardin à Auguste Valensin, Bruno de Solages, Henri de Lubac, André Ravier – 1919-1955*, Editions Aubier-Montaigne, Paris, 1974, p. 323).

an appeal for another kind of peace that is of another substance and reality, as we will see later in this book.

CHAPTER FOUR

THE BATTLEFIELD

Enlightened leaders are clear, straightforward, and challenging. When they need to send people to war, they will tell them as well as the country they lead: this is the battlefield, this is the mission, this is the strategy, and only victory is expected. However, victory cannot be assured if the strategy is lacking, the mission is not clear, and the battlefield is the wrong one. One may win a battle in the wrong battlefield, but never the war.

It is astonishing to realize how many times throughout history we picked the wrong battlefield for our war. How can one reach a permanent peace if one picks the wrong place to fight?

In August 18, 1940, Teilhard de Chardin wrote in a letter to a friend: "I am more and more convinced that the real battlefield, today, is not in Dover, Egypt, or Rumania, but in Man's mind and soul."[1] Teilhard was writing this during WWII. There is no doubt that, if he was writing today, he would replace the words "Dover, Egypt, or Rumania" with Iraq, Syria, Afghanistan, and/or any other country where wars are taking place or will take place in the future. The sentence that Teilhard wrote will remain correct in any case. Wars will never cease if we continue to fight in the wrong places.

The ground of the battle

Teilhard was not ambiguous or hesitant or difficult to understand when he wanted to indicate where the battle was supposed to take place. He clearly and straightforwardly stated: "It is… in the depths of the soul that the battle will be decided…. And then, struck at its source, the conflict will die of its own accord, never to break out again."[2] Isn't this what the UNESCO Charter, in substance, said as well as many other thinkers?[3]

---

[1] LTF, p. 149 -- *Accomplir l'homme*, p. 179.
[2] AE, pp. 19-20 -- VII, p. 26.
[3] The Constitution of UNESCO, signed on 16 November 1945, starts with these words: "Since wars begin in the minds of men, it is in the minds of men that the

Therefore, the first thing to do, if we truly want peace, is to work on the right battleground – the self. The famous "Know thyself" of Socrates still reverberates throughout the centuries, and his other bold statement, "The unexamined life is not worth living," still makes headline among those who want to make a difference in this world. Indeed, these courageous people who truly want to make a difference start with themselves, for this is where a change in consciousness takes place first. Teilhard was no exception. He wrote:

> ... I took the lamp and, leaving the zone of everyday occupations and relationships where everything seems clear, I went down into my inmost self, to the deep abyss whence I feel dimly that my power of action emanates. But as I moved further and further away from the conventional certainties by which social life is superficially illuminated, I became aware that I was losing contact with myself. At each step of the descent a new person was disclosed within me of whose name I was no longer sure, and who no longer obeyed me. And when I had to stop my exploration because the path faded from beneath my steps, I found a bottomless abyss at my feet, and out of it came – arising I know not from where – the current which I dare to call *my* life.[4]

---

defences of peace must be constructed." Michael N. Nagler offered the following observation: "Whatever else the 'new age' paradigm may have accomplished, or failed to, it has made it easier to talk about the baffling problem of large conflicts by making it somewhat more natural to bear in mind their connection with consciousness. Consciousness is within, but not limited to, the individual. However vast, however complex and 'out there' the war system may finally play itself out, it is crucial to remember that 'wars begin in the minds of men.' Emerson had long ago foreshadowed this truism of the UNESCO Charter in his musing about the Concord armory that I've often quoted. 'It is really a thought that built this portentous war establishment, and a thought shall also melt it away.'" (Michael N. Nagler, *Is There No Other Way? The Search for a Nonviolent Future* (Berkeley, CA: Berkeley Hills Books, 2001), p. 221). Stephen G. Cary also said: "We must move beyond the naïve but satisfying illusion that "we" are good and "they" are evil—that the devil always lives somewhere else: now in Berlin and Tokyo; now in Moscow, Hanoi, and Beijing; now in Belgrade and Kabul; but never in Washington. The devil lives in the hearts of all of God's children, and until we take responsibility to try to lift up that which is good in us and cast out that which is bad, the scourge of terrorism will continue to torment us." (Quoted in *Practicing Peace: A Devotional Walk through the Quaker Tradition*, by Catherine Whitmire (Notre Dame, IN: Sorin Books, 2007), pp. 163-164).

[4] DM, pp. 76-7 -- IV, p. 75.

Then Teilhard decided to return to the light of external reality again to find himself dizzy because of "the supreme improbability, the tremendous unlikelihood of finding myself existing in the heart of a world that has survived and succeeded in being a world."[5] Then, in the depth of this "night," he saw God right there, and he exclaimed, full of joy: "It is you yourself whom I find, you who makes me participate in your being, you who moulds me."[6]

At this deeper level of our life, a "comm-union" with God and the world is taking place. Realizing the obviousness of such a reality leaves profound and tremendous consequences in our consciousness. We cannot be defined except in relationship with God, others, and the world. Our true self is essentially relational; it is a loving force.

What is at stake in such a context is the very way of thinking. In fact, we cannot continue to think that God is "out there" and not "here."

God is no longer "out there"

Most of the time, it seems, we find ourselves afraid to deal directly with God, wishing, knowingly or unknowingly, that we could just close our eyes and escape from this reality. Some of us prefer to deny that God exists, and some others find it much easier to replace God by the "gods" they can handle. To get to meet God in the street, for example, or in any other specific place for that matter is a catastrophe, because, if we do, nothing would remain the same. Instantly, we will discover that we have lived in lies and more lies most of, if not all of, our life.

To let God be God in our lives requires considerable effort and courage to let go of the god-idols that include the god we make of ourselves and of absolute prejudices and biases. Taken seriously, this kind of work is truly destructive, obliterating, and demolishing – therefore, it is a deconstruction project first. One needs to un-block all that was preventing the sun from penetrating the room, then open the window if one wants light and the fresh air.

When we allow the living God to permeate our lives, God will turn all our ideas about Him upside down. He is not restricted to our definitions, formulas, and rites. He doesn't come necessarily in the form of the known. We may know about Him, but we rarely know Him. It is precisely here, when we identify God with our concept of Him, that God becomes an idol similar to the other idols we've created.

---

[5] DM, p. 77 -- IV, p. 77.
[6] DM, p. 78 -- IV, p. 78.

The long history of humanity teaches us that wars and quarrels between religions have been very often caused, among other things, by clinging to words, formulas, structures, rites, institutions, interpretations of factual events, doctrines.... The truth is that God is not "out there" in one particular place, definition, or interpretation we choose for Him. God is not an unattainable abstraction we create. God is right here in this world He created and in anyone that we like or we don't like. Teilhard has this penetrating statement which condenses a whole theology in one sentence. He wrote: "Since my dignity as a man, O God, forbids me to close my eyes to this – like an animal or a child – that I may not succumb to the temptation to curse the universe and Him who made it, teach me to adore it by seeing you concealed within it."[7] He also prayed: "Grant that I may see you, even and above all, in the souls of my brothers, at their most personal, and most true, and most distant."[8]

Authentic theology is an incarnational theology.

People's orthodoxy should not be judged by whether or not they agree with the correct formulas and the rights words created very often by our biased minds, but by how much love they have in their hearts and actions. In fact, it is a heresy to reduce God to an object we possess or manipulate according to our own circumstances. If we pretend to know God and yet stay the same, we just reduce God to an object of mental truth. God is much more than that. One may prove God's existence to someone who does not believe in God's existence and he or she will feel satisfaction by doing that. One may give a good lesson of history, or an impeccable lesson in doctrine and ethics, or a convincing lesson on compared religions and all the students pass the test and succeed. But nothing would have changed just because the best arguments were presented. The perfect and coherent definitions were like the forts of olden days. These forts served a purpose, and now, even if they are out of use, they managed to leave behind all kinds of militia, mercenaries, fighters, and "holy" warriors.

God is the most dangerous being who ever existed. When God is an abstract definition and a set of rules and regulations, he becomes a killer. This god-idol becomes a reason that justifies all the cruelties we are able to commit. But if God enters our lives as the flame of love, the fire of purification, the energy of transformation, and the generator of change, He will certainly provide us the right tools to kill the god-idols, uproot our false notions of Him, and deconstruct our false certainties and biases. God and gods do not exist together. We cannot worship both. The choice is

---

[7] DM, p. 137 -- IV, p. 172.
[8] DM, p. 145 -- IV, p. 185.

made within – in our minds, hearts, and souls – and the battlefield takes place there also. The violence that we experience outside is only the mirror of what is going on inside. That is why peace in the world is not going to happen if we do not have peace within first.

Growing by subtraction

It is easier to wander than to stay put, to talk than to be silent, to gain than to lose, and to add than to subtract. That is why most of us prefer to be elsewhere than to be home; being home forces us to face reality as it is when being elsewhere helps us to escape that reality. No wonder people find a convenient escape in "drugs" such as wealth, power, sex, ideologies, politics, possessions, institutions, and all that drives them from their true selves and God. Reality can be very painful. It is safer to hide it, to forget it, to pretend that it does not exist, and to be drunk and not think about it. Why can't we be at ease at home, relaxed, still, alone, and silent? That is because, whenever we are only with ourselves, we feel empty as if we are nobody, and we get scared and dizzy in front of an abyss.

In front of this abyss we realize that our false self is losing ground. Our false self is what we see in the eyes of others – the fake version of ourselves. Their opinions become our identities. Their values become our garments. Their behaviors become our models for action. Their lifestyles become our faces. Their ways of thinking become the inspiration of ours, without realizing that this could be the most sophisticated mask we can put on. That is why we become what we are not – by-products of others. That is why it is very difficult, if not impossible, to reconcile the false self with the true self.

Liberation from the false self is needed. When we go that deep, and we see everything in its existential purity, without hidden motives and without pretending what we are not, we will discover, as Teilhard put it, that

> Man is essentially the same in all of us, and we have only to look sufficiently deeply within ourselves to find a common substratum of aspirations and illumination. To put it in a way which already expresses my fundamental thesis: 'It is through that which is most incommunicably personal in us that we make contact with the universe,'[9]

and we will discover that everything is related to everything else in a profound unity. Teilhard also said:

---

[9] CE, pp. 97-8 -- X, p. 118.

> I believe I can distinguish in the Universe a *profound*, essential *Unity*, a unity burdened with imperfections, a unity still sadly 'pulverulent,' but a real unity within which every 'chosen' substance gains increasing solidity.[10]

Then we will recognize ourselves in others and others in ourselves. We are of the same essence even if the majority of us count on the addition operation to survive while the others are more inspired by the spirituality of subtraction.

In a practical manner, and for the sake of peace, let us try this exercise. Let us find a very quiet place and just be silent. Silence is universal. In a sense, language limits reality. When we talk, we are immediately identified. We talk as "American," "French," "Chinese," "Catholic," "Protestant," "Buddhist," "Jewish," "Muslim," "Atheist," "Republican," "Democrat," "Communist," "Conservative," "Liberal," or whatever one happens to be. The words we use may point to the light, but they are not the light. They can never be absolute. Let us subtract these and similar words, and all that they represent, from our dictionary for awhile, and just be silent. In silence we will feel more whole and more universal.

If truth can grow by the addition of knowledge, it can grow also by the subtraction of the so-called certainties of the false selves such as our piles of possessions, our pride, our ambition, our ego, etc. So, let us empty ourselves from all that is not us and allow ourselves to be just in silence with our true selves only. You will see, like I saw, that your silence, my silence, and the silence of others is one single silence. It is like the same air we all breathe and the same light we all enjoy. We then realize that we all have the same entity and we all have the same needs. The new reality we are seeing now is the fruit of silence and not "words." In silence we see things as they are. Teilhard recommended that "It is essential to see – to see things as they are and to see them really and intensely."[11]

The transfigured perception

The way to see things as they are is to see them in a way that is different from the way we are used to seeing them. Now we see them with a mystical eye – the way of the heart and soul.

While retaining confidence in reason, logic, syllogism, theories, and concepts, we may have to try something else. To transcend reason doesn't

---

[10] HM, p. 199 -- XII, p. 298.
[11] DM, p. 53 -- IV, p. 44.

mean to contradict reason. Logic knows only a part of reality. There are other parts of reality that are known by other insights and by the intuitions of the heart.

Let us think vertically this time by going down further and further, breaking through the many levels of consciousness, to the center of the soul and the core of our being. If we are sincere in this journey, we will realize that we are going to lose what we are not, and then we will reach the point where we are in tune with ourselves, with others, with the universe, and with God. It is the original blessing of unity, which is the mere simplicity that is beyond the opposites, the prejudices, and the biases. This is where there is no longer room for any idealistic philosophy that seeks to transfer everyday life to the celestial realm, and make our temporal existence unworthy or used for a materialistic way of living that denies any value to a metaphysical outlook. All this is gone. Our old categories are worn out. Our earlier thinkers, including Plato, Aristotle, Hegel, Kant, Marx, Nietzsche, Sartre, and many others do not satisfy our minds anymore and do not give peace of heart. Neither do our systems and ways of living. Teilhard wasn't too shy to write, for example: "We are locked up in a prison where we cannot breathe. We must have air. We do not want fascist fronts, or a popular front – but a *human front*."[12]

Enlightened people see the truth and follow it no matter the cost. Teilhard was one of these enlightened people and, like them, he was an outsider to the establishment. He was a "desert" man, like Buddha, Abraham, Socrates, Moses, Al-Hallaj, and Jesus Himself. True people discomfort us. Near true people, lies become evident. They are like a "prophet." They are like Nathan who pointed the "sword-finger" at King David and said, "You are the man!"[13] A true man, like Teilhard was, is never afraid to tell the truth because he is never afraid of peace. For peace is first of all a reconciliation with oneself and with existence itself. We are not going to meet God in the street to love Him. But we will meet another person, we will meet a tree, a mountain, a rock, a bird.... We should love God in all that is. "The world is full of God," said Teilhard. "For if it were empty, the world would long ago have died of disgust."[14]

A transfigured self makes all the difference. Mountains are mountains and rivers are rivers, according to a Zen wisdom. Then mountains are no longer mountains and rivers are no longer rivers. Then mountains are mountains again and rivers are rivers again. Even though the first and last lines of this wisdom seem the same, in reality they are not. The difference

---

[12] SC, p. 144 -- IX, p. 185.
[13] 2 Samuel 12:7.
[14] LTF, p. 57 -- *Accomplir l'homme*, p. 73.

is between a mundane view and an enlightened view. When we are enlightened and transfigured, we may still look the same as before and the things we look at seem also the same as before, but in reality we are no longer the same, and the things we look at are no longer the same either. Teilhard put it this way:

> It is essential to see – to see things as they are and to see them really and intensely .... We shall be astonished at the extent and the intimacy of our relationship with the universe.[15]

> Everything that is active, that moves or breathes, every physical, astral, or animate energy, every fragment of force, every spark of life, is equally sacred; for, in the humblest atom and the most brilliant star, in the lowest insect and the finest intelligence, there is the radiant smile and thrill of the *same Absolute*.[16]

---

[15] DM, pp. 58-9 -- IV, pp. 44-5.
[16] WTW, p. 28 -- XII, p. 34.

PART II

THE REVOLUTION OF THE INCARNATION

CHAPTER FIVE

THE REVOLUTION OF THE INCARNATION

If, for Teilhard de Chardin, "Both in nature and in function, Christ gathers up in himself and consummates the totality and fullness of humanity"[1] because, as St. Paul and St. John put it, "Christ is all in all"[2] and "All things came into being through him, and without him not one thing came into being,"[3] what does this mean for us here and now? It means that Christ is the very Center that activates the whole cosmos and creation to the greatest possible consciousness, that the intrinsic orientation toward Point Omega[4] may become the source of energy and inspiration for our lives and activities in our temporary existence, and that faith in the Christ as the goal of history must be the most efficient motivation for our work together in building the future so that peace on earth may prevail.

In us, therefore, must coincide both the love for Christ as the goal of world history and the love for our task on this earth as a way to achieve that goal. Teilhard talked many times about his two passions: passion for God and passion for the world.[5] He did not hesitate to say for example:

---

[1] SC, p. 164 -- IX, p. 209.
[2] Colossians 3:11.
[3] John 1:3.
[4] The Omega-Point will be mentioned many times in this book and it will be explained from different angles. As a preliminary introduction to it, this is how Oliver Rabut saw it. He wrote: "The Omega-Point stands in the first place for the end of evolution, as compared with its beginning (alpha). It means, then, as Teilhard sees it, the human superorganism which will one day come into being, after the 'second point of reflection'. In yet a third sense, the word stands for God, the pre-existing Centre of this superorganism. Finally, it denotes Christ – Christ bound up with the cosmos, when at last he takes possession of the final human unity and supernaturalizes it." See Olivier Rabut, O.P., *Teilhard de Chardin: A Critical Study* (New York: Sheed and Ward Ltd, 1961), p. 115.
[5] See, for example, PierreTeilhard de Chardin, *The Making of the Mind: Letters from a Soldier-Priest 1914-1919*, New York: Harper and Row, Publishers, 1961),

"Today I believe probably more profoundly than ever in God, and certainly more than ever in the world"[6] and "... we can reconcile... the love of God and the healthy love of the world."[7]

But is such a reconciliation possible? Was this possible?

Dichotomous Mind

The sacred/secular dichotomy goes back very far in time; to the dualistic belief that was in Zoroastrianism (Persia); to the philosophical thoughts of Pythagoras, Empedocles, Heraclitus, Permenides, Plato and others (Greek World); to the Jewish and Christian Gnosticism (Roman Empire); to Manichaeism (Persia and Roman Empire); to Bogomilism (Byzantine Empire); to Catharism (Medieval Europe); and to others in Christianity or other religions that may have influenced Christianity.

In modern times, the French philosopher René Descartes is largely responsible for this kind of worldview in the Western thought. Indeed, Cartesianism aims at separating all that is spiritual from all that is material.

Although certain nuances can be noticed among those who believe in the dualism approach, the dualistic point of view is generally characterized by the thought that, from the beginning, life and the universe are run by two principles: good and evil, light and darkness, spirit and matter, mind and body, and all that is related to this dichotomy.

The reality is that one does not need to be a philosopher or a sophisticated intellectual to embrace a dualistic point of view and live it in a very practical way. Aware of it or not, we seem to be able to develop such an attitude at any time, in any place, with any social group or any system. Racism, discrimination, believers and non-believers, thinkers by reaction and biased positions, the have-and-have-nots, all kinds of "we" and "they" approaches, are just a few examples to illustrate our dichotomous way of life. These mentioned and forced either/or options may be sharpened and deepened into sometimes unbridgeable oppositions according to particular personal or historical circumstances.

The two principles approach has affected most of the systems we live by and also most of world religions, Christianity included. Indeed, Christians, at times, did not walk the talk. With regard to the body, just as an example, while Christianity has the highest theological evaluation, it

---

p. 165 -- *Genèse d'une pensée: Lettres 1914-1919*, (Paris: Bernard Grasset Editeur, 1961), p. 213.
[6] CE, p. 97 -- X, p. 118.
[7] DM, p. 53 -- IV, p. 36.

has not given too much attention to it as a legitimate contributor to spiritual growth. This is another dichotomy between theory and practice.

Moreover, most of the religious traditions, especially perhaps the Christian tradition, have always struggled with two choices. The first one was to withdraw from the world into a closer circle and a safer haven where the corrupt world was not allowed to step in, spoil, and destroy. The second one was to accommodate the world, compromise, and just go with the flow of the culture of the day.

For centuries, those two choices somehow managed to survive in spite of their darkest sides. Indeed, both of them not only may have been motivated by fear or defensiveness, but also, and more importantly, they may not be based on solid scriptural ground. Both of them seemed to have ignored, or at least to have forgotten—not necessarily in theory but certainly in practice—that the Incarnation has happened and that the implications of this Incarnation are enormous, critical, structural, and existential. It is so because, when grounded in Christ, all things have their true reality. "All things came into being through him, and without him not one thing came into being"[8] Also, "In him we live and move and have our being."[9]

Does, and can, a dichotomy approach still make sense? What validity does it have anyway?

The Revolution of the Incarnation

The Incarnation event gave the answer to the dichotomy dilemma, and made all the difference.[10] "And the Word became flesh and lived among us, and we have seen his glory, the glory as of a father's only son, full of grace and truth."[11] This is how John described the Incarnation of the Son of God—Jesus Christ—as being divine and human.

---

[8] John 1:3.
[9] Acts 17:28.
[10] Thomas King wrote: "The Incarnation could be identified as the central truth of Christian faith, and throughout the Christian Ages theologians presented this in the language of the times. The very system of dates, whereby the ages before Christ's birth were identified as B.C. and the ages after as A.D., was one attempt to show the centrality of the Incarnation." See Thomas M. King, S.J., *Teilhard de Chardin* (Wilmington, Delaware: Michael Glazier, Inc., 1988, 'The Way of the Christian Mystics'), p. 49.
[11] John 1:14.

Here was God among us showing us how God looks and how being human is supposed to be[12] so that we would be able "to walk just as he walked"[13] and be Christ-like.

In this Jesus, we see "the image of the invisible God."[14] In this incarnate God, who was true flesh and blood, and who ate, drank, walked, slept, suffered and died, we see the God who can be touched, talked to, listened to, and have dinner with. He was the Word among us and He remains among us with the mission He confided to us. Jesus told His disciples, "As the Father has sent me, so I send you."[15] Therefore, as followers of Christ, we are on a mission to be Christ-like and incarnate His word within ourselves, and everywhere to the end of the world and to the end of time.

Saturated with words, the world does not need more abstract words—not even of the "right" words. The world needs more of the words-made-flesh. We may have the best systems in place and listen to the most beautiful and eloquent speeches, but if we don't see the incarnation of these words, these words will remain intellectual exercises. Saint Francis of Assisi said it best in an unforgettable line: "Preach the Gospel at all times, and only when necessary use words." And, to paraphrase G.K. Chesterton, he observed that the best argument for Christianity is Christians and the strongest argument against Christianity is also Christians. In the final analysis, it is not mere words that change people; it is people who change people.

The truth is that Christ's presence is supposed to be incarnated in and through us in every situation and at any moment of our life—twenty-four hours a day, seven days a week, four weeks a month, twelve months a

---

[12] In such a context, we find the following observation written by Raimon Panikkar: "The spiritual and the celestial are not on one side, and the material and political on the other; time is not now and eternity later; the isolated individual is not in opposition to the undifferentiated collectivity. Jesus was neither a political liberator nor an ascetic who denied the world, much less a member of the clergy, but simply a being (we do not have any other word) who lived the fullness of the human. What Jesus did was to participate in the affairs of the earth and the vicissitudes of men and women, while knowing that it is the obligation of each of us to assume our responsibilities so that the common effort will achieve a greater justice. But this human fullness also includes participation in the divine – thereby recalling what we are called to become." (Raimon Panikkar, *Christophany: The Fullness of Man*, trans. by Alfred Dilascia (Maryknoll, N.Y.: Orbis Books, 2004), pp. 188-189).
[13] 1 John 2:6.
[14] Colossians 1:15.
[15] John 20:21.

year, and this to the end of our life. In such a case, the sacred/secular dichotomy that haunted our thoughts throughout the centuries is a very questionable way of thinking, if not wrong altogether, precisely because of the Incarnation. The Incarnation should have radically changed the way we think, but very often we remain attached to our own ways.[16] Jesus showed God's presence in the way He lived and did things, but we very often don't do as Jesus did.

As a result of the Incarnation, when Jesus took the world as part of himself, no one was, and is, supposed to dismiss this world as something undesirable—only sin should be dismissed. In virtue of the Incarnation, life in this world has radically changed; the divine energy penetrated it and made it sacred.[17] Matter became holy. Flesh became holy and, as St Paul says, "Do you not know that your body is a temple of the Holy Spirit within you, which you have from God, and that you are not your own?"[18] All human endeavors became holy, and again as St Paul says, "Whether you eat or drink, or whatever you do, do everything for the glory of God."[19] "Whatever [we] do" means all our human activities that include feasting, fasting, exercising, resting, suffering, laughing, crying, feeding the hungry, visiting the sick, clothing the naked, sheltering the homeless, burying the dead, and working to change structures of discrimination, injustice, violence, and all kinds of poverty. Therefore, all that we are and do is the stuff of our spiritual growth and constitutes a path to our sanctification.

---

[16] We have our own ways and we seem to have our own Christs as well. "Today more than ever before," wrote Ursual King, "we are aware of the many Christs of Christianity, the many faces of Jesus expressed in different ages and cultures. By comparison, classical Chalcedonian Christology is rather exclusive and monolithic, not leaving room for the pluralistic Christologies we need in order to account for the different Christs experienced by faith – not only the Christ of dogma, but the Christ of piety and devotion, the Christ of ascetics and mystics, the Christ of political and social radicalism, the Christ of peace and justice, the Christ of love and forgiveness, the Christ of healing and reconciliation, the Christ of transformation and renewal." See Ursula King, *Christ in All Things: Exploring Spirituality with Teilhard de Chardin* (Maryknoll, NY: Orbis Books, 1997), p. 64.

[17] Emile Rideau wrote in this context: "Bien plus que juridique ou contractuel, le lien qui rattache le Christ au monde est ainsi *physique*, c'est-à-dire ultra-concret. Par conséquent, tout est divinement valorisé et consacré dans le Christ : la matière, la vie, l'histoire humaine et les valeurs de l'homme. » See Emile Rideau, S.J., *Teilhard Oui ou Non* (Paris : Librairie Fayard, 1967, 'Jalons'), p. 82.

[18] 1 Corinthians 6:19.

[19] 1 Corinthians 10:31.

Becoming flesh for the life of the world, the Word of God has been, therefore, totally involved in this very world. If the Lord is here,[20] we cannot live as if He is not here. Since He is here, He therefore is not "there," somewhere in the far space and time, indifferent, aloof, and abstract. He is here, in you and me, and He is continuing the creation of the world through you and me. Can we imagine what a responsibility this is!

The truth is that Christianity is not a system of dis-embodiment—this would be a distortion of its doctrine and mission, and would lead to more discrimination, injustice, violence, and morbidity. Christianity is a continuous Christmas—a continuous embodiment of God's work. When Jesus talked about the kingdom of God, He did not mean some kind of inner, ethical, peaceful state of consciousness only, He also meant a non-violent and just social reality that is healthy at all levels—politically, economically, psychologically, and especially spiritually. Jesus himself embodied this reality, practiced it, taught it, and invited His followers to do the same—"'As the Father has sent me, so I send you.' When He had said this, He breathed on them and said to them, 'Receive the Holy Spirit.'"[21] Consequently, an authentic Christian spirituality is an incarnated and embodied spirituality that encompasses the whole of life—the individual person, society, politics, environment, soul, mind, heart, body, daily activities… everything, and nothing should be left out of reach. Our prayer and mission should be a comprehensive one. All things belong to the One who created them and saw that they were good.[22]

Christianity is not a system among other systems; it is a way of thinking and living for every system—in its theory and practice—that exists. We should not and we cannot in conscience separate our "faith" from the rest of our "life." Except sin, Jesus embraced all human condition in his person. We should do the same. Everything should be holy and should lead to holiness. Everything belongs. We live one reality made of "heaven" and "earth," "private" and "public," "eternal" and "temporal," "invisible" and "visible," "sacred" and "secular," "faith" and "work." If we want to absolutely maintain the dualistic position on understanding things and live by the dichotomy approach, we knowingly or unknowingly belittle the choice that God has made by taking our human condition and, at the same time, we doubt the ability of Christ to change what He came to change. Doesn't this smell of heresy? The biblical message is different. *All*

---

[20] Genesis (28:16) says: "Surely the Lord is in this place, and [we] did not know it."
[21] John 6:21-22.
[22] See Genesis 1.

that was created before the Fall event was sacred. Then *all* fell. Then *all* is being redeemed. The Incarnation—the direct involvement of God in human history—did it. Therefore, it is imperative to think and live incarnationally. We are now deeply involved. There is no way we can be just neutral. Our faith does not allow it. Our faith is to be lived in all that we do. We have an official mandate and that is to be "salt of the earth"[23] and "light of the world."[24] And this is also how the Word continues to incarnate. God's clear commitment to the world by the Incarnation continues through His presence in us and through us. If we say we love others as He first loved us, then we must incarnate that love among them in the footsteps of the incarnated Son of God in the way He did it. Still, prayer is very important, but a good understanding of prayer must include our involvement in our social order. The grace of God uses our minds, hearts, and hands to make "Thy kingdom come" a reality. This is the ongoing process of God's self-immersion in this world.

The problem of our world today is not that we seem to be too incarnated—materialistic to the extreme. The real problem is that we are not incarnated enough; we don't incarnate the Invisible in the visible. This is the very root-cause of our crises. If we live incarnationally, we show forth God's presence in our lives and actions like Jesus did. Being incarnational is more than being just a "Christian"; it is being "Christ-like."

To such an incarnational spirituality, Teilhard was one of the most passionate heralds, prophets, advocates, and messengers. On this, he may even have passed everyone before him.

In fact, Teilhard sees only one reality—"spirit-matter." He says, for example: "There is neither spirit nor matter in the world; the 'stuff of the universe' is *spirit-matter*."[25] This suggests, in Christian terms, that a true life of holiness consists in a personal relationship with God through matter, "a communion... with God through the world,"[26] and "*It is through the fulfillment of the world* that we reach Christ."[27] No wonder he could even write:

---

[23] Matthew 5:13.
[24] Matthew 5:14.
[25] HE, pp. 57-58 -- VI, p. 74.
[26] CE, p. 93 -- X, p. 111.
[27] WTW, p. 300 -- XII, p. 443. Not far from this kind of reasoning, Raimon Panikkar observed: "... if the mystery of Christ is not our very own, if christophany means no more than the archaeology of the past or the eschatology of the future, it might as well be considered a museum piece. The cry for a new spirituality is a cry of the Spirit which, according to tradition, is the very Spirit of

> Matter, you in whom I find both seduction and strength, you in whom I find blandishment and virility, you who can enrich and destroy, I surrender myself to your mighty layers, with faith in the heavenly influences which have sweetened and purified your waters. The virtue of Christ has passed into you. Let your attractions lead me forward, let your sap be the food that nourishes me; let your resistance give me toughness; let your robberies and inroads give me freedom. And finally, let your whole being lead me towards Godhead.[28]

Teilhard wants to see nature and human endeavor incorporated into the kingdom of God by "christifying"[29] them. This conviction is certain in Teilhard's mind, and he talked about it many times throughout his writings, insisting that "In virtue of the fundamental unity of being in the world, we may already say of every upright man that everything he does on earth is ordered, more or less directly, to the spiritualization of the universe."[30]

Teilhard's approach is about a life-enhancing partnership between the other-worldly spirituality of a former age and this-worldly spirituality of this age. It is about wholeness, integration, and fulfillment. A happy life is a healthy life and a holy life. It entails increasing actualization of all spiritual, emotional, intellectual, and physical potential. It embraces the world the way Christ embraced it. It sees the world as a place where a loving God meets people, a place of grace, and a place where one lives a truly human, authentic, and fulfilled life. It is the eyewitness for, and the hands of, a God-at-work in the world. It is the encounter of the divine in the daily living, right here, right now. It makes visible the realm of the invisible. It is contemplation in action. It is the integration of being and doing into a living reality. It is the reliable path to peace.

Christ himself.... The christophany *from within* which we are timidly suggesting constitutes the deepest interiority of all of us, the abyss in which, in each one of us, there is a meeting between the finite and the infinite, the material and the spiritual, the cosmic and the divine. The christophany of the third millennium is a summons to us to live this experience." (Raimon Panikkar, *Christophany: The Fullness of Man*, trans. by Alfred Dilascia (Maryknoll, N.Y.: Orbis Books, 2004), p.189).

[28] DM, pp. 110-111 -- IV, pp. 128-29.
[29] See HM, p. 47 -- XIII, p. 58; AE, p. 263 -- VII, p. 272.
[30] WTW, p. 258 -- XII, pp. 374-75.

CHAPTER SIX

THE COSMIC IMPORTANCE OF THE INCARNATION

The well-known "Felix culpa" (Happy fault) of St. Augustine of Hippo (354-430) is still reverberating throughout the centuries and it will continue to reverberate as long as there are human beings. St. Augustine and the theologians and philosophers before and after him are almost unanimous in considering that Adam and Eve committed the Original Sin, and that sin was so grave that it necessitated the Incarnation (God becoming a man) and the Redemption (by the brutal suffering of Jesus) so that we can be granted our Salvation. The "Felix culpa" was indeed a "happy fault" because God came and straightened out our sin in the most glorious way.

It is true that the Incarnation is understood as a reaction to a particular event – the Fall of Adam and Eve into sin. But should the Incarnation be understood only as a reaction to the Original Sin, or is there more to the story?

The Incarnation as a Cosmic Event

While the Incarnation clearly has soteriological implications for the salvation of humanity by divine intervention, it is also a cosmic event. Indeed, it is in God's plan to perfect creation and to unite all things in the eternal reality[1] – "a plan for the fullness of time, to gather up all things in him, things in heaven and things on earth,"[2] as St. Paul wrote. More than

---

[1] Sister Maria Gratia Martin commented: « By His Incarnation, therefore, Christ becomes the organic or physical Center of the universe in the sense that the universe even on the natural level is dependent on Him for fulfillment and for the energies by which it progresses toward that fulfillment." See Sister Maria Gratia Martin, I.H.M., *The Spirituality of Teilhard de Chardin* (New York, NY: Newman Press, 1968), p. 62.
[2] Ephesians 1:10.

any other theology, the Eastern theology seems to develop this conviction. For example, St. Maximus the Confessor did not hesitate to say:

> After the transgression [of the divine will] one can no more explain the end by the beginning, but only the beginning by the end.
> ... man could not know his origin which was behind him. He thus tried to know his end which lay in front of him. In this way he might learn to know through the end that beginning which he had broken with, since he did not know the end through the beginning.
> ... in uniting Himself with every man, in a manner known by Him alone, God awakes in man the sensibility which corresponds to the degree of his preparedness to receive Him, who at the end of time will be all in all.[3]

Such a theology is teaching us that Christ is not only related to the beginning of the universe, but also to its end and purpose. From this point of view, it becomes imperative to consider the Incarnation from its broader implications that include its teleological[4] meaning. Still, forgiveness of sin and salvation are a central part of the Incarnation, but it is more than that. The Incarnation is no longer simply a reaction to the Fall of humanity,[5] but

---

[3] Quoted by Lars Thunberg in *Man and the Cosmos: The Vision of St. Maximus the Confessor*, (Crestwood, NY: St. Vladimir's Seminary Press, 1985), pp. 69, 68. Moreover, Archpriest G. Florovsky wrote: "St. Maximus the Confessor (580-662) seems to be the only Father who was directly concerned with the problem, although not in the same setting as the later theologians in the West. He stated plainly that the Incarnation should be regarded as an absolute and primary purpose of God in the act of Creation. The nature of the Incarnation, of this union of the Divine majesty with human frailty, is indeed an unfathomable mystery, but we can at least grasp the reason and the purpose of this supreme mystery, its logos and skopos. And this original reason, or the ultimate purpose, was, in the opinion of St. Maximus, precisely the Incarnation itself and then our own incorporation into the Body of the Incarnate One. The phrasing of St. Maximus is straight and clear. The 60th questio ad Thalassium, is a commentary on I Peter, 1:19-20: "[Christ was] like a blameless and spotless lamb, who was foreordained from the foundation of the world." (See: http://www.freerepublic.com/focus/religion/1866256/posts).

[4] Teleology, (from Greek *telos*, "end," and *logos*, "reason"), explanation by reference to some purpose, end, goal, or function. Traditionally, it was also described as final causality, in contrast with explanation solely in terms of efficient causes (the origin of a change or a state of rest in something). (http://www.britannica.com/topic/teleology).

[5] Sœur Ina Bergeron and Anne-Marie Ernst observed : « Si l'Incarnation/Création se presentent aux yeux de Teilhard comme deux aspects d'un seul acte, elles en appellent un troisième : la Redemption. Pour Dieu 'créer, c'est unir', et 's'unir la création en Omega-Christ'. Se profile alors un point plus délicat : le mal 'dont

it is its destiny as well. Understood this way, the Incarnation becomes also a necessity that allows us to appreciate the full scope of God's redemptive plan. Professor Peter Kreeft helps us to understand this point. He says:

> Jesus is not merely the universe's savior; He is the universe's purpose. The Incarnation was not a last-minute fix-it operation. And it was not undone in the Ascension. He is still incarnate, still with us. He is with us in different ways. He is with us through the material things, for He created them and He sanctified all matter by incarnating Himself in matter.[6]

We can therefore say that the Incarnation was not an isolated and one-time event. It was and still is an ongoing process that is carried out by each human being.

"The Unceasing Operation of the Incarnation"[7]

For Teilhard de Chardin, the divine Omega was the ultimate source of being, and being cannot be without origin and without purpose. From both ends – the beginning and the purpose or the goal – the Christ Omega was visibly manifested, by uniting divinity and humanity, in the Incarnation. For Teilhard, "And the Word became flesh and lived among us"[8] was summarized and realized in the body-person of Jesus of Nazareth who is the physical-personal Center for all that exists. Then, Teilhard employed passages from St. John and St. Paul to support his idea of Christ as the

---

l'ampleur même nous transcende', écrit Teilhard. Concomitante à l'acte créateur et raison d'être du créé, l'incarnation ne peut plus apparaître comme la conséquence d'une faute originelle, exigeant passion et mort sur la croix ; mais passion et mort sur la croix deviennent les conséquences de l'incarnation. Changement de perspective dans le respect du dogme et les événements de l'histoire. » See Sœur Ina Bergeron and Anne-Marie Erns*t, Le Christ Universel et l'Evolution* (Paris : Les Editions du Cerf, 1986), p. 77.

[6] See http://thechristianwatershed.com/2014/03/16/the-cosmic-importance-of-the-incarnation/ - Here also we find a quotation from St. Maximus the Confessor that says: "Because of Christ–or rather, the whole mystery of Christ [i.e., the Incarnation]–all the ages of time and the beings within those ages have received their beginning and end in Christ. For the union between a limit of the ages and limitlessness, between measure and immeasurability, between finitude and infinity, between Creator and creation, between rest and motion, was conceived before the ages. This union has been manifested in Christ at the end of time, and in itself brings God's foreknowledge to fulfillment . . ."

[7] MD, p. 62 -- IV, p. 51.
[8] John 1:14.

Center and as cosmic Christ. For example: "all things came into being through him, and without him not one thing came into being"[9]; "He himself is before all things, and in him all things hold together"[10]; "For in him the whole fullness of deity dwells bodily, and you have come to fullness in him"[11]; "Christ is all in all."[12] This means, for Teilhard, that "Both in nature and in function, Christ gathers up in himself and consummates the totality and the fullness of humanity"[13] and

> (...) through the unceasing operation of the Incarnation, the divine so thoroughly permeates all our creaturely energies that, in order to meet it and lay hold on it, we could not find a more fitting setting than that of our action.[14]

This also means that Christ, as personal Center, activates the whole cosmos and creation to the greatest possible consciousness, and He awakens men and women to their responsibilities and active role in the evolution, drawing them to the highest degree of sanctity and the deepest union with Him. "Everything that is good in the universe (that is, everything that goes towards unification through effort) is gathered up by the Incarnate Word as a nourishment that it assimilates, transforms and divinises."[15] This is the "Super-Christ"[16] who leads to "Super-humanity."[17]

---

[9] John 1:3.
[10] Colossians 1:17.
[11] Colossians 2:9-10.
[12] Colossians 3:11.
[13] SC, p. 164 -- IX, p. 209. Teilhard also wrote : "The man who habitually lives in the society of the elements of this world, who personally experiences the overwhelming immensity of things and their wretched dissociation, that man, I am certain, becomes more acutely conscious than anyone of the tremendous need for unity that continually drives the universe further ahead, and of the fantastic future that awaits it. No one understands so fully as the man who is absorbed in the study of matter, to what a degree Christ, through his Incarnation, is interior to the world, rooted in the world even in the heart of the tiniest atom." (SC, p. 36 -- IX, p. 62).
[14] MD, p. 62 -- IV, p. 51.
[15] SC, p. 59 -- IX, p. 88. In footnote, Teilhard added: "In short, Christ, understood in this sense, is the milieu in which and through which the (abstract) attribute of the *divine immensity* is concretely realised for us."
[16] Teilhard explains: "By Super-Christ I most certainly do not mean *another* Christ, a second Christ different from and greater than the first. I mean *the same* Christ, the Christ of all time, revealing himself to us in a form and in dimensions, with an urgency and area of contact, that are enlarged and given new force. We can readily appreciate that the appearance in Christian consciousness of a Christ so

This is also what divinization is about, since we are "participants of the divine nature,"[18] as St. Peter said, and since the psalmist said it too, "I say, 'you are gods, children of the Most High.'"[19]

If the word "divinization" that is very dear to Teilhard seems to be more or less absent in modern theological writings, it had, nevertheless, a long and rich history in the early centuries of the Church, especially with the Greek Fathers. For St. Basil the Great, for example, a human being has received the order to become god, and for St. Athanasius, God became a human being so that that the human being becomes god. The early Fathers created a special tern for this. They called it *theosis* or "deification," or "divinization" – the term used by Teilhard. Needless to say that Teilhard was very comfortable with this kind of theology and way of thinking. Indeed, the Greek Fathers were famously known for seeing in the Incarnation not only the redemption of the human race, but also the broader gift of God to humankind—the gift of deification. Saint Maximus the Confessor goes as far as to see deification as the consequence, if not even the purpose, of the Incarnation.

These great early Fathers based their teachings mainly on three premises: The creation of humankind in the image of God, the Incarnation of the Word of God, and the indwelling Holy Trinity's strength in the soul.

Humankind's supreme destiny—being in the image of God that was restored by the Incarnation—was made possible again by the gift of the Holy Spirit, who exists and operates in the Church, in the soul of every faithful person, and in all things. For, as Saint Maximus the Confessor believes, the divine "Logos" wishes to effect the mystery of His incarnation always, and in all things.

The deification the Fathers are talking about is not the result of a mechanical commutation of humanity, but a profound ontological regeneration of our human nature that happened by, and through, the hypostasis of the incarnate "Logos" of God, and continues to happen when we truly live "in Christ." And, as Thomas Merton explains,

> To live "in Christ" is to live in a mystery equal to that of the Incarnation and similar to it. For as Christ unites in His one Person the two natures of God and of man, so too in making us His friends He dwells in us, uniting us intimately to Himself…. A "new being" is brought into existence. I

---

magnified will immediately result in the appearance in human consciousness of Super-humanity" (SC, p. 164 IX, pp. 208-9).

[17] Ibid.
[18] 2 Peter 1:4.
[19] Psalm 82:6; see also John 10:34.

become a "new man" and this new man, spiritually and mystically one identity, is at once Christ and myself.... The union of the Christian with Christ is not just a similarity of inclination and feeling, a mutual consent of minds and wills. It has a more radical, more mysterious and supernatural quality: it is a mystical union in which Christ Himself becomes the source and principle of divine life in me.[20]

This is, in essence, what *Theosis* or deification is about. Teilhard called it "divinization" and/or "Christification."

Saint Paul insists much on "Christification." In his letter to the Colossians, for example, he wrote: "He is the image of the invisible God, the firstborn of all creation. For in him all things in heaven and on earth were created, things visible and invisible, whether thrones or dominions or rulers or powers—all things have been created through him and for him. He himself is before all things, and in him all things hold together."[21] Then, he called everyone to become "mature in Christ,"[22] to acquire "the mind of Christ,"[23] "until all of us come...to maturity, to the measure of the full stature of Christ,"[24] and until one can truly say, "It is no longer I who live, but it is Christ who lives in me."[25] Thomas Merton has an interesting explanation of this line of Saint Paul. He wrote:

> Christ living in me is at the same time Himself and myself. From the moment that I am united to Him "in one spirit" there is no longer any contradiction implied by the fact that we are different persons.... This union is not merely a moral union, or an agreement of wills, nor merely a psychological union which flows from that fact that I keep Him in my thoughts. Christ mystically identifies His members with Himself by giving them His Holy Spirit.[26]

When Saint Paul uses such a direct, strong language, he is not talking about some external behavior, or ethical improvement, or pious sentiments. He speaks about an ontological transformation of self by becoming Christ—being "Christified"—for the faithful "have come to

---

[20] Thomas Merton, *New Seeds of Contemplation*, (New York, N.Y.: New Directions Books, 1961), pp. 158-59.
[21] Colossians 1:15-17.
[22] Colossians 1:28.
[23] 1 Corinthians 2:16.
[24] Ephesians 4:13.
[25] Galatians 3:20.
[26] Thomas Merton, *The New Man*, (New York, N.Y.: The Noonday Press, a division of Farrar, Straus and Giroux, 1961) pp. 168-69.

fullness in him"[27] and "in him all things hold together."[28]

This is also how history is seen. Indeed, history is much more than a biological, dialectical, or societal process. Since the ontological origin of humankind is being in Christ and in the realization of being in Christ is the journey from the "in the image" to the original source, history, then, should be understood as the development of humanity—and the whole creation for that matter—toward divinity. This operation is mainly inwardly, effectuated by God's grace. Saint Gregory of Nyssa wrote:

> For this is the safest way to protect the good things you enjoy: by realizing how much your Creator has honored you above all other creatures. He did not make the heavens in His image, nor the moon, the sun, the beauty of the stars, nor anything else which surpasses all understanding. You alone are a similitude of eternal Beauty, and if you look at Him, you will become what He is, imitating Him who shines within you, whose glory is reflected in your purity. Nothing in all creation can equal your grandeur. All the heavens can fit in the palm of God's hand... and though He is so great... you can wholly embrace him. He dwells within you... He pervades your entire being.[29]

Therefore, having been made "in the image of God,"[30] humankind has profound theological roots and structures that explain why a true understanding of a human being must be related to this very theocentric origin. Again, Thomas Merton has an interesting line here. He wrote: "If my true spiritual identity is found in my identification with Christ, then to know myself fully, I must know Christ. And to know Christ I must know

---

[27] Colossians 2:10.
[28] Colossians 1:17.
[29] Quoted by Archbishop Cyril Salim Bustros in "Characteristics of Byzantine Spirituality," Sophia, Fall 2006, p. 24.
[30] St. Gregory of Nyssa says: "... I think that the entire plenitude of humanity was included by the God of all, by His power of foreknowledge, as it were in one body, and that this is what the text teaches us which says, 'God created man, in the image of God created He him.' For the image is not in part of our nature, nor is the grace in any one of the things found in that nature, but this power extends equally to all the race; and a sign of this is that mind is implanted alike in all. For all have the power of understanding and deliberating and of all else whereby the Divine nature finds its image in that which was made according to it. The man that was manifested at the first creation of the world and he that shall be after the consummation of all, are alike; they equally bear in themselves the Divine image." [See *The Cosmic Christ: From Paul to Teilhard*, by George A. Maloney, S.J., (New York: Sheed and Ward, Inc., 1968), p. 269.]

the Father, for Christ is the Image of the Father."[31] In this context, living according to God allows a person to reach out into infinity—deification. Living as if God does not exist is intrinsically a denial and a destruction of oneself.

Humanity and the entire universe become the ultimate sacrament that God uses to convey His grace in a process of deification—an unceasing Incarnation. In the process of our deification, nothing is left behind. Nothing of what makes us human is denied, despised, lost, or ignored. God transforms everything. God is not a static and fixed statement in the book; God continues to reveal Himself in the structures of human life. God continues to incarnate so that we are able to continue to "become participants of the divine nature."[32] Teilhard would say:

> Little by little, stage by stage, everything is finally linked to the supreme centre *in quo omnia constant*. The streams which flow from this centre operate not only within the higher reaches of the world, where human activities take place in a distinctively supernatural and meritorious form. In order to save and establish these sublime forces, the power of the Word Incarnate penetrates matter itself; it goes down into the deepest depths of the lower forces. And the Incarnation will be complete only when the part of chosen substance contained in every object – given spiritual import once in our souls and a second time with our souls in Jesus – shall have rejoined the final centre of its completion. *Quid est quod ascendit, nisi quod prius descendit, ut repleret omnia?*[33]

The Continuous "Good News" of the Incarnation

For Teilhard, the Incarnation has changed everything, and forever. We should no longer think, live, and act as if the Incarnation never happened. The Incarnation is the "Good News" of change and restoration. Teilhard wrote:

> The Incarnation is a making new, a restoration, of *all* the universe's forces and powers; Christ is the Instrument, the Centre, the End, of the *whole* of animate and material creation; Through Him, *everything* is created, sanctified, and vivified. This is the constant and general teaching of St John and St Paul (that most 'cosmic' of sacred writers), and it has passed

---

[31] Thomas Merton, *The New Man*, (New York, N.Y.: The Noonday Press, a division of Farrar, Straus and Giroux, 1961), p. 170.
[32] 2 Peter 1:4.
[33] DM, pp. 61-2 -- IV, pp. 49-50.

into the most solemn formulas of the Liturgy: and yet we repeat it, and generations to come will go on repeating it, without ever being able to grasp or appreciate its profound and mysterious significance, bound up as it is with understanding of the universe.[34]

He also wrote:

(...) by virtue of the Creation and, still more, of the Incarnation, *nothing* here below *is profane* for those who know how to see. On the contrary, everything is sacred to the men who can distinguish that portion of chosen being which is subject to Christ's drawing power in the process of consummation.[35]

However, the "Good News" of the Incarnation was not easy to swallow – at least the way it happened. The same difficulty still exists for the people of today. Yes, at Christmas, we go to church, we celebrate, we decorate, we put lights everywhere, we make sure to have the tree, the gifts, and the appropriate foods and most fitting clothes, but we often forget Christ who is the "reason for the Season," as it is often said. Why? Because soon after the angel announced to the shepherds, "I am bringing you good news of great joy for all the people: to you is born this day in the city of David a Savior, who is the Messiah, the Lord,"[36] life on earth took a new turn; reality became more complicated and still is more than ever.

In fact, the "good news" was not easy to accept and to digest. In one way or another people throughout the centuries until this very day had great difficulty with understanding the mystery of the Incarnation; either Jesus was divine or human, but not both/and at the same time. The "fully divine and fully human" notion was not conceivable; since matter was considered as evil, how could the Son of God have a body? Furthermore, if God could not be depicted, and if the name of Yahweh could not even be pronounced, as was often the case in the Old Testament—then how could God incarnate in a body that could be seen with physical eyes?

So, the Incarnation was a scandal for the Jews, a foolish thing for the Greeks, and a real problem for the followers of Ebionism, Manicheism, Arianism, Nestorianism, Monophysitism, Docetism, Monothelitism, Apollinarianism, Adoptionism, Gnosticism, and other schools of thought and movements. Salvation, in such contexts, should have been the result of some kind of "dis-incarnation," rather than of incarnation.

---

[34] WTW, p. 58 -- XII, p. 68.
[35] MD, p. 66 -- IV, p. 56.
[36] Luke 2:10-11.

But, the fact is that in the lowly stable of Bethlehem, God, who before had been only heard of, feared, and talked about, could now be seen, touched, and loved as a baby. Jesus was under the care of His mother, Mary, and her husband, Joseph. He became approachable, accessible, available, vulnerable, lovable, and touchable.

Instead of welcoming the "good news" about Jesus' birth, many people were rather bothered by a God who became "living flesh," because it seemed that people could deal more easily with a distant God and unseen realities. In fact, they could handle principles, dogmas, systems, and ideas more easily than handle God as a living person. What was God doing in Jesus, the little baby, born in Bethlehem?

However, no matter how logical and plausible they are, impersonal ideas that are vague, general, and simply academic can never replace the irresistible force of the one who said, "And I, when I am lifted up from the earth, will draw all people to myself."[37] No wonder one could shout with François Mauriac, "Once you get to know Christ, you cannot be cured of him."

God is not an abstract concept—this would have been easy to handle. But God, as Christ in our daily life and in everyone we meet, is challenging to our lives. No philosophy, not even theology, constitutes a threat until we live it.

If God became fully human, the followers of Christ must embrace His way and become fully human as He was. They must embrace His Church despite its human brokenness, weakness, and sin. In following Christ, they need to learn how to love their neighbors[38] and their enemies,[39] and forgive seventy times seven times.[40] Pope Benedict XVI wrote: "Love of God and love of neighbour have become one: in the least of the brethren we find Jesus himself, and in Jesus we find God."[41] This is how we celebrate the birth of Christ all over again.

Christmas did not happen only once some two thousand years ago, but it is an everyday event—a continuous Christmas that happens again and again.[42] Every time we "incarnate" what Jesus told us to do, it is Christmas.

---

[37] John 12:32.
[38] See Matthew 5:34.
[39] See Luke 6:27.
[40] See Matthew 18:22.
[41] http://w2.vatican.va/content/benedict-xvi/en/encyclicals/documents/hf_ben-xvi_enc_20051225_deus-caritas-est.html, Pope Benedict XVI, Encyclical Letter *Deus Caritas Est,* No.15, (25 December, 2005).
[42] Teilhard wrote: "Christmas, which might have been thought to turn our gaze towards the past, has only fixed it further in the future. The Messiah, who appeared

Every time we stir more love in others, it is Christmas. Every time we let the Holy Spirit be active in our lives as well as in the lives of others, it is Christmas. Christmas is a continuous celebration—the very soul of Christmas decorations and the very joy of those who delight in decorating. Christmas is the meaning of all things. Christmas is eternal; its eternity should be measured not by time, but by meaning and intensity of being. God has always been with us waiting for our consent, like Mary, to be born in the manger of our soul.

Christmas is this vulnerable baby in the stable. Christmas is this innocent child, this blooming flower, this beautiful mountain. Christmas is a loaf of bread when we are hungry, a cup of water when we are thirsty, a doctor and a nurse when we are sick, a harbor when a storm strikes. Christmas is our loving fathers, mothers, brothers, sisters, friends, leaders, guides, teachers, comforters, burden-bearers, and our heart-fixers. Christmas is our lawyers and judges who know how to work for justice and fairness. Christmas is our priests who are always ready to serve. Christmas is each and every one of them, right here, right now. "In Jesus' birth," wrote Ronald Rolheiser, "something fundamental has changed. God has given us the power, literally, to keep each other out of hell."[43] We are "part of God's ongoing incarnation," continued Rolheiser, "... The word has started to become flesh and it needs to continue to take flesh in that God must now be transubstantiated not only into the bread of the Eucharist but, even more important, into human faces."[44]

---

for a moment in our midst, only allowed himself to be seen and touched for a moment before vanishing once again, more luminous and ineffable than ever, into the depths of the future. He came. Yet now we must expect him–no longer a small chosen group among us, but all men—once again and more than ever. The Lord Jesus will only come soon if we ardently expect him. It is an accumulation of desires that should cause the Pleroma to burst upon us" (MD, p. 151 -- IV, p. 197). Then recognizing the reality of things, Teilhard complained: "We persist in saying that we keep vigil in expectation of the Master. But in reality we should have to admit, if we were sincere, *that we no longer expect anything*" (MD, p. 152 -- IV, p. 198).

[43] Ronald Rolheiser, *The Holy Longing: The Search for a Christian Spirituality*, (New York, NY: Doubleday, a division of Random House, Inc., 1999), p. 92.

[44] Ibid., p. 70, 103. Rolheiser wrote also in this same book, *The Holy Longing*: "If God is incarnate in ordinary life then we should seek God, first of all, within ordinary life. Too often, even though we know this theoretically, practically we still look for God in the extraordinary.... The task of taking God to others is not that of handing somebody a Bible or some religious literature, but of transubstantiating God, the way we do with the food we eat. We have to digest something and turn it, physically, into the flesh or our own bodies so it becomes

God is not just "out there." God is "in here." God is everywhere. God has never been absent; God was unrecognized. The Word of God made flesh corrects this shortsighted and deformed vision of ours by making us see God in all aspects of our lives. Salvation neither excludes anyone nor any dimension of life—be it psychological, social, political, economic, cultural, physical, or any other. Salvation is not the result of "disincarnation," but of incarnation. When we follow Christ, we do not follow just a character from past history; we follow the living Christ who is in us, with us, among us, and who is the very life of our lives. Our religious and ethical behaviors, then, cannot be measured by their conformity to merely theoretical opinions, but by their transcendent and immanent dimensions found in the "good news" brought by the Incarnation. We want religious meaning more than religious magic, connections more than politically correct answers, and wonder and awe more than predetermined conclusions.

Even though it is exciting to realize that the living God—the most magnetic guiding force there is—is in our midst here and now, it is also scary because this means that we cannot stay the same. We have to change and things have to change. Jesus, the New Adam, has inaugurated the new creation. We are supposed to be this new creation. The incarnated Christ is the very soul of the newness and change.

Christ is the meaning of all reality—the reality of how to be human included. Indeed Christianity is not opposed to humanity; it is the perfection of humanity by realizing that we are God's children. Then we would know what is relevant and what is irrelevant in our human life. Thomas Merton put it beautifully this way: "If Christ is the revelation of the whole meaning of man, if this meaning of man's life is solely and entirely to be found in the fact that *man is a child of God*, then everything in my life becomes relevant or irrelevant in proportion as it tends to my growth as a member of Christ, as a child of God, and to the extension of Christ in the world of man through his Church."[45]

If we strip down the traditional poetry, imagery, magic, decorations, and all the stories wrapped around Christmas, we will get to the essential and incredible reality of the mystery itself. The Incarnation is the end of the dichotomous dualism. Jesus, the God-Man is the new reality. He leads us to the deeper unity behind all appearances of what is related to

---

part of what we look like. If we would do this with the word of God, others would not have to read the Bible to see what God is like, they would need only to look at our faces and our lives to see God." (Pp. 100, 102).

[45] Thomas Merton, *Love and Living*, Edited by Naomi Burton Stone & Brother Patrick Hart, (New York: A Harvest/HBJ Book, Harcourt Brace Jovanovich, Publishers, 1985), p. 231.

self/others, spirit/matter, contemplation/action, Christ/neighbor, and spiritual life and ordinary life. The foundational reality of everything is God; not a God-concept, hypothetical and imagined, but a God who has a human face—a "God-with-us."

The early Fathers of the Church believed that God became human, so that humans could become god. For Saint Augustine, we became partakers of God's divinity, and for Saint Thomas Aquinas, we became the children of God.

What a responsibility! With the Incarnation at the center, human nature took on such dignity that it was possible for God to act through it; thus our unlimited potential. At the meeting point of "fully divine and fully human," nothing would seem impossible. Only the encounter with Christ can solve the problem of finite and infinite, limited and unlimited, and transient and eternal.

By becoming more divine we become more human. Also, if we are not divinized enough, chances are that we will become less human because our unlimited potential remains unrealized. "The truth is," declared the Second Vatican Council, "that only in the mystery of the incarnated Word does the mystery of man take on light,"[46] and it is the role of the Church, the body of Christ, to continue the enfleshment of the Word—enfleshment that is by its very nature perpetual, progressive, and universal—into the farthest reaches of the world and until the end of time. Jesus promised: "Remember, I am with you always, to the end of the age."[47]

Over two thousand years ago, the mystery of Jesus' birth radically changed the order of things, and an overturning of false values and ways of thinking should have happened—but on many occasions, then and now, it didn't. The critical question is this: Do we live our lives as if the first Christmas never happened?

The birth of Christ is our birth to a new way of thinking and living—the way of Christ who "is the same yesterday and today and forever"[48]; Christ is the cosmic Christ, as Teilhard saw, and he is "the term of even the natural evolution of living beings." Teilhard explained:

> And since Christ was born, and ceased to grow, and died, *everything has continued in motion because he has not yet attained the fullness of his form.* He has not gathered about Him the last folds of the garment of flesh

---

[46] http://www.vatican.va/archive/hist_councils/ii_vatican_council/documents/vat-ii_const_19651207_gaudium-et-spes_en.html - Pastoral Constitution on the Church in the Modern World (December 7, 1965), *Gaudium et Spes*, Chap. 1, No. 22.
[47] Matthew 28:20.
[48] Hebrews 13:8.

and love woven for him by his faithful. *The mystical Christ has not reached the peak of his growth – nor, therefore, has the cosmic Christ.* Of both we may say that *they are* and at the same time *are becoming*: and it is in the continuation of this engendering that there lies the ultimate driving force behind all created activity. By the Incarnation, which redeemed man, the very Becoming of the Universe, too, has been transformed. Christ is the term *of even the natural* evolution of living beings;[49] evolution is holy. There we have *the truth that makes free*, the divinely prepared cure for faithful but ardently moved minds that suffer because they cannot reconcile in themselves two almost equally imperative and vital impulses, faith in the world and faith in God.[50]

Teilhard de Chardin can be called the apostle of the Incarnate God who is in the work of evolving our world, our human family, and our individual and collective consciousness. Indeed, not only "The heavens are telling the glory of God,"[51] but we should do the same by living lives that are deepening and "completing" the Incarnation of God. The human person is and should be considered, as he or she truly is, the meeting place of heaven and earth. Our destinies and the destinies of the world and all that the world contains are so wrapped together that we will live together or we will die together. But no, we cannot die, promised Teilhard. We are living the mystery of the Incarnated God who will pull everything to him in the Christ Omega.

---

[49] The footnote says: "Once the universe (nature) is an evolution, we may say with regard to evolution what St. Thomas, speaking of the supernatural, said with regard to nature: *Non est aliquid naturae, sed naturae finis* – it is not something that belongs to nature, but nature's (final) end. (WTW, p. 59 -- XII, p. 69.)
[50] WTW, p. 59 -- XII, p. 69.
[51] Psalm 19:1.

CHAPTER SEVEN

THE DIVINE MILIEU: OUR HOME

Teilhard de Chardin wrote a book called *The Divine Milieu*. Although it was written during the years of 1926-1927, it was not officially published until 1957. This book became one of the 20th century's greatest books of spirituality, and because of its deep influence on our understanding of our relationships with God and the world, we can now say that it became a spiritual classic.[1]

The word "milieu" suggests words like "environment," "surroundings," "atmosphere," "context," "ambiance," and especially center or "Centre," as Teilhard used it. As the Centre, this milieu has "the absolute and final power to unite (and consequently to complete) all beings within its breasts. In the divine *milieu*, all the elements of the universe *touch each other* by that which is most inward and ultimate in them,"[2] creating "an atmosphere ever more luminous and ever more changed with God. It is in him and in him alone that the reckless vow of all love is realized: to lose oneself in what one loves, to sink oneself in it more and more."[3] "Diaphany" – from its Greek roots "to appear through" – would mean the appearing, or the transparency, of God in and through the universe that is illuminated from within by the light of Christ. When we have the right eyes to see, we will see Christ shining in a diaphany, through the cosmos and in matter. The presence of Christ in the world is not static but dynamic and transforming. He is not just a passive point of convergence, but a driving force that leads matter to its evolutionary destination in the process of Christogenesis.

---

[1] See Jean Maalouf, *The Divine Milieu: A Spiritual Classic for Today and Tomorrow*, (American Teilhard Association for the Future of Man, Inc., "Teilhard Studies" Number 38, Autumn 1999). See also: Louis M. Savary, *Teilhard de Chardin The Divine Milieu Explained: A Spirituality for the 21st Century*, (Mahwah, New Jersey: Paulist Press, 2007).
[2] MD, p. 114 -- IV, p. 137.
[3] MD, p. 132 -- IV, p. 165.

Christ in all things and all things in Christ

To see Christ in all things is to recognize Christ as the divine element, the core, the heart, and the center of every particle.[4] Christ is present in every potentiality, in every growth, in every evolution toward the fullness of life which is the fullness of Christ himself, "the way, and the truth, and the life."[5] Filled with the "Cosmic Christ"[6] – "Christ the Evolver,"[7] "the Omega or energizing focal point of the process,"[8] as Ewert H. Cousins would say – all matter becomes a dynamic energy, full of promise and potential. On the same wavelength, Thomas Merton had this comment: "Christ, in Teilhard de Chardin, is not merely the Risen Lord dwelling in heaven, he is also above all the Mystical Christ, living and working in mankind."[9] This suggests that Christ must have been working and will continue to work with us and through us. "What a serious responsibility for Christians," wrote George A. Maloney, "to take the lead in all fields of human endeavors, knowing with certainty of God's revelation in Christ Jesus through His Body, the Church, that the world is already 'Christic.' Yet we are called to fashion the universe still more into the total cosmic

---

[4] Henri de Lubac wrote: « To the believer who lives by his faith, this world is not one-dimensional. It has a mysterious background. It is not opaque, but ever increasingly transparent.... Everything in this world, things and events, and human relationships, had for père Teilhard a sacramental character. When some years later he was thinking of treating the subject of *Le Milieu Divin* with a slightly different emphasis, he proposed ... to give the new essay the title 'Sacrament of the World'" See Henri de Lubac, S.J., *The Religion of Teilhard de Chardin* (Garden City, N.Y: Image Books, a Division of Doubleday & Company, Inc., 1968), pp. 35-36.
[5] John 14:6.
[6] WTW, p. 57 -- XII, p. 67.
[7] SC, p. 165 -- IX, p. 210.
[8] Ewert H. Cousins wrote: "Pierre Teilhard de Chardin reflects the revolution in biology effected by Darwin's theory of evolution. A paleontologist who spent many years on field trips in the Orient, Teilhard developed a worldview that made evolution central. From the atom to man, the entire universe is evolving toward increased consciousness. By reading the past, we can discern the direction of evolution and obtain guidelines for the creative action toward building the future. Teilhard interpreted the Christian message in terms of evolution and saw Christ as the Omega or energizing focal point of the process." 'Introduction' in *Hope and the Future of Man*, edited by Ewert H. Cousins, (Philadelphia: Fortress Press, 1973, p. IX).
[9] Thomas Merton, *Love and Living*, (New York: Harcourt Brace Jovanovich, 1985, p. 176).

Christ."[10] The truth is that when we see all things in Christ we can see Christ in all things. Then, we become participants in the mystery of Christ. Unlike some spiritual writers who recommend a partial or even a total withdrawal from the world, Teilhard, who sees Christ in all things, recommends a total participation in everyday tasks. Everyone is responsible for the progress of a universe united in Christ.

Our communion with God's will, which is also our participation in the fullness of the mystery of Christ and our participation in the divine plan for the world, leads to the conviction that the everyday activity of life has great value, and nothing can be totally profane.[11] The followers of Christ's mission is to divinize the world in Christ, that is, to unify all things in themselves and to unify themselves with Christ. Their lives cannot be a passive resignation, or a fearful denial, or an indifferent withdrawal, or an awkward escape. Their lives are supposed to be an active conformation to the Incarnated Christ who, crucified and resurrected, remains with us in the Eucharist and in the Spirit, and who, through us, continues to work in the world. He is not only the starting point but also the final point – the point of attraction and the final achievement. The risen Christ, for Teilhard, draws the entire world to Himself as an extension and continuation of the mission of the historical Jesus but under another mode of presence. Teilhard wrote:

> The mystical Christ, the universal Christ of St. Paul, has neither meaning nor value in our eyes except as an expansion of the Christ who was born of Mary and who died on the cross. The former essentially draws his fundamental quality of undeniability and concreteness from the latter. However far we may be drawn into the divine spaces opened up to us by Christian mysticism, we never depart from the Jesus of the Gospels. On the contrary, we feel a growing need to enfold ourselves ever more firmly within his human truth.[12]

The mystical body of Christ is a physical reality. Physical here does not refer to dead matter in the sense of materialist, but to an ontological and alive reality. It reflects the sense of "life" as used by St. John[13] and which St. Paul implied when characterizing the Church as the Body of

---

[10] George A. Maloney, S.J., *Mysticism and the New Age*, (New York: Alba House, 1991, p. 120).
[11] See MD, p. 66 -- IV, p. 56.
[12] MD, p. 117 -- IV, p. 141.
[13] See John 1:4; 10:10; 6:33, 63.

Christ.[14] In his book, *Teilhard de Chardin*, Thomas M. King, S.J, explained:

> Teilhard would insist on speaking on the physical presence of God in the world, and he would tell of this God in terms of radiation, force, gravity and tangibility. He acknowledged that many people would not find this language acceptable, but it was the language of experience and the only language in which he could feel at home.[15]

It is within the context of the Divine Milieu, the Body of Christ, that God in Christ acts upon the evolution, transformation, and unification of all things. This is a project of the here and now. Pope Francis said it so well when he stated, "The Lord Jesus is not only the destination point of our earthly pilgrimage, but also a constant presence in our lives. That's why when we speak of the future and project ourselves toward it, it is always to lead us back to the present."[16]

We often talk about the Parousia[17] to mean the second coming of Christ or to the judgment that is the final episode of the cycles of generations and civilizations wherein human beings have the chance to work for their salvation. For Teilhard, the Parousia means a final step of growth and a pinnacle of unification that is the ultimate point of convergence – the "Omega Point." It is Christ who, through evolution and history, leads this growth of the world toward unity.[18] Teilhard saw Christ in and via the mechanism of evolution as the guiding influence over the cosmos. Christ is the world Omega point: its plan, fulfillment, and final end.

Teilhard's vision was rooted in, and centered on, Christ. At the same time, however, being in Christ is not different from being in the world. "The world," as Professor Ian G. Barbour wrote, "converges to a spiritual

---

[14] See Ephesians 4:11-12; 5:33; Colossians 1:18.
[15] Thomas M. King, S.J., *Teilhard de Chardin*, (Wilmington, DE: Michael Glazier, 1988, p. 48).
[16] Pope Francis, Angelus Address, Rome, November 15, 2015.
[17] The word "Parousia" was used many times in the New Testament to mean the "bodily presence" (for example, 2 Corinthians 10:10), the coming of the blameless one (for example, 1 Thessalonians 2:9), and the Second Coming of Christ and the coming of the "Day of the God" (for example, 2 Peter 3:12). See also Matthew 24:3, 27, 37, 39; 1 Corinthians 15:23; 1 Thessalonians 2:19; 3:13; 4:15; 5:23; 2 Thessalonians 2:1, 8, 9; James 5:7, 8; 2 Peter 1:16; 3:4,12; 1 John 2:28. Therefore, this word is not limited to the final return of Christ.
[18] See DM, pp. 110, 124, 150-155 – IV, pp. 12-128, 151-152, 195-202.

union with God in Christ, whose relation to the world is organic and not merely juridical and extrinsic."[19] Also Professor Ewert H. Cousins noted:

> The cosmic presence of Christ in the world is not static, merely an object of detached contemplation. On the contrary, the cosmic Christ is dynamic, drawing all individuals and the universe as a whole to a creative unity. It is here that Teilhard's vision reveals its distinctive features. He attempts to reformulate Christian belief within an evolving world. He was thoroughly convinced that this was the paramount theological task of our time.[20]

"Communion with God through earth"

Teilhard started his essay, "Cosmic Life," with this line: "There is a communion with God, and a communion with earth, and a communion with God through earth."[21] Then, in the last page of this essay, he wrote: "Lord Jesus, you are the centre towards which all things are moving: if it be possible, make a place for us all in the company of those elect and holy ones whom your loving care has liberated one by one from the chaos of our present existence and who now are being slowly incorporated into you in the unity of the new earth."[22]

These lines, written by Teilhard in 1916 – early in his life and career as a writer – can be considered as a prelude to *The Divine Milieu*, written about ten years later, and also to the largest part of his other writings.

Teilhard never compromised in his passion for God or in his passion for the world. He never found himself compelled to choose either God or the world.[23] "Teilhard..." observed Beatrice Bruteau, "was a unique type of mystic, driven as he was by a simultaneous love for God and for the

---

[19] Ian G. Barbour, "Teilhard's Process Metaphysics," in *Process Theology*, edited by Ewert H. Cousins, (New York: Newman Press, 1971, p. 347).
[20] Ewert H. Cousins, "Process Models in Culture, Philosophy, and Theology," in *Process Theology*, edited by Ewert H. Cousins, (New York: Newman Press, 1971, pp. 16-17).
[21] WTW, p.14 -- XII, p. 19.
[22] WTW, p. 70 -- XII, p. 81.
[23] In his essay, "Christology and Evolution," written in 1933, Teilhard wrote: "It used to appear that there were only two attitudes mathematically possible for man: to love heaven or to love earth. With a new view of space, a third road is opening up: to make our way to heaven *through* earth. There is a communion (the true communion) with God through the world, and to surrender oneself to it is not to take the impossible step or trying to serve two masters." (CE, p. 93 – X, p. 111).

world."[24] He wanted to reach God through the world. But he had to do this in his own unique way. Let us discern his way and his spiritual journey throughout the text and context of his book, *The Divine Milieu.*

Teilhard's concern, first of all, was to find a harmonious integration between spirit and matter, the inner and the outer, activity and contemplation. Central to this process was the divinization of activities and passivities.

Teilhard was a great Christian mystic both in the traditional sense of mysticism and in his wanting all mysticism to be totally involved in the development and progress of the modern world. Although he cherished solitude, his mysticism was not one associated with the wilderness tradition of deserts and mountain tops. Rather, it encouraged involvement in the factory, the classroom, the workshop, the laboratory, and the marketplace. In his prayerful attitude, he "was united with matter, and through matter with Christ,"[25] as William Johnston said. He sought to unify the different aspects of reality rather than dividing, separating, splitting, and segregating them. He did not believe in dualism and dichotomy. Commenting on this position, Ian G. Barbour rightly observed:

> Teilhard reacts not only against the mind-matter dualism, but against the dichotomy of matter and spirit which Christian thinkers have supported. Here he adopts a biblical view of the unity of man as a whole being and rejects the assumption that matter and spirit are separate substances or antagonistic principles.[26]

Indeed, for Teilhard, "Pure spirituality is as inconceivable as pure materiality,"[27] "There is neither spirit nor matter in the world; the 'stuff of the universe' is *spirit-matter*,"[28] "We are no longer surrounded by a physical realm and a moral realm. There is only the *physico-moral*,"[29] and "The essence of Christianity is neither more nor less than a belief in the unification of the world in God by the Incarnation."[30] Teilhard's

---

[24] Beatrice Bruteau, *Evolution Toward Divinity: Teilhard de Chardin and the Hindu Traditions*, (Wheaton, Illinois: The Theosophical Publishing House, 1974, p. 15).
[25] William Johnston, *The Still Point*, (New York: Fordham University Press, 1970, p. 164).
[26] Ian G. Barbour, "Teilhard's Process Metaphysics," in *Process Theology*, edited by Ewert H. Cousins, (New York: Newman Press, 1971, p. 331).
[27] HE, p. 58 -- VI, p. 75.
[28] HE, pp. 57-58 -- VI, p. 74.
[29] HE, p. 72 -- VI, p. 90.
[30] HE, p. 91 -- VI, p. 113.

mysticism, therefore, sought spirit in and through matter and thus was engaged with the development of the world and the dynamics of an ever-changing society. We might call it a mysticism-in-action spirituality, one that inspires men and women in all the areas of their lives, rather than an introspective and soul-searching type of spirituality that focuses, mainly and above all, on the concerns of the individual. No matter how important private devotions, religious life in cloisters, and ritual prayers in chapels are -- and they are very important, indeed – in a sense, they no longer completely satisfy the spiritual needs of our contemporaries. Teilhard is convinced that spirituality should live and grow in the marketplace and in every corner of ordinary life.[31] This is truly "a spirituality-of-being-in-the-world."[32]

The human Endeavor

Emile Rideau, S.J., a leading figure in Teilhardian studies and one who knew Teilhard personally, contends that Teilhard's spirituality relates human activity very closely to the realization of the Kingdom of God, that is to the divinzation of the human being as well as the universe.[33] Indeed,

---

[31] Teilhard seemed to be willing to distance himself from the Thomas à Kempis' book, *Imitation of Christ*, that was one of the best-known 15th century classics of devotional literature that considered life on earth rather a misery. Claude Cuénot, Agrégé de l'Université Docteur ès lettres, who wrote major works on Teilhard, went so far as to say: "Il y a bien des années déjà que les hommes se laissent influencer par ce beau livre de spiritualité qu'est *Le Milieu Divin* composé par Teilhard en 1926-1927 et qui semble bien destiné a supplanter l'*Imitation* et à prolonger les *Exercices* de Saint Ignace... (« La Spiritualité de Teilhard de Chardin, » in *Le Message Spirituel de Teilhard de Chardin*, Seuil, Paris, 1969, p. 17).

[32] Ursula King, *Christ in All Things: Exploring Spirituality with Teilhard de Chardin*, (Maryknoll, N.Y.: Orbis Books, 1997, p. 157).

[33] Emile Rideau wrote: « [La spiritualité de Teilhard] a le mérite unique, l'originalité impérissable, de relier fortement l'activité humaine à l'existence religieuse, à la poursuite et à la réalisation du Royaume de Dieu : d'affirmer le sérieux de l'acte humain et de l'histoire humaine, dans leur vocation divine. Se refusant à une dissociation mortelle, Teilhard ulilise à fond toutes les ressources du mystère de l'Incarnation pour inviter à une présence totale au monde, à une sanctification des valeurs terrestres : la vocation majeure du chrétien est de contribuer, de toutes ses forces au Plan de Dieu, qui est la divinisation de l'homme et de l'univers, le triomphe du Christ dans l'histoire par la Plénitude du Corps mystique. » (Emile Rideau, *La Pensée du Père Teilhad de Chardin*, Seuil, Paris, 1965, p. 474).

Teilhard showed us, time and again, how important our contribution in building the earth was. In *The Divine Milieu*, he talked about "the sanctification of human endeavour"[34] as well as "the humanisation of Christian endeavour,"[35] although he realistically conceded:

> One thing is infinitely disappointing, I grant you: far too many Christians are insufficiently conscious of the 'divine' responsibilities of their lives, and live like other men, giving only half of themselves, never experiencing the spur or the intoxication of advancing God's kingdom in every domain of mankind. But do not blame anything but our weakness: our faith imposes on us the right and the duty to throw ourselves into the things of the earth.[36]

In such a context, the spirituality of Teilhard should be considered as an incarnational spirituality. All Teilhard's works strongly affirm Christian faith in the mystery of the Incarnation, and he sees this mystery as an ongoing universal process. While he linked it to the historical Jesus, the Word made flesh, the Incarnation of Christ is extended to the entire cosmos. It is an element in the whole process of created reality – a reality that needs to be completed, fulfilled, and redeemed. In that sense, everything "is the body and blood of the Word."[37] This is why Christianity, being the religion of both Incarnation and evolution as ongoing events, must also be a "religion of action."[38] Teilhard stated:

> Through the unceasing operation of the Incarnation, the divine so thoroughly permeates all our creaturely energies, that, in order to meet it and lay hold on it, we could not find a more fitting setting than that of our action.... By virtue of the Creation and, still more, of the Incarnation, *nothing* here below *is profane* for those who know how to see. On the contrary, everything is sacred to the men who can distinguish that portion of chosen being which subject to Christ's drawing power in the process of consummation.[39]

---

[34] MD, p. 65 -- IV, p. 55.
[35] MD, p. 68 -- IV, p. 59.
[36] MD, p. 69 -- IV, p. 61.
[37] HU, p. 28 -- HU, p. 39.
[38] SC, p. 112 -- IX, p. 145.
[39] MD, pp. 62, 66 -- IV, pp. 51, 56.

"Christogenesis"[40]

Teilhard sees Christ as the center and the ultimate purpose of the universe, and nothing can be created without going through Him, for He entirely participates in the life of the universe. He is the evolutive principle. Consequently, the creation, incarnation, and redemption were not single events that were completed once and for all; they constitute together the fullness of existence – the "pleroma."[41] With this view, Teilhard seems to be inspired by the Prologue of John, John 17, and Revelation 1:8, while he was trying to throw light on understanding these texts.

The creation-incarnation-redemption process is an ongoing process that leads to "deification," as the Greek Fathers, whose works were known and loved by Teilhard, would say. With this approach, Teilhard was clearly distancing his spirituality from that practiced by certain Christians who were still under the influence of an everlasting Platonism and a certain comfortable dualism, to embrace the idea of Christogenesis – the next phase of evolution that was also termed by him the Omega Point. "Cosmogenesis," Teilhard wrote, "reveals itself, along the line of its main axis, first as Biogenesis and then Noogenesis, and finally culminates in the Christogenesis which every Christian venerates."[42] Then, he added:

> And then there appears to the dazzled eyes of the believer the eucharistic mystery itself, extended infinitely into a veritable universal transubstantiation, in which the words of the Consecration are applied not only to the sacrificial bread and wine but, mark you, to the whole mass of joys and sufferings produced by the Convergence of the World as it progresses.
> And it is then, too, that there follow in consequence the possibilities of a universal Communion.[43]

Such an understanding highlights for us the cosmic aspect of Christ within an evolutionary universe. For Teilhard, Christ is the organic centre of evolution and it is His love that draws the Cosmogenesis ever onward and upward. He is the Alpha and Omega – the beginning and the end of the process of cosmic evolution and He "radiates his influence throughout the

---

[40] HM, p. 90 -- XIII, p. 104.
[41] This term generally refers to the totality of divine powers. It is, from a theological point of view, a state of perfect fullness, especially of God's being – "all in all" (1 Corinthians 15-28).
[42] HM, p. 94 -- XIII, p. 109.
[43] HM, p. 94 -- XIII, p. 109.

whole mass of nature,"[44] because He is its animating energy at every point along the way.

Through Christ, a radical transformation has happened – a transformation from consmogenesis to Christogenesis. This vision of Christ's presence as the motor and the enlivener of the evolutionary process was not for Teilhard a mere theory, but the very reality of his mission that was to universalize Christ and to christify the universe.[45] Seen from this point of view, the universe becomes the milieu – the Divine Milieu or the Christic Milieu – that is transparent or diaphanous to the action of God.

To live in such a divine milieu – the universe permeated through and through by the omniprece of God[46] – is to live a divinization in progress and a mysticism in action. Then, our peace is God's peace, and this is what present and future generations are longing for, and where their true happiness is found.

---

[44] CE, p. 88 -- X, p. 107.
[45] See HM, p. 90 -- XIII, p. 105.
[46] Sœur Ina Bergeron and Anne-Marie Ernst wrote: "Qu'est-ce que le milieu divin? C'est un centre, c'est une atmosphère chargée de Dieu.... 'C'est une atmosphère si nous voulons, toujours plus lumineuse et plus chargée de Dieu. En Lui, et en Lui seul, se réalise le vœu fou de tout amour : se perdre dans ce qu'on aime et s'y enfoncer de plus en plus' (IV, p. 165) ». See Sœur Ina Bergeron and Anne-Marie Ernst, *Le Christ Universel et l'Evolution* (Paris : Les Editions du Cerf, 1986), p.107.

CHAPTER EIGHT

THE THIRD WAY

It seems easier to keep heaven separate from earth than to try to unify them in one single reality. For intellectual and even practical reasons, we have done this for centuries. But is heaven really separate from earth, and earth from heaven? Do we really have to choose either this or that?

Teilhard de Chardin did not think we had to choose and he invited us to abandon this dilemma and adopt a third way – the way of "both/and" instead of "either/or." As early as 1916, when he still was in his thirties, he started his essay, *Cosmic Life*, with this line, "There is a communion with God, and a communion with earth, and a communion with God through earth."[1] This was, we can perhaps say, the principle that he must have lived by.[2]

No wonder Teilhard sees no separation or opposition between spirit and matter. For him, "There is neither spirit nor matter in the world; the 'stuff of the universe' is *spirit-matter*,"[3] and "Pure spirituality is as inconceivable as pure materiality."[4]

Teilhard is drawing our attention to what reality truly is. The physical and the spiritual are only ideas and creations of our imagination. They are poles of our existence. They are like two banks of a river. Can a river flow with one bank? Teilhard is not rejecting one pole to emphasize the other. What he is saying is that any division, opposition, or separation is not real.

---

[1] WIW, p. 14 -- XII, p. 19.
[2] Ursula King explained: "These two attitudes – communion with earth and communion with God – are regarded as incomplete: only the synthesis of both is acceptable. This synthesis of 'communion with God through earth' is not simply a combination of two different attractions but something of a new order altogether. The initial experience of 'cosmic consciousness', the love of the earth and all its realities, is prolonged and transformed through the experience of God as both an immanent and transcendent presence." See Ursula King, *Towards a New Mysticism: Teilhard de Chardin and Eastern Religions* (New York: The Seabury Press, 1981), p.111.
[3] HE, pp. 57-8 -- VI, p. 74.
[4] HE, p. 58 -- VI, p. 75.

What is real is a direct grasp and simultaneous experience of the unity of the invisible and the visible, the noumenal and the phenomenal, the subject and the object, the ultimate and the immediate. In fact, we know what we know about life through synthesis more than we know it through analysis. It is not by cutting the throat of a nightingale that we will grasp the secret of its beautiful voice. When we analyze, we practice science. Science helps to solve a problem. But life is not a problem. Life is a mystery. Analysis can be violent, but synthesis is more peaceful. Things start to make more sense when they are attached to the whole. Then even opposites are not necessarily opposite; they rather are complementary.

Mystical Evolution

How can we describe the world we live in? How can we describe our human realities and various activities? Are they "sacred" or "profane"? This was and still is an everlasting question.

Teilhard had his answer.[5] It was, "There is a communion with God, and a communion with earth, and a communion with God through earth."[6] "The communion with God" stands for a God and a religion separated from this world. The transcendent would be the concern while the caring attention to this world is kept at a minimal level. "The communion with earth" refers, on the contrary, to a monistic pantheism, purely and simply. While distancing himself from both attitudes, Teilhard suggests the third way: a synthesis of both – "a communion with God through earth." [7]

---

[5] The God-universe relationship was a central theme in the life and writings of Teilhard de Chardin. N.M. Wildiers, among many others who think the same, describes Teilhard's life and thoughts this way: « Le problème des rapports entre Dieu et l'Univers est effectivement le problème central de la vie spirituelle de Teilhard de Chardin. C'est uniquement de ce point de vue que l'on peut saisir l'unité et la cohérence de son œuvre si vaste. Ce problème initial est le point de départ de tous les grands thèmes qu'il a traités dans ses écrits.» See N.M. Wildiers, Teilhard de Chardin (Paris: Editions Universitaires, 1960, 'Classiques du XXe Siècle'), p.12.

[6] WTW, p. 14 -- XII, p. 19.

[7] F.C. Happold observed the following: "[Teilhard's] *mystic way is thus one very different from the* via negative *of Dionysius and St John of the Cross. For him union with God was not through withdrawal from the activity of the world but through a dedicated, integrated, and subliminated absorption in it. At the end of his life he said:* 'Throughout *my life, by means of my life, the world has little by little caught fire in my sight until, aflame all around me, it has become almost luminous from within.... Such has been my experience in contact with the earth – the diaphany of the Divine at the heart of a universe on fire.... Christ; the heart; a*

Such a synthesis is not an attempt to combine two different attractions in a sort of compromise, but to describe a reality of another order, that is different and original. The earthly realities are transformed by the experience of God as the most active presence, in both ways immanence and transcendence – God being within these realities and at the same time as being beyond them. This is, indeed, the most intimate and powerful way of relating God and the world, of reconciling the sacred and the profane,[8] and of linking mystical spirituality to human growth and social development.

The world, then, becomes "The Divine Milieu" where everything is sacred in a "divine matter"[9] and where the "diaphany" transforms everything and gives a new meaning to everything. It is the encounter of "physics" and "mysticism," the encounter of "stillness" and "evolution," and the encounter of "contemplation" and "action." Teilhard was above all concerned with developing a "science of human energetic"[10] that emphasized the mystical consequences of evolution, which is, after all, "the discovery of God":

> Driven by the necessity to build up the unity of the world, we may perhaps, come in the end to see that the great work dimly guessed at and pursued by science is simply the discovery of God.[11]

and "the rise of a God":

> And what does this mean except, finally, that the planetisation of Mankind, if it is to come properly into effect, presupposes, in addition to the enclosing Earth, and to the organization and condensation human thought, yet another factor? I mean the rise on our inward horizon of a cosmic

---

fire; capable of penetrating everywhere and, gradually, spreading everywhere" (Italics by author). See F.C. Happold, *Mysticism: A Study and an Anthology* (New York, N.Y.: Penguin Books Ltd, 1963, 1964, 1970), p. 394.

[8] In the context of the sacred and the profane, James W. Skehan, reminding us the "Ignatius's goal" that permeated deeply Teilhard's perspective, wrote: "Because of Jesus' Incarnation, all matter in the universe has become sacred, and all of our activities partake of the sacred. As a result, the distinction between the sacred and the profane fades away. Cultivating a spirit of reverence will allow us to strive for Ignatius's goal to 'seek and find God in all things.'" See James W. Skehan, SJ, *Praying with Teilhard de Chardin* (Winona, MN: Saint Mary's Press, 2001, 'Companions for the Journey'), p. 69.

[9] WTW, p. 29 -- XII, p. 36.

[10] PM, p. 283 -- I, p. 315.

[11] SC, p. 146 -- IX, p. 187.

spiritual centre, a supreme pole of consciousness, upon which all the separate consciousnesses of the world may converge and within which they may love one another, *the rise of a God.*[12]

Therefore, there is a goal for evolution. Teilhard, as a scientist and a person of faith, sees the convergence of science and mysticism and affirms the existence of the Omega point which is the Prime Mover ahead, a loving personal center of attraction. That is why religion becomes of primary importance in our life. Religion, for Teilhard, possesses the dynamic capacity of assuring us of the fundamental energy for action at the personal level and at the social level. Religion is supposed to teach that love of God and love of the world should be inseparable.

The "Secular Society" and the Mystical Mind

What we nowadays call a "secular society" is, in a sense, an impossibility. The Absolute is always there in our lives and in the world.[13] Teilhard wrote:

> Everything that is active, that moves or breathes, every physical, astral, or animate energy, every fragment of force, every spark of life, is equally sacred; for, in the humblest atom and the most brilliant star, in the lowest insect and the finest intelligence, there is the radiant smile and thrill of the *same Absolute.*[14]

---

[12] FM, pp. 124-25 -- V, p. 153.

[13] In the context of the "absolutes" that seem to have divided Teilhard, Thomas King observed: "Thus, through the *ascent of matter* (evolution) and the *descent of God* (the Incarnation), Teilhard saw the two "Absolutes" that once divided his allegiance come into conjunction to form the Body of Christ. A great Soul, the soul of Christ, was seen to be animating the universe, the Body; the universe was responding by rising into unity." See Thomas M. King, S.J., *Teilhard de Chardin* (Wilmington, Delaware: Michael Glazier, Inc., 1988, 'The Way of the Christian Mystics'), p. 30. Also, Sister Maria Gratia Martin wrote: "Teilhard's efforts to resolve this conflict in no way represent a compromise between two opposing loves, God and the world, it is rather a perfect illustration of 'faith seeking understanding' in order to believe more ardently in the Christ of Colossians in whom 'all things were created' and in whom 'all things hold together' [Col. 1:16, 17 – RSV]. His thought focused, therefore, on a fundamental vision of the co-extension of Christ with the universe...." See Sister Maria Gratia Martin, I.H.M., *The Spirituality of Teilhard de Chardin* (New York, NY: Newman Press, 1968), p. 3.

[14] WTW, p. 28 -- XII, p. 34.

Thus, the development of society is always related to the development of our understanding of our connections with the divine, and vice versa. The "mystical temperature" of humanity is rising and is providing human beings with the deepest springs of energy for action, interaction, and transformation at all levels – individual, social, religious, vertical, and horizontal.

In truth, and despite all the arguments in its favor, there is no such a thing called "secular society." There is always a mystical society – a society made of "spirit-matter."

True mysticism does no longer value a dualistic mentality. It rather advocates the spirit-in-and-through-matter mentality. Spirit and matter are no longer seen as separate or opposed, for, as Teilhard wrote, "Rightly speaking, there are no sacred and profane things,"[15] and, "*Nothing* here below is *profane* for those who know how to see."[16]

There are very practical consequences for the interdependence of the sacred and the profane; we move away from utopian ideals to the here and now reality. A mystical mentality must provide humanity with a spirituality to cope with today's problems, today's responsibilities, and today's choices. Mysticism has lost its privacy in order to leaven society as a whole and alter our individual behaviors accordingly. A "mysticism of escape," that is the flight from involvement with the things of this world, should be replaced by a "mysticism of evolution," that is a complete readiness to take responsibility for action; the period of transformation is in the making. Teilhard wrote:

> We now have to accept it as proven that mankind has just entered into what is probably the most extensive period of transformation it has known since its birth. The seat of the evil we are suffering from is to be found in the very foundations of thought on earth. Something in the general structure of Spirit: it is a new type of life that is beginning.[17]

In this sense, and whether we know it or not, and whether we want to admit it or not, the mystical mentality is highly political. Can one imagine a more political act than the act of transforming the consciousness that will transform the very structures of society?

The ending of dichotomy may also mean that the separation of the fields of knowledge, that existed for a long time, does no longer apply, and it becomes now both outdated and inadequate. The truth is that any big

---

[15] TF, p. 72 -- XI, p. 78.
[16] DM, p. 66 -- IV, p. 56.
[17] SC, pp. 128-9 -- IX, pp. 169-70.

decision we make is a decision based on science, economics, history, philosophy, religion, law, etc., and it is so because reality is always comprehensive and complex. That is why it will be a kind of deformation of reality to focus too much on one field, and do things as if the other fields do not matter or even do not exist. It is not because this or that action is legal, for example, one can do it without taking into account whether this action is right or wrong. It is not because statistically speaking everybody does it that we can do it, too, without taking into account whether what we do is legal or not, or whether it benefits others or brings harm to them. Reality is not that simple.

Every thinker, to be true and real, must pass the "mystical test" of the all. He or she must refuse to be in the service of the ideologies that profess restrictions, limitations, exclusion, and the rejection of possibilities. By refusing to adhere to such ideologies, thinkers release themselves from the utopian "heaven" of seeking power for personal protection and self-interest, and they sweep away the insane notion of the survival of the strongest and the fittest. Then it will make sense to talk about inter-sympathy, unanimity, solidarity, personalization, team spirit, unification, and communion, as Teilhard suggested. Then the one is exalted and the all is united.

The mystical way of thinking transcends the individual's needs to reach the social needs. It is closely concerned with the areas of development – at all levels – of society. No wonder Teilhard sees the future in a synthesis of the rational and the mystical.[18] That is why it does not seem possible to imagine a reality that is not theological.

---

[18] Commenting on Teilhard's synthesis, Robert Faricy wrote: "Teilhard's understanding of the natural order and the order of grace is that they are in synthesis, and must be brought more into synthesis in Christian life.... There is, then, an intrinsic and necessary mutual complementary between Christian faith and faith in man, in progress, in the world. In his clearest presentation of the problem and the need for synthesis between the two faiths, Teilhard writes that at the source of the modern religious crisis lies a conflict of faith, a conflict between man's upward impulse of worship and his forward impulse towards involvement in building the world. The 'upward' and the 'forward' are, in reality, the two mutually complementary components of a complete Christianity; Christian faith is whole only when it is a synthesis of faith in God and faith in man. See Robert Faricy, S.J., *The Spirituality of Teilhard de Chardin* (Minneapolis, Minnesota: Winston Press – Collins Publishers, 1981), pp. 38, 41-42.

Mysticism and Peace

What does the mystical way mean for peace? It means that love is the real bond which can provide an impulse for human unity and peace that is more compelling than any external force of unification. Teilhard is convinced that the evolution of humanity toward greater unity "will never materialize unless we full develop within ourselves the exceptionally strong unifying powers exerted by inter-human sympathy and religious forces."[19]

In such a case, the mystic is not a dreamer who wants to escape the world. The mystic is rather the determined realist who aims to change the world and bring peace and unity. The mysticism that fosters a unitive experience, is a mysticism in which a reconciliation with God, with oneself, and with others has to occur, and it does. In mysticism, there a sense of integration.[20] No wonder, then, inter-action, inter-connection, inter-dependence, and inter-being become a natural process between the elements and the whole. Here, the whole is exalted while the elements are united and personalized. The more humanity is a whole, the more the countries are independent. The more humanity is one, the more the units that make the whole are inter-dependent. It is not a kind of identification or a fusion, but a personalization. The expression that became very dear to Teilhard was "union differentiates."[21]

How does a mystical mind help, at the practical level, to bring peace to the world?

From a mystical eye, it would be inadequate, as it has been mentioned above, to separate the fields of knowledge – science, religion, philosophy, history, anthropology, economics, literature, politics.... In fact, there is no dividing line between them. All important decisions should be rooted in all

---

[19] Quoted by Ursula King, *Toward a New Mysticism: Teilhard de Chardin and Eastern Religions,* (New York: Seabury Press, 1980), p. 179.

[20] Thomas Merton seems to describe best this state of being. He wrote: "Final integration is a state of transcultural maturity far beyond social adjustment, which always implies partiality and compromise. The person who is 'fully born' has an entirely 'inner experience of life.' [Such a person] apprehends his life fully and wholly from an inner ground that is at once more universal than the empirical ego and yet entirely his own. [Such an individual] is in a certain sense 'cosmic' and 'universal [person].' He/she has attained a deeper, fuller identity than that of his limited ego-self which is only a fragment of his being. He/she is in a certain sense identified with everybody." See Thomas Merton, *Contemplation in a World of Action* (Garden City, NY: Image Books – A Division of Doubleday & Company, Inc., 1965, 1973), p. 225.

[21] PM, p. 262 -- I, p. 291; also VI, pp. 80-81, 129, 179; VII, p. 122; X, p. 200.

of them. A good decision is the fruit of synthesis. Again Teilhard's insights prove to be right.

Consequently, one of the ways of reaching the peace we want, is to consider including in our programs of schooling the mystical notion of the interaction between the one and the many, the synthesis between the without and the within, and the reconciliation between faith and reason. As a corollary to this, we should not give any academic degree on the basis of a separate field of knowledge. A Ph.D. candidate in literature, for example, should not be awarded the degree until he or she proves competency in knowing how a business operates. A Ph.D. candidate in political science should not be awarded the degree until he or she proves competency in metaphysics. A Ph.D. candidate in international affairs should not be awarded the degree until he or she proves competency in anthropology, philosophy, theology, and languages. And so on.

What such a program does is to train the student to grow with the idea that everything is connected with, and needs, everything else, and that everything is interacting, everything is converging, everything is inter-being, and everyone is needed and belongs to the whole. Peace does not mean the abolition of variety or diversity. Peace means convergence. Peace means mystical union.

Furthermore, and this could be the most difficult part to realize, but at the same time the most fascinating and rewarding, there will be no permanent peace unless we "see" God in the world.[22] The following prayer is one of many prayers that Teilhard wrote to describe this longing:

---

[22] What is called "The world" has, after Teilhard, a different connotation. Christopher F. Mooney remarked: "We might note… the growing importance of Teilhard's overriding concern for what he calls quite simply 'the world.' This constitutes, I think, his single most significant contribution to modern Christian spirituality. For since spirituality in its broadest sense is a style of approach to God, and attitude toward life, each era must have its own, with its own set of images and its own motivations corresponding to the Christian needs of a given time. Thus, in the apostolic era it was the Parousia which fired the Christian imagination; in a later era the blood of the martyrs; still later the quarrels between Protestant and Catholic; and in recent centuries the intense missionary activity of Christians. Today what motivates people is 'the world.' Christians want to feel they can reach God through the world, through the whole scientific, technological, humanistic enterprise. But not until Teilhard appeared on the scene has anyone succeeded in showing them how. He is the only one who has given this vivid image of modern man a completely Christian explanation." See Christopher F. Mooney, S.J., *The Making of Man: Essays in the Christian Spirit* (New York, N.Y.: Paulist Press, 1971), p. 148.

Since my dignity as a man, O God, forbids me to close my eyes to this – like an animal or a child – that I may succumb to the temptation to curse the universe and him who made it, teach me to adore it by seeing you concealed within it.[23]

Elsewhere, he also wrote: "The world is full of God. For if it were empty, the world would long ago have died of disgust."[24]

    A profound change in our way of thinking has to occur, if we are serious about making peace in the world. The battlefield is not out there; it is in our mind, heart, and soul. If we refuse to know where the battlefield is, we will never have peace. We, then, will continue to fight the wrong war, with the wrong enemy, in the wrong place, and at the wrong time.

---

[23] DM, p. 137 -- IV, p. 172.
[24] LTF, p. 57 -- *Accomplir l'homme*, p. 73.

PART III

THE BIRTH OF A NEW CONSCIOUSNESS

Chapter Nine

A Transformed Consciousness

"*In Eo Vivimus*" (In Him We Live) is the title of the introduction that Teilhard wrote for his book, *The Divine Milieu*. This little quote taken from St. Paul when he addressed the Greek people describes the in-depth core of Teilhard's spirituality and philosophy of life. It also gives the right tone to what he brings to the table that is different and makes him somewhat paradoxically unique. Indeed, for centuries, theologians and philosophers were debating whether God was transcendent who was "out there" or "up there" in the "Our Father who art in heaven," or he was immanent who dwelled within each one of us, right here, right now. While seeing the validity of these perspectives, Teilhard opted for St. Paul's affirmation, "In him we live and move and have our being,"[1] and concluded that "[God] will penetrate [the universe] as a ray of light does a crystal; and, with the help of the great layers of creation, he will become for you universally perceptible and active – very near and very distant at one and the same time."[2] No wonder he could also summarize his conviction with the striking line, "There is a communion with God, and a communion with earth, and a communion with God through earth."[3] No wonder Louis M. Savary could insightfully and rightly write:

> Teilhard says we could build a new spirituality that finds God's imprint and spirit in everything happening today if only we had the ability to "see him" – to see Christ at the heart of the world and to see God's pervasive and perceptible presence all around us, as easily as we can sense the atmosphere we breathe.
> In all our human experiences, what we do and what we undergo, God is waiting for us in everything we touch or that touches us. Everything in

---

[1] Acts 17:28.
[2] DM, p. 47 -- IV, p. 26.
[3] WTW, p. 14 -- XII, p. 19.

the whole world is swimming in a sea of God. In him we live and move and have our being.[4]

In a world that operates according to the mind of Christ, people would have clear references for discerning right from wrong. So, in vain we would go on searching for the truth in a philosophy, a political system, or even a "religion." It is not there. And it is not in what "you" think it is either, nor is it in what "I" think, nor in what "we" think, nor in what "they" think. It is not there. The truth is found in the word of God who said, "I am the Lord your God.... You shall have no other gods before me,"[5] and in the Son of God who said, "I am the way, and the truth, and the life"[6]—the Christ who summed everything in one word, *LOVE:* "'You shall love the Lord your God with all your heart, and with all your soul, and with all your mind, and with all your strength.... You shall love your neighbor as yourself."[7] If we say we love others, then we must incarnate this love toward them. In doing that, we will prove God's continuous involvement in human history, for then our hands will be God's, always ready to do God's work.

God still has human skin and still walks the earth among us, touches us, listens to us, hugs us, looks deeply through our eyes into our brain, heart, and soul, and heals us, as Jesus did; "Truly I tell you, just as you did it to one of the least of these who are members of my family, you did it to me."[8]

When God's eyes become our eyes, his ears our ears, his will our will, his hands our hands, it becomes up to us, in a sense, to co-create a world according to God's desire and will. Let us take a close look at our hands. What a responsibility is in our hands! "A new creation" is in the making.

God was visible in Jesus and is still visible in the other who is Christ in disguise, as Mother Teresa of Calcutta would like to say. God once acted through Jesus and he now acts through those who imitate Jesus, think like Jesus, act like Jesus, and be like Jesus; being Jesus Christ – the "Super-Christ" in the words of Teilhard, who explained:

> By Super-Christ I most certainly do not mean *another* Christ, a second Christ different from and greater than the first. I mean *the same* Christ, the

---

[4] Louis M Savary, *Teihard de Chardin The Divine Milieu Explained : A Spirituality for the 21st Century*, (Mahwah, NJ: Paulist Press, 2007), p. 11.
[5] Exodus 20:2,3.
[6] John 14:6.
[7] Mark 12:30-31.
[8] Matthew 25:40.

Christ of all time, revealing himself to us in a form and in dimensions, with an urgency and area of contact, that are enlarged and given new force. We can readily appreciate that the appearance in Christian consciousness of a Christ so magnified will immediately result in the appearance in human consciousness of Super-humanity.[9]

With such a consciousness,[10] our eyes will start to see things differently. Of course, we can still see everything the way we have always done before, but with new dimensions this time, and new quality of observation and perception. A deep transformation has happened, producing a renewal in the way we think, live, and act. In this context, it is good to remember the Declaration of the Parliament of the World's Religions in which we read the following lines:

> Historical experience demonstrates the following: Earth cannot be changed for the better unless we achieve a transformation in the consciousness of individuals and in public life. The possibilities for transformation have already been glimpsed in areas such as war and peace, economy, and ecology, where in recent decades fundamental changes have taken place. This transformation must also be achieved in the areas of ethics and values! Every individual has intrinsic dignity and inalienable rights, and each also has an inescapable responsibility for what she or he does and does not do. All our decisions and deeds, even our omissions and failures, have consequences.... Earth cannot be changed for the better unless the consciousness of individuals is changed. We pledge to work for such transformation in individual and collective consciousness, for the awakening of our spiritual powers through reflection, meditation, prayer, or positive thinking, for a conversion of the heart. Together we can move mountains![11]

Maturing to reach such a state of consciousness[12] makes us see our differences, opposites, and even contradictions as ingredients for

---

[9] SC, p. 164 -- IX, pp. 208-209.
[10] When Teilhard uses the word "consciousness," he does not use it as synonym of thought only. It is rather "taken in its widest sense to indicate every kind of psychism, from the rudimentary forms of interior perception imaginable to the human phenomenon of reflective thought." See PM, p. 57, note 1 -- I, p. 53, note 1.
[11] Hans Küng and Karl-Josef Kuschel, ed., *A Global Ethic: The Declaration of the Parliament of the World's Religions* (New York, N. Y.: The Continuum Publishing Company, 1993), pp. 34, 36.
[12] This is how Wayne Teasdale described consciousness : "All that we experience – or know, think, imagine, remember, feel, and dream – we experience because we are first *aware*. For us, everything requires and depends on consciousness to be.

complementarity and synthesis. Consequently, even the mere idea of the need to obtain weapons for killing becomes ridiculous, outrageous, and completely unnecessary and inappropriate. Now we can use our differences to complement what was lacking and complete what we couldn't achieve. Mikhail Gorbachev saw that "Each generation inherits from its predecessors the material and spiritual wealth of civilization. And each generation is responsible for preserving this inheritance and developing it for the succeeding generations."[13]

Teilhard recognized though that individual setbacks are possible and could be expected, especially when external socializing forces are at work trying an artificial union when the true union is much deeper. Ursula King explained:

> There are certain socializing forces at work in our contemporary world, numerous attempts to establish stronger and more effective social, political, and economic communities. Yet Teilhard regarded the attempts of existing political systems, whether they be democracy, socialism, communism, or fascism, to promote a better society as insufficient. Whatever social integration they may have achieved has largely been through external coercion. Their attempts do not yet represent the true union of people through the forces of love and attraction.[14]

The perception of an external world, the existence of others, even the fact of our own bodies, are presented and represented to us through the agency of our consciousness. Consciousness is the inside, outside, and farside of reality; it is the height, breadth, and transcendent beyond. Consciousness is the locus of reality. Even the fact that we have a brain is mediated to us through our awareness of it; our perception of the brain, as of all other perceptions, occurs in our thought and awareness." See Wayne Teasdale, *The Mystic Heart: Discovering a Universal Spirituality in the World's Religion* (Novato, CA: New World Library, 1999), pp. 65-66.

[13] Mikhail Gorbachev in Michael Collopy and Jason Gardner, ed., *Architects of Peace: Visions of Hope in Words and Images* (Novato, CA: New World Library, 2000), p. 29. In the same place (pp. 28-29), Mikhail Gorbachev said also: "The roots of the current crisis of civilization lie within humanity itself. Our intellectual and moral development is lagging behind the rapidly changing conditions of our existence, and we are finding it difficult to adjust psychologically to the pace of change. *Only by renouncing selfishness and attempts to outsmart one another to gain an advantage at the expense of others can we hope to ensure the survival of humankind* and the further development of our civilization."

[14] Ursula King, *The Spirit of One Earth: Reflections on Teilhard de Chardin and Global Spirituality* (New York, N.Y.: Paragon House, 1989), pp.54-55.

It is true that, very often, we go seeking God in monasteries, retreat centers, books, theories, systems, the far sky, and in the extraordinary—of course, he is there since he is everywhere. But he is also much closer to home. He is incarnate in the ordinary events of our daily life. He lives in the here and now of a family, a community, a nation—this very world. God is not only in heaven. God is also on earth. St. John describes this incarnate God by using very revealing words. He wrote: "Those who say, 'I love God,' and hate their brothers or sisters, are liars; for those who do not love a brother or sister whom they have seen, cannot love God whom they have not seen."[15] This means, in substance, that God has a human face: loving God requires loving others. But to be able to do that, one must "incarnate" God in himself or herself first. Then it wouldn't be enough to read, or to hear someone telling us about what God wants. Now we want our eyes to be God's eyes so that we can look at things the way God looks at them. No wonder we would discover something that was invisible to us and to others, and we would realize that everything is sacred because "The earth is the Lord's and all that is in it, the world, and those who live in it."[16]

The reality of external changes happens as the fruit of inner transformation first. This is where real and genuine changes should start. Wayne Teasdale wrote insightfully:

> The spiritual journey changes us to the core of our being. If it didn't, it wouldn't be real. This quality of inner change is what I understand by the term *transformation*: a radical reordering and alteration of our character, and all our old habits of thought, feeling, and action.
>
> Spirituality is always meant to make us better by unlocking our potential for divinity, to be *like* God in some participatory way. This is what the Christian theologians of the early Orthodox church called theosis, or deification, becoming like God. It is what Eastern traditions mean when they speak of awakening the Buddha-nature within us, or the Atman. If spirituality does not offer access to actualizing our potential for this higher form of life, which is what we are made for, then what ultimate value can it possibly have for us?[17]

There is no doubt that the way we live our realities affects to a certain degree our consciousness. But our consciousness affects our life and

---

[15] 1 John 4:20.
[16] Psalm 24:1.
[17] Wayne Teasdale, *The Mystic Heart: Discovering a Universal Spirituality in the World's Religion* (Novato, CA: New World Library, 1999), p. 144.

reality to a much higher degree.[18] A transformed consciousness, we can even say, created the new reality. As our understanding increases, ignorance dissipates. As our consciousness becomes "mind of Christ," we become Christ-like. Then a completely different set of emotions, imagination, character, will, behavior, lifestyle, action, and relationship with others will emerge with a new set of values and references for truth, love, and peace. Everything is now oriented toward Christ. Teilhard saw that "Every process of material growth in the universe is ultimately directed towards spirit, and every process of spiritual growth towards Christ."[19]

We do not understand the mystery of the Incarnation if we do not see the immensity of its implications. Divinity in human nature means the full potentiality and openness of our nature to the possibility of what the Greek Fathers termed "deification" or, as Teilhard called it, "divinization."[20]

In order to do that, a birth of a new consciousness—"the mind of Christ"[21]—is needed. Then the entire world will be uplifted.

Imagine a world without ugly wars, terrorism, and violence of any sort. Imagine a society without poisoned racism, dishonesty, adultery, and gender confusion. Imagine a leadership without malignant political correctness, intellectual intimidation, and self-serving interest. Imagine a community without insane "religion,"[22] a double-face way of living, and self-destructive lifestyles and behaviors. Imagine a nation without a leadership deficit, a budget deficit, and character deficit. Imagine a world

---

[18] Teilhard talked often, especially in his book *The Phenomenon of Man*, about the "without" and the "within" of things. Christopher Mooney wrote the following insightful explanation. He said: "The overreaching desire of Teilhard to see through the world of people and things and find God is the reason why he is at such pains to show that material evolution is ultimately oriented toward growth of the spiritual. Thus the function he assigns to his law of complexity-consciousness is that of allowing the 'within' of things to emerge, to promote growth in 'consciousness,' by the interplay of radial and tangential energy. Unlike many physical scientists, Teilhard refused to see in the law of entropy a gloomy prediction that the universe will one day run down completely and stop. Such a law, he felt, told us only about the 'without' of things and left untouched the world of spirit 'within.'" See Christopher F. Mooney, S.J., *The Making of Man: Essays in the Christian Spirit* (New York, N.Y.: Paulist Press, 1971), p.135.
[19] SC, p. 68 -- IX, p. 96.
[20] See for example DM, p. 49, 74 -- IV, p. 29, 69.
[21] 1 Corinthians 2:16.
[22] A bad interpretation of religion can be very dangerous and destructive. God cannot be limited to our very often self-serving interpretations; God is infinitely larger than what our minds can perceive.

without the counterfeit gods of money, power, prestige, pleasure, and the never-ending greed forever "more." Imagine a world without intentional or unintentional lies, without seen or unseen robberies, and without palpable or hidden hypocrisy. Imagine a world "where righteousness is at home,"[23] where Yes is Yes and No is No,[24] and where truth is known—a truth that makes us free.[25] Such a world is not a world that has undertaken a sheepish reform of a sort, or even some kind of cosmetic surgery. This is a new world altogether because "I am making all thing new"[26] for "a new creation is everything."[27] Wouldn't it be the world that we were waiting for, as St. Peter says, "In accordance with his promise, we wait for new heavens and a new earth"[28]? It would and it will because, as David Grumett put it, "Teilhard's metaphysics is inevitably theological and profoundly political. It challenges the assumptions about how the world is and what it should become, assumptions that are held by most scientists and other powerful interest groups in society.... Teilhard makes clear that in evolution's human phase, morality, religion, politics, and social issues take center stage. These are the new drivers of evolution...."[29] Who can say that the theological is not also political!

With a transformed consciousness that can be also called a higher consciousness, we begin to be aware of the gift of being co-creators—the great gift that God has given us; we now see how much we are able to participate in creating the divine reality we are still longing to see in the world around us.

A transformed consciousness signals a radical change in life because of the change in the chain of command that happens in the mind; the negative programming embedded in our subconscious and conscious mind are replaced by positive and empowering re-programming that effects a new way of living our life and all life; the defense mechanisms of denial, regression, acting out, repression, rationalization, projection are replaced by sublimation, reconciliation, and peace and love. A transformed consciousness dissolves the numbness, illusions, and self-interests of our "big" egos; it frees us to become co-creators of our destiny by making us

---

[23] 2 Peter 3:13.
[24] See Matthew 5:37.
[25] See John 8:32.
[26] Revelation 21:5.
[27] Galatians 6:15.
[28] 2 Peter 2:13.
[29] David Grumett, "Metaphysics, Morality, and Politics" in Ilia Delio, ed., *From Teilhard to Omega: Co-creating an Unfinished Universe* (Maryknoll, N. Y.: Orbis Books, 2015), p. 115.

all and together form a "human front"[30] – "one solid block"[31] – capable of moving the universe forward and upward toward its divine destiny.

A transformed consciousness is not a naïve idealism; it is what the book of Proverbs said, "For as he thinketh in his heart, so is he."[32] A thought that is allied to a clear and unmistakable purpose becomes unmistakably a driving force toward achievement. In his book, *As a Man Thinketh*, James Allen offered this advice: "Cherish your visions; cherish your ideals; cherish the music that stirs in your heart, the beauty that forms in your mind, the loveliness that drapes your purest thoughts, for out of them will grow all delightful conditions, all heavenly environment; of these, if you but remain true to them, your world will at last be built."[33]

A transformed consciousness allows us to "see" the world we want to build, and pass to action and build it. This is what Teilhard meant to convey through his writings and especially through his essays under the title, "Building the Earth."[34]

---

[30] SC, p. 142 -- IX, p. 184.
[31] HM, p. 185 -- XII, p. 267.
[32] Proverbs 23:7.
[33] James Allen, *As a Man Thinketh* (Philadelphia, PA: Running Press, 1989), pp. 74-75.
[34] See Teilhard de Chardin, *Building the Earth* (Wilkes-Barre, PA: Dimension Books, 1965) or (New York, N.Y.: Avon Books – A division of the Hearst Corporation, 1969). This book contains the following essays: "We Must Save Mankind," "The Spirit of Earth," "Human Energy," "Thoughts on Progress," "On the Possible Basis of a Common Credo." Then, for the Avon Books edition, another essay was added: "The Psychological Conditions of Human Unification."

Chapter Ten

The Unitive Consciousness

The unification of humanity was one of Teilhard's main concerns. He quoted with conviction and enthusiasm the declaration of President Wilson that says: "I feel that the time has come when men must forget their local attachments and unite in a single great enterprise that will unite all free men for ever, so to become a single body of free minds [.] (President Wilson, 2 January 1910)."[1]

Teilhard saw some kind of unity, to start with, in the people's duties that are no longer directed toward the individual only, but also toward society and the international community. He wrote:

> ... The ever vaster organizations that are being formed (or disclosed) in the World are tending to produce a new category of duties; and room must be made for these alongside the old commandments. Morality has hitherto been individualistic (the relations of individuals to individuals). In future more explicit emphasis will have to be laid on Man's obligations to collective bodies and even to the Universe: on political duties, social duties, international duties – on (if I may be allowed the expression) cosmic duties, first among which stands the Law of Word and Research.[2]

Teilhard welcomed the creation of the United Nations and wished to see greater and greater numbers of organizations with international missions. But he did not believe in the possibility of an international government, at least not in the near future. His preference was rather leaning toward an internationalism that is incarnated in the growing interdependence in the economic, technological, intellectual, and spiritual fields, and also in the cooperation of everyone with the international organizations of research. "[Teilhard,]" wrote Frederick C. Copleston,

---

[1] HM, p. 213 -- XII, pp. 402-3.
[2] HM, p. 220 -- XII, p. 422.

"was acutely aware of the world as a whole, of the human race as a whole, and of our common vocation."[3]

Moreover, planetary unity – "Commonwealth"[4] – should not be taken, in Teilhard's view, as a juridical concept.[5] It is rather a dynamic understanding which requires necessarily an ultimate point of evolution and maturation. Planetary unity also means a general ecumenism, not only between Christians, but between Christians and all other faiths and even with those who do not believe in anything, for even these can, in a sense, present an opportunity for deepening one's own religion. So, different religions, different cultures, different races and ethnic groups join together to make one mature humanity. Teilhard wrote: "Races, peoples and nations consolidate one another and complete one another by mutual

---

[3] Frederick C. Copleston, S.J., "Teilhard de Chardin and a Global Outlook" in Thomas King, S.J. & James F. Salmon, S.J., ed., *Teilhard and the Unity of Knowledge*, 'The Georgetown University Centennial Symposium', (New York/Ramsey: NJ.: Paulist Press, 1983), p. 8.

[4] For Benjamin T. Hourani, "A new synthesis anticipating a Commonwealth rather than an Empire must be based on the simple extrapolation – the eventual unification of mankind, a notion which in its simplicity could elude us for a long time. Teilhard arrives at this extrapolation through the effects of his law of complexity-consciousness and the eventual folding of humanity upon itself as it completes the planetization of the earth. He sees the old systems and 'ways of life' to be the immobilists' fort. The new spirit of the earth, Teilhard believed cannot be contained by building power condominiums nor could the Darwinian ethos stem the tide for being welling up in the heart of the human mass." See Benjamin T. Hourani, "Teilhard's Political Ecumene: Empire or Commonwealth," in Leo Zonneveld and Robert Muller, ed., *The Desire to Be Human*, "International Teilhard Compendium" Centenary volume (Netherlands: Mirananda Publishers b.v. Wassenaar, 1983), p. 225.

[5] Thomas King helps explain the unification that Teilhard is talking about from a philosophical point of view. He wrote: "Teilhard would further argue that this process of interrelating will finally result in a single unified organism extending throughout the universe, an organism with a single unified form. Presently this unified Form is only the *goal* toward which all things are moving—thus, in Aristotelian terms, this unity could better be seen as a single Final Cause rather than as a single Formal Cause. But, apart from this reservation, one could say that Teilhard is proposing a modified philosophy of hylomorphism, a hylomorphism that is extended through time. For Teilhard, there was in the beginning only the radical plurality of matter and there will be at the end only the perfect unity of Form. This perfect form will be the form of the universal Christ and it will give a final unity to the cosmos." Thomas M. King, *Teilhard's Mysticism of Knowing* (New York, N.Y.: The Seabury Press, 1981), pp. 10-11.

fecundation."[6] Ursula King wrote about this unity Teilhard is talking about,

> Teilhard always saw the need for greater unity and often perceived promising efforts toward greater human unification, despite increased difficulties and tensions. It was not uniformity and unity achieved through absorption and fusion he envisaged, but a unity of complexity with respect for pluralistic differences. True unity was not wrought through outside pressures and mere expediency; it had to be worked for and animated by the powers and energies of love.[7]

The kind of unification Teilhard is talking about has its own laws and requirements. He elaborated his unifying vision mainly in his theory of "*Creative Union*"[8] in which he defined the relation between the one and the many. For him, unification and differentiation go together and are the fundamental basis for understanding all realities – spiritual, material, and relational between individuals and individuals and between individuals and God.

In the process of unification, the idea of convergence is central in Teilhard's vision.[9] One can see convergence in all areas of human activities today. In spite of evident discrepancies, disturbances, suffering, injustice, hatred, and bloodshed, movements have been created for greater economic, political, cultural, and spiritual unity among the people of the world. Never before was humanity so aware of its oneness. This is a profound change of age, indeed. As early as 1923, Teilhard could write:

---

[6] PM, p. 242 -- I, p. 269. Numerous are the texts in Teilhard's writings that talk about the interdependence and the convergence of people, cultures, and religions. See, for example: VP, pp. 206-7 -- III, pp. 290-91; VP, p. 208 -- III, p. 293; PM, p. 244 -- I, p. 271; AE, pp. 240-41 -- VII, p. 249; AE, p. 239 -- VII, p. 248; AE, p. 240 -- VII, p. 248.

[7] Ursula King, *Spirit of Fire: The Life and Vision of Teilhard de Chardin* (Maryknoll, N.Y.: Orbis Books, 1996, 1998), p. 202.

[8] See WTW, pp. 151-176 -- XII, pp. 193-224.

[9] Jean-Marc Moschetta wrote : « Teilhard proposait de 'substituer à une métaphysique de l'*Esse*, une métaphysique de l'*Unire*' [CE, p. 227 - X, p. 271]. L'idée était d'interpréter l'histoire de l'univers comme un mouvement d'unification convergente dont le point focal est le Christ. Cette option métaphysique a pour fondement une conviction théologique qui est que le 'Christ universel' est ce qui relie entre eux les divers éléments du cosmos. » See Jean Marc Moschetta, « Le Christ cosmique chez Teilhard : Fondement d'une 'écologie intégrale' in *Teilhard Aujourd'hui : Vers une écologie intégrale, l'apport de Pierre Teilhard de Chardin* (Saint-Léger Editions, mars 2016), p. 66.

"We are standing, at the present moment, not only at a change of century and civilization, but at a *change of epoch*."[10]

A new path is on the horizon. A synthesis based not in reduction, common denominators and compromises, but in differentiation and personalization, will overcome oppositions and differences. Teilhard spoke of two forces that were responsible for such a change; one external and one internal.

Under the pressure of external conditions, humanity is coming closer and closer to forming one world and one civilization, and Teilhard asks, "Is not the world tending to become one so quickly these days that certain differences between countries are disappearing?"[11]

Through technology we are witnessing the convergence of individuals and groups from many places in the world. Humanity forms, at the present time, a simple village whose residents think, talk, and deal with each other through electronic devices.

Even though they are compelling and constraining, such external forces are not able to bring about real and organic unity between people. For this, nothing can replace the spiritual energies of inner affinity – the internal forces. Teilhard talks about "a sort of living affinity towards the splendid realization of some foreseen unity,"[12] the inner bonds of love,[13] and the mutual and profound attraction that he explained this way:

> Prompted by some favouring influence, the elements of mankind should succeed in making effective a profound force of mutual attraction, deeper and more powerful than the surface-repulsion which causes them to diverge. Forced upon one another by the dimensions and mechanics of the earth, men will purposefully bring to life a common soul in this vast body.[14]

With such a "common soul," a new consciousness and a different state of mind – a "Mind [that allows to] see things from a broad angle,"[15] as Teilhard says – will emerge, and we will start to see the universal realities that are without frontiers. Teilhard wrote:

> Humanity was sleeping – it is still sleeping – imprisoned in the narrow joys of its little closed loves. A tremendous spiritual power is slumbering in the

---

[10] VP, p. 75 -- III, p. 107.
[11] LTF, p. 105 -- *Accomplir l'homme*, p.128.
[12] VP, p, 78 -- III, p. 110.
[13] See chap. "Fire on Earth" of this book.
[14] FM, p. 76 -- V, p. 98.
[15] LZ, p. 75 -- *Lettres à Léontine Zanta*, p. 82.

depths of our multitude, which will manifest itself only when we have learnt to *break down the barriers* of our egoisms and, by a fundamental recasting of our outlook, raise ourselves up to the habitual and practical vision of universal realities.[16]

The Universal realities and the Global mind

These universal realities that Teilhard talked about are many. He talked, for example, about the "sense of the earth,"[17] the "spirit of the earth,"[18] the "sense of man,"[19] the "sense of the species,"[20] the "sense of the universal,"[21] "the human,"[22] the "cosmic sense,"[23] the "stuff of the universe,"[24] the "sense of humanity,"[25] the "'front-line' of humanity,"[26] the "common faith,"[27] the "common soul of humanity,"[28] "a child and citizen of the Earth,"[29] etc.

Underneath all these appellations, there is one common reality, though, and that is the human being. "What we see taking place in the world today," Teilhard wrote, "is not merely the multiplication of *men* but the continued shaping of *Man*."[30] The more one "sees" deeply, the more universal, unifying, and unified one becomes. Then, one goes beyond all limitations, frontiers, separations, divisions, and discriminations to reach each and everyone.

To have a universal consciousness, forsaking the individualistic mentality, is what Teilhard is recommending. This is a way to peace, too. In 1942, when the world was plunged in the catastrophic WWII, Teilhard, paradoxically and ironically, wrote these penetrating words: "… let your thought and action be 'universal', which is to say 'total'. And tomorrow,

---

[16] DM, p.146 -- IV, p. 186.
[17] HE, p. 31 -- VI, p. 39.
[18] HE, p. 32 -- VI, p. 39.
[19] TF, p. 13 -- XI, p. 21.
[20] FM, p. 253 -- V, p. 315.
[21] AE, p. 176 -- VII, p. 182.
[22] AE, p. 376 -- VII, p. 399.
[23] AE, p. 218 -- VII, p. 227.
[24] HE, p. 58 -- VI, p. 74.
[25] HE, p. 78 -- VI, p. 97.
[26] HE, p. 136 -- VI, p. 171.
[27] TF, p. 203 -- XI, p. 217.
[28] HE, p. 137 -- VI, p. 171.
[29] LTF, p. 44 -- *Accomplir l'homme*, p. 56.
[30] FM, p. 275 -- V, p. 342.

maybe, you will find to your surprise that all opposition has disappeared and you can 'love' one another."[31]

Peace is a state of mind, and also a mind at peace; thinking and feeling right, without fear, without paranoia or neurosis, and globally. For a global mind embraces societies, nations, races, religions, continents, and "strangers" with all their differences. A global mind recognizes the value of each individual and each "category" as a way of being human, but it also sees what connects us to the human family and holds us together such as: everyone is a human being; everyone has rights and duties; everyone has needs and aspirations. A global mind is non-reductionist. It celebrates the uniqueness of individuals and the particularity, originality, and difference of each culture, but, at the same time, finds that we are so much related, linked, and interconnected.[32]

Moreover, a global mind is a prerequisite for global peace. A global mind does not think in terms of "*Homo homini lupus*" (man is wolf to man) philosophy, nor in terms of the survival of the fittest, the strongest, the richest, and the most powerful and influential. A global mind recognizes that such ways of thinking lead undoubtedly to aggression and wars. When our mind is not at peace, we create the conditions for wars. We are already at war, at least psychologically.

Furthermore, a lack of meaning for our lives, because of the failure to have a purpose and a direction, will make us lose ties with the world. That makes us lose faith, hope, and self-respect for and in ourselves, and harmony, understanding, and love with and for others. To create peace is to create a state of mind that creates peace. A global mind thinks synthesis, transformation, evolution, universality, unification, diaphany, divinization, fuller being, conciliation, and love.

---

[31] AE, p. 95 -- VII, p. 101.

[32] Someone like His Holiness the Dalai Lama, for example, cannot agree more. He said: "Many of the world's problems and conflicts arise because we have lost sight of the basic humanity that binds us all together as a human family. We tend to forget that despite the diversity of race, religion, ideology, and so forth, people are equal in their basic wish for peace and happiness. ... A new way of thinking has become the necessary condition for responsible living and acting. If we maintain obsolete values and beliefs, a fragmented consciousness, and a self-centered spirit, we will continue to hold to outdated goals and behaviors. Such an attitude by a large number of people would block the entire transition to an interdependent yet peaceful and cooperative global society." See Michael Collopy and Jason Gardner, ed., *Architects of Peace: Visions of Hope in Words and Images* (Novato, CA: New World Library, 2000), p. 175.

Teilhard remains an incontestable master of this school of thought. But isn't this a utopian approach to reality? While recognizing the difficulty, Teilhard says:

> Mankind, the spirit of the earth, the synthesis of individuals and peoples, the paradoxical conciliation of the element with the whole, and of unity with multitude – all these are called Utopian and yet they are biologically necessary. And for them to be incarnated in the world all we may well need is to imagine our power of loving developing until it embraces the total of men and of the earth.[33]

That is because "Driven by the forces of love, the fragments of the world seek each other so that the World may come to being."[34] "We know we inter-are,"[35] as Thick Nhat Hanh summarized it so well. We usually celebrate independence, and that is great. But aren't we supposed to celebrate interdependence,[36] in its true sense, also? Isn't "isolationism"[37] ontologically and existentially impossible anyway?

---

[33] PM, p. 266 -- I, p. 295.
[34] PM, pp. 264-65 -- I, p. 294.
[35] Thick Nhat Hanh, *Love in Action: Writing on Nonviolent Social Change*, ed., by Arnold Kotler (Berkeley, CA: Parallax Press, 1993), p. 137. See also Thick Nhat Hanh, *Peace Is Every Step: The Path of Mindfulness in Everyday Life*, ed., by Arnold Kotler (New York: Bantam Books, 1991), p. 96.
[36] Wayne Teasdale said about interdependence: "Interdependence is an inescapable fact of our contemporary world. Not only is it a prevailing condition that dominates international commerce, cultural exchange, and scientific collaboration, it is a value that promotes stable global peace. The more the bonds of interconnectedness define the shape and scope of the future, the less likely they will be ruptured. The more interdependent we are, the more we will safeguard the system of the universal society." Wayne Teasdale, *The Mystic Heart: Discovering a Universal Spirituality in the World's Religions* (Novato, CA: New World Library, 1999), p. 5.
[37] Arthur C. Cochrane wrote: "ontologically there is no such thing as an isolated, solitary individual. To be sure, one can deny his or her co-humanity. One can live as a hermit or as a superman. Yet in so doing we cannot annul our relationship with others. We have been created in a horizontal relationship through Christ with and for our fellow human beings." Arthur C. Cochrane, *The Mystery of Peace* (Elgin, IL: Brethren Press, 1986), p. 15.

"Citizen of the earth"[38]

It is interesting to see that Teilhard, on many occasions, confided to his friends that he would like to be a "citizen of the earth." In one of these letters, he wrote:

> would like to express the thoughts of a man who, having finally penetrated the partitions and ceilings of little countries, little coteries, little sects, rises above all these categories and finds himself a child and citizen of the earth.[39]

To another friend, he wrote:

> dream of a kind of "Book of the earth" in which I could let myself speak not as Frenchman, nor as a member of a particular division, but as a Man or simply as "terrestrial."[40]

When one sees the big picture, one usually has a better view of the essential. From far away, one has a more comprehensive perspective. Teilhard complained to another friend with these words:

> But mind you see things from a broad angle! Here, around the Pacific, you couldn't believe how petty our little European disputes appear. I hope that we are gradually approaching a time when men will be capable of loving "nothing but the earth." Anything else is too small for us, you see. And even the earth, when we have encircled it with our union, will send us off to the love of what is greater still.[41]

When one transcends the familiar, the ordinary, and the "business-as-usual" habit, to see things from a distance, one acquires a different perspective. Don't we remember what happened, for example, to the people who went to the moon for the first time? The higher they traveled,

---

[38] LTF, p. 44 -- *Accomplir l'homme*, p. 56.
[39] LTF, p. 44 -- *Accomplir l'homme*, p. 56.
[40] On 12 October 1926, Teilhard wrote M. l'Abbe Gaudefroy: "Je rêve d'une espèce de 'Livre de la Terre' où je me laisserais parler, non comme Français, ni comme élément d'un compartiment quelconque, mais comme Homme, ou come 'terrestre' simplement. Je voudrais dire la confiance, les ambitions, la plénitude, et aussi les déceptions, les inquiétudes, l'espèce de vertige, de celui qui prend conscience des destinées et des intérêts de la Terre (Humanité) tout entière.... – Si j'arrivais à mettre cela debout, il me semble que ce serait un peu comme le livre de ma vie » (LI, pp. 52-53).
[41] LZ, p. 75 -- *Lettres à Léontine Zanta*, p. 82.

the less clear the frontiers between countries and continents and other things became; now where are Canada, India, China, the United States…, now where are America, Europe, Asia…, now where are the countries who are democratic, dictatorial, socialist…, now where are the Christians, the Muslims, the Buddhists…, now where are those who speak English, Spanish, French, Arabic…? All boundaries seem to have disappeared. No lines of any kind were to be found; no red lines, no green lines, no dividing lines. Only one earth remains – a beautiful and radiating earth. For the first time, they became existentially aware of the fact that their maps did not carry the whole truth.

That was very interesting and compelling. It shows how our perspective changes when we see things from different angles, and from a deeper or higher level, or from a distance. Maps – all kinds of maps – are human-made. They can be made again and again. We may even choose to live without them at all if our vision is that we are "citizens of the same earth," we are brothers and sisters in the same journey of life, and we feel at home everywhere.

CHAPTER ELEVEN

"UNION DIFFERENTIATES"

Yes, humanity ought to be united. But how do we, collectively, answer this call? Would it be by creating a common enemy to fight against? Could the horror of common disasters that may happen with or without warning be a reason for closer collaboration? Would the fear of losing what we already possess be a good reason for reconciliation? Even though these reasons, and other similar reasons, may play a role in the unification process, they cannot be the main reason, for the main reason remains the intensification of being – a greater sense of being. It is this kind of feeling that nourished the hearts of the most famous conquerors of the seas and the far lands, the most determined explorers and adventurers, and the most talented leaders and thinkers and inventors of all times. Peace also is a conquest. Teilhard wrote: "'Peace' cannot mean anything but a *higher process of conquest*."[1] This, in order to happen, requires the intensification of being -- being more – because "Fuller being is closer union,"[2] as Teilhard said.

"Union Differentiates"[3]

True peace can exist and increase only through people's psychic powers; by being more intensely human. The truth is that, when we talk about intensification, we are talking at the same time about the differentiation of the individual and also about the unification with society. The more the self is, the more it is unified with others. The more others are united as a group, the more the self is articulated. Teilhard's concept here is worth emphasizing. He wrote: "In any domain – whether it be the cells of a body, the members of a society or the elements of spiritual synthesis – *union differentiates*."[4]

---

[1] LTF, p. 146 -- *Accomplir l'homme*, p. 176
[2] PM, p. 31 -- I, p. 25.
[3] PM, p. 262 -- I, p. 291; also VI, pp. 80-81, 129, 179; VII, p. 122; X, p. 200.
[4] PM, p. 262 -- I, p. 291; also VI, pp. 80-81, 129, 179; VII, p. 122; X, p. 200.

Teilhard de Chardin, wrote Bede Griffiths,

> ... always emphasized the principle that union differentiates. We become more ourselves as we enter more deeply into relationship with others. In our ordinary consciousness we are all separated in time and space, but as we go beyond the limitations of time and space we experience our oneness with others. We do not lose our sense of separation and division and discover our integral oneness in the One Reality.[5]

There are, according to Teilhard, two forms of unity. One type requires the fusion of all the elements in order to form that unity. The other is the organic unity that makes the individual difference be heightened rather than be the cause for it to vanish and disappear. It is this second type that must constitute the noosphere that Teilhard talked about. "For Teilhard," wrote Thomas King, "the unity of a living being does not dissolve its constituent parts; rather, it intensifies them.... The elements become more themselves the more they come together; this union accentuates the individual identities."[6] Therefore, union does not swallow individuality and destroy identity. In union, the energy flows from center to center,[7] and, as Teilhard put it,

---

[5] See Bede Griffiths, *A New Vision of Reality: Western Science, Eastern Mysticism and Christian Faith* (Springfield, Illinois: Templegate Publishers, 1989), p. 94. Also, it is interesting to note here how Bede Griffiths describes the principle of differentiation in the Eastern perspective. He wrote: "Again, within the void, within the Ultimate, there is a stir, there is a principle of differentiation, and this is fundamental. If there is no principle of differentiation, which is the basic point missing in Shankara, then one has absolute non-duality, pure *advaita*. In the void of Mahayana Buddhism, on the other hand, the principle of differentiation is recognised. The universe is regarded as coming out through this principle of differentiation. But, at the very moment that it comes out, in the instant that it differentiates, it returns to unity. This, of course, is not in time. It is an eternal movement outwards and an eternal movement of return, all within the Ultimate." See Bede Griffiths, *A New Vision of Reality: Western Science, Eastern Mysticism and Christian Faith* (Springfield, Illinois: Templegate Publishers, 1989), pp. 158-159.
[6] Thomas M. King, S.J., *Teilhard de Chardin* (Wilmington, Delaware: Michael Glazier, Inc., 1988, 'The Way of the Christian Mystics'), p.77.
[7] André Devaux wrote: "Teilhard always clearly distinguishes the union of *dissolution* and the union of *differentiation*. Rather than a real union, the first is an absorption in which the element is assimilated in the all, like salt dissolving in the sea. Such a 'unification of coercion' opens the way to sheer totalitarianism and Teilhard rejects it unequivocally. Entirely different is the authentic union which, far from destroying the differences, exalts the originality of each of the elements

Following the confluent orbits of their centres, the grains of consciousness do not tend to lose their outlines and blend, but, on the contrary, to accentuate the depth and incommunicability of their egos. The more "other" they become in conjunction, the more they find themselves as "self."[8]

Teilhard's concept of union is for growth and fulfillment. In it, the very existence of the individuals is guaranteed by the all, and the very existence of the all is secured by the individuals. Far from being lost in the all, the individuals will become more "themselves" and much more authentic because they are allowed more autonomy, and the all becomes richer and stronger because of the rich and strong interaction of the individuals with the all. Fulfilled individuals make a solid union. A solid union makes fulfilled individuals. "Fuller being is closer union."[9] "True union does not stifle or confuse its elements; it super-differentiates them in unity."[10]

What does this mean for peace? If the principle "the more the element is, the more the union will be and vice versa" is correct, then the union and the element do not destroy each other but enrich each other.[11] They need each other, they make peace with each other, and they fulfill each other. This means that, when each individual works harder to perfect the self, when each ethnic group works harder to live its particular identity, and when a nation works harder to be what makes it different and glorious and proud of its own history, the union of the all becomes not only richer but

---

which it brings together 'center to center.'" See André Devaux. *Teilhard and Womanhood* (New York, N.Y: Paulist Press Deus Books, 1968), p. 6.
[8] PM, p. 262 -- I, p. 291.
[9] PM, p. 31 -- I, p. 25.
[10] HE, p. 42 -- VI, p. 52; see also II, p. 368; V, p. 74; VI, pp. 80, 129; VII, p. 122; IX, p. 74; XIII, p. 168.
[11] Bede Griffiths offered this remarkable theological explanation. He wrote: "Here, as Pierre Teilhard de Chardin emphasises, 'union differentiates.' This means that the more we are united with others, the more we become ourselves. So each is in the other and in the One who unites all the others together. The basis of this is the Christian understanding of the Trinity. The Father is in the Son in a total self-giving to the Son, and the 'I' of the Son is one with the Father. Similarly, in the Holy Spirit the 'I' of the Father and the 'I' of the Son are united in the 'I' of the Spirit. It is a total interrelationship of unity; in other words, total non-duality and yet with this profound differentiation. That is also what we experience in our lives in the experience of love, when we can share and participate in the identity of the other. The ultimate state is when we all reach that state of pure identity in difference." See Bede Griffiths, *A New Vision of Reality: Western Science, Eastern Mysticism and Christian Faith* (Springfield, Illinois: Templegate Publishers, 1989), pp. 173-174.

also it will find ways to help the elements that constitute the whole more themselves and more fulfilled. The interaction becomes so organic that it would seem a critical condition for their very existence. Moreover, it becomes a "Creative Union,"[12] as Teilhard called it. Kathleen Duffy explained:

> The process of Creative Union, the desire and tendency in nature to become more, has been driving the evolutionary process from the beginning. It has been keeping nature in search of new ways to adapt to the changing environment. This process impressed Teilhard. He noted that whenever elements do interact and unite, they become something new with greater potential. He describes this phenomenon succinctly: 'union differentiates' (HP, 186). When elements unite they become more than they were by themselves as they participate in a higher form of being. Examples of this abound: water molecules have properties different from those of the hydrogen and oxygen atoms from which they are formed; the union of sperm with egg generates a zygote that, in both form and potential, is quite unlike the components from which the new cell is made.[13]

This kind of union is not going to be a simple collectivization of the consciousness of different societies. Teilhard described the emerging collective consciousness as being an intensification of "being as group" which works not by absorbing the elements, but by interacting with the elements from center to center in a very complex manner. The greater the complexification, the greater the individualization. It is when a global consciousness is, that the forces of divergences give way to the forces of convergence. Teilhard remarked that "Races, peoples, and nations consolidate one another and complete one another by mutual fecundation."[14]

No matter how justifiable policies of isolation, hostility, or colonialism had been in the past, they are no longer suitable, in this age of ours, for our human evolution and for the development of consciousness. We belong now to the international community and the international community belongs to us. We are citizens of the world and the world is what we make of it. We are not mutually exclusive but profoundly interdependent. We are here to be together and, in a complex way, we affect each other very deeply at the level of the consciousness and of the spirit. For Teilhard, "The higher the degree of complexity in a living

---

[12] WTW, p. 153 – XII, p. 193.
[13] Kathleen Duffy, SSJ, Teilhard's Mysticism: Seeing the Inner Face of Evolution (Maryknoll, N.Y.: Orbis books, 2014), p. 61.
[14] PM, p. 242 -- I, p. 269.

creature, the higher its consciousness; and vice versa."[15] Complexity is not confusion; it is a symphony. A single note is simple and has its meaning when it joins other notes. With the other notes things become complex. The higher the complexity, the more beautiful the symphony would be. In a society, harmony between the individuals does not necessarily require unanimity. It rather requires a formation of a "human front."[16]

"Human front"

A common pursuit of the same truth has the capacity to bring people together. But Teilhard sees more than that. He says: "*In the course of genesis*, knowledge links together not only brains but inevitably hearts as well."[17]

In fact, there is an affective warmth, as Teilhard thinks, between those who have the same goals, ideals, or fields of research. Here Teilhard sees, against all pessimism and skepticism, a real chance for action – a creation of a "human front" charged with the mission of finding solutions for modern problems. With such an atmosphere of cooperation and coordination, a transformation in the psychological milieu becomes possible. What looked utopian yesterday will not remain utopian tomorrow.[18]

Create the right environment and the right atmosphere – the right milieu, Teilhard would say – and peace will come as an inevitable by-product. Therefore, we need to revise the way we think in the first place. In order to do that, we need, first, to abolish these "iron laws" that control and direct our minds. Teilhard explains:

> Under colour of realism (or sometimes of metaphysics) we are ceaselessly reminded that man is by nature held in a certain number of circles which he will never be able to break: the eternal conflict between master and slave – the organic necessity of wars – the functional inconceivability of humanity not divided within itself. And how many more? But how can one fail to see that, to justify conservatism and pessimism, all these alleged "iron laws" systematically ignore the possibility of transformation *modifying the psychological circumstances* in which history has hitherto developed.[19]

---

[15] FM, p. 116 -- V, p. 144.
[16] Teilhard wrote: "We are locked up in a prison where we cannot breathe. We must have air. We do not want fascist fronts, or a popular front – but a *human front*" (SC, p. 145 -- IX, p. 185).
[17] AM, p. 256 -- II, p. 353.
[18] See AM, p. 258 -- II, pp. 254-55.
[19] AM, pp. 257-58 -- II, p. 354.

We also need to abandon our "old ideologies and categories" (such as democracy, fascism, communism, socialism, etc.), and engage in a new movement based on universalism, futurism, and personalism.[20]

Moreover, we should "renounce the comfort of familiar narrowness"[21] and embrace the large horizons of humanity. Teilhard foresees a lot of changes all over the world, and he is interested in them all. These changes can constitute an opportunity for creating a common objective and a universal ideal on the scale of the whole earth,[22] precisely because of a possible unanimity that "can only result from a common passion for some reality or ultimate realization,"[23] observes Teilhard. For Teilhard unanimity means unanimity; he does not want to exclude anyone. There ought to be a collective push for a spiritual renewal. This is how he describes this "all together" work:

> The outcome of the world, the gates of the future, the entry into the super-human – these are not thrown open to a few of the privileged nor to one chosen people to the exclusion of all others. They will open only to an advance of *all together*, in direction in which *all together** can join and find completion in a spiritual renovation of the earth....[24]

In this context, we cannot but notice the overlapping of the different activities that is continuously growing. We see this at any level of human activities – cultural, military, economic, medical, spiritual.... There is a kind of constant interaction between events which, in the past, were thought to have nothing to do with each other. Consequently, it no longer seems right to analyze a situation from within the specific field in which it appears to be. Here, complexification and globality would prove to be a great support for peace, precisely because of the interdependent reality they advocate. The positive side of such a reality is that there is a mutual growth, and not mutual elimination, between the many and the one; by itself this constitutes an enormous step for peace in the world.

---

[20]See LT, p. 228 and Teilhard de Chardin, *Lettres inédites,: Lettres à l'Abbé Gaudefroy et l'Abbé Breuil*, Le Rocher, 1988, p. 114.

[21] PM, p. 226 -- I, p. 251.

[22] See LTF, p. 135 -- *Accomplir l'homme*, p. 162.

[23] On 20 January 1953, Teilhard wrote to Jeanne Mortier: "Vous avez cent fois raison : il n'y a aucun principe constructeur dans la doctrine de la 'non-violence', -- aucune foi, et donc aucun dynamisme. La non-violence est simplement la face négative de l'*unanimité*. Et l'unanimité ne peut résulter que de la passion commune pour quelque réalité ou réalisation suprême » (LM, p. 123).

[24] PM, pp. 244-45 -- I, pp. 271-72. -- * In footnote: "Even if they do so only under the influence of a few, an *élite*."

Furthermore, it is worth noticing also that, today and from now on, it is, and it will be, hard to be isolated. A certain common psychological "network" seems to be in place, in spite of all the differences we might have. A new civilization is rising – the Universal Human. Teilhard summarized this idea in one line. He wrote: "What is no more than national may well disappear, but what is human cannot be lost."[25]

Indeed, the human – the universal that is in everyone of us – has no borders of any kind, no frontiers, and no demarcation lines. It has only bonds. One feels at home everywhere and with anyone. The universal has no boundaries and no enemies. Enmity, then wars, start with selfishness and the desire to separate and be fragmented. The fragmentation view – the inner one as well as the external one – is a major cause of confusion and frustration at a personal level, and of political disorder and violence at a social level. Only when we feel real interrelation and connection with everyone and everything, and live organically and mystically in and with the whole, will the risk of war be reduced, if not completely eliminated. "It is the whole that will have the last word,"[26] reminds Teilhard.

Therefore, if we get stuck in a problem, if we lose the reason for doing things, or if we think that violence is the only remaining tool for finding a solution, let us look at the situation from a larger perspective. Let us link it to the whole where it really belongs, feel the mystical oneness in everything and with everyone, and feel how much every separate thing and every unique individual are important for the whole and how important the whole is for all the elements that form it. Magically, new insights and new options and solutions will emerge and become available to us. What cannot be reached through ordinary cognition can be grasped with the whole being.

This is to say that the bottom line for winning a cause is not to shift weapons from these hands to those hands, but to shift to another state of consciousness altogether in which opposites are complementary, contradictions are a dynamic synthesis, and the many find themselves on the same human front. In such a state of consciousness, the crude feeling of a need for a weapon becomes just outrageous, ridiculous, and unthinkable.

---

[25] SC, p. 131 -- IX, p. 172.
[26] AE, p. 51 -- VII, p. 58.

Chapter Twelve

The Cyberpeace Way

At any moment of the day or the night, we find ourselves submerged in an ocean of information. Thoughts, images, suggestions, publicities, instructions, recommendations, dictations, speculations, manipulations … are more than one can really absorb and handle. All kinds of electronic devices are used to carry them through our senses to our minds. People seem to adapt and even enjoy the continuous noise that is going on, be it the TV, the radio, the computer, and all the other gadgets. Life is becoming a constant whirlwind of activities dictated by the media, and people do not feel any embarrassment if they choose their activities according to what is trending on their favorite electronic device. It seems that what really counts for them is what is fashionable, and not necessarily what they really like, or what they know in their hearts they are supposed to consider and do.

So, whether we like this overwhelming information age or not, we are in it for better or worse. It is the electronic revolution that triggered it big and far. But how has this happened? Maybe this is the time to reconsider the noosphere concept that was so dear to Teilhard de Chardin.

The Noosphere

The word "noosphere" – literally, "mind-sphere" (from the Greek "noos" – or "nous" – and "sphaira") – was a term that was used originally by French philosopher Edouard Leroy, Russian geochemist Vladimir Vernadsky, and especially Jesuit paleontologist and mystic Pierre Teilhard de Chardin who has made it one of the most important themes of his vision.

As a paleontologist, Teilhard observed, throughout the very long history of creation, how the earth was transformed from a dead planet into a living world – a "biosphere." As a mystic, he saw that the next step was going to take the "biosphere" into a "noosphere" that is led by the mind, thought, and intention – a kind of thinking sphere that can be called global or collective consciousness. In this long evolving process, Teilhard kept perceiving the unity of all things. He talked, for example, about "*fundamental unity... unity of homogeneity... collective unity...* the unimaginable reality of collective bonds."[1] He also talked about "a cosmic sense of 'oneness'"[2] and about "the *milieu* in which all is made one."[3] Moreover, he affirmed elsewhere: "Time and space are organically joined again so as to weave, together, the stuff of the universe,"[4] and "We are, at this very moment, passing through a change of age... Beneath a change of age lies a change of thought."[5]

The very idea of the noosphere is intriguing and fascinating.[6] Although it seems like a science fiction idea, many people want it to be true because they see it growing close to awakening. Teilhard is certain of it. He sees it as an evolution towards understanding one's own reality: "Man discovers that *he is nothing else than evolution become conscious of*

---

[1] PM, pp. 41, 42 -- I, pp, 35, 36.
[2] TF, p. 209 -- XI, p. 227.
[3] HM, p. 125 – XIII, p. 147.
[4] PM, p. 218 – I, p. 241.
[5] PM, p. 214, 215 – I, pp. 237, 238.
[6] Many thinkers, for generations now, expressed interest in the idea of the noosphere. Moreover, some theologians in particular went as far as to consider the description of the noosphere presented by Teilhard as consistent with the millennial Christian theology. For example, this is how Pope Benedict XVI talked about it. He wrote: "And so we can now say that the goal of worship and the goal of creation as a whole are one and the same—divinization, a world of freedom and love. But this means that the historical makes its appearance in the cosmic. The cosmos is not a kind of closed building, a stationary container in which history may by chance take place. It is itself movement, from its one beginning to its one end. In a sense, creation *is* history.

This can be understood in several ways. For example, against the background of the modern evolutionary world view, Teilhard de Chardin depicted the cosmos as a process of ascent, a series of unions. From very simple beginnings the path leads to ever greater and more complex unities, in which multiplicity is not abolished but merged into a growing synthesis, leading to the "Noosphere", in which spirit and its understanding embrace the whole and are blended into a kind of living organism. Invoking the epistles to the Ephesians and Colossians, Teilhard looks on Christ as the energy that strives toward the Noosphere and finally incorporates everything in its "fullness'. From here Teilhard went on to give a new meaning to Christian worship: the transubstantiated Host is the anticipation of the transformation and divinization of matter in the christological "fullness". In his view, the Eucharist provides the movement of the cosmos with its direction; it anticipates its goal and at the same time urges it on." (Joseph Cardinal Ratzinger [Pope Benedict XVI]. *The Spirit of the Liturgy* (San Francisco: Ignatius Press. 2000), pp. 28-29.

itself.... The consciousness of each of us is evolution looking at itself and reflecting upon itself."[7] He also sees it as something much bigger than the self: "Man is not the center of the universe as once we thought in our simplicity, but something much more wonderful – the arrow pointing the way to the final unification of the world in terms of life."[8]

Teilhard is convinced that such an evolution that goes from geogenesis to biogenesis and now to noogenesis gives hope. He wants humanity to cling to hope. He wants to see humanity transcending the barriers that obstruct human unity and peace. He wants humanity to keep going toward a "super-life." He wrote: "... there is for us, in the future, under some form or another, at least collective, not only survival but also *super-life.*"[9]

Teilhard, the mystic, envisions life moving towards unification and maturing in the mystical Christ who is waiting to gather to himself "the last folds of the garment of flesh and love woven for him by his faithful" because he "*has not yet attained the fullness of his form*" and "*reached the peak of his growth.*"[10] "Christ is the term *of even the natural* evolution of living beings."[11] This is, in Teilhard's view, the Omega point towards which the evolution is moving.[12] "Omega," the last letter in the Greek alphabet, refers to the final stage of evolution where the All absorbs all. Teilhard wrote:

---

[7] PM, p. 221 – I, pp. 244, 245.

[8] PH, p. 224 – I, pp. 248-49.

[9] PH, p. 234 – I, p. 259.

[10] FM, p. 320 -- V, p. 397.

[11] FM, p. 320 -- V, p. 397. Teilhard wrote also: "Nevertheless, however efficacious this newly born faith of Man in the ultra-human may prove to be, it seems that Man's urge towards *Some Thing* ahead of him cannot achieve its full fruition except by combining with another and still more fundamental aspiration – one from above, urging him towards *Some One*." (FM, p. 302 – V, p. 374).

[12] Pope Francis concurred with Teilhard in seeing the maturity of all things in God. He wrote: "The Ultimate destiny of the universe is in the fullness of God, which has already been attained by the risen Christ, the measure of the maturity of all things... all creatures are moving forward with us and through us towards a common point of arrival, which is God, in that transcendent fullness where the risen Christ embraces and illumines all things" (*Laudato Si: On Care for Our Common Home*, #83). See also Pope Benedict XVI, *Homily for the Celebration of Vespers in Aosta* (July 24, 2009) and Pope John Paul II, *Letter to the Reverend George Coyne* (June 1, 1988).

Christian tradition is unanimous that there is more in the total Christ than Man and God. There is also He who, in his 'theandric' being, gathers up the whole of Creation. *In quo omnia constant.*

Hitherto, and in spite of the dominant position accorded to it by St Paul in his view of the World, this third aspect or function – we might even say, in a true sense of the words, this third 'nature' of Christ (neither human nor divine, but cosmic) – has not noticeably attracted the explicit attention of the faithful or of theologians.[13]

Teilhard sees clearly the continuous Incarnation of Christ in the creation. "For where two or three are gathered in my name, I am there among them."[14] "Now you are the body of Christ and individually members of it."[15] God is integrated in humanity more than ever. But this also means that we should feel responsible as well for the creation and consider that, as Teilhard put it:

> Any increase that I can bring upon myself or upon things is translated into some increase in my power to love and some progress in Christ's blessed hold upon the universe. Our work appears to us, in the main, as a way of earning our daily bread. But its essential virtue is on a higher level: through it we complete in ourselves the subject of the divine union; and through it again we somehow make to grow in stature the divine term of the one with whom we are united, our Lord Jesus Christ.[16]

But why and how are we able to effect this increase upon ourselves and upon others? Teilhard finds the answer in Christ. He explained it this way:

> Christ consumes with his glance my entire being. And with that same glance, that same presence, he enters into those who are around me and whom I love. Thanks to him therefore I am united with them, as in a divine *milieu*, through their inmost selves, and I can act upon them with all the resources of my being.
>
> Christ *binds* us and *reveals* us to one another.[17]

Teilhard's hope for the human future is founded in the noogenesis and in the future of the noosphere. Since the direction of the evolution, according to him, is clear and it is leading humanity toward a kind of higher and more perfect unity, then peace is also coming and it is

---

[13] HM, p. 93 -- XIII, p. 107.
[14] Matthew 18:20.
[15] 1 Corinthians 12:27.
[16] DM, p. 63 – IV, p. 52.
[17] WTW, pp. 110-11 – XII, p. 149.

inevitable. However, the path that leads there remains a long and rocky path. Teilhard recognized the difficulties and the struggles that humanity will continue to endure during that journey. The final line of his *"The Phenomenon of Man"* is: "In one manner or the other it still remains true that, even in the view of the mere biologist, the human epic resembles nothing so much as a way of the Cross."[18]

The emergence of the noosphere – the sum total of the ever increasing human knowledge and experience of all times – is seen by Teilhard at a peak mystical moment that is the Omega Point. This moment is no other than the result of the interactions between the all-powerful attraction of the Omega Point and of the increasing activity of human networks creating a highly complex thinking layer over the earth. In that huge global information network, the Internet can be seen as the electronic linking means in that noosphere prior to the mystical moment of the Omega Point. Here we can say that there is no doubt that Teilhard was, if not the inventor, the direct inspiring thinker for the invention of the Internet. We all know how much the Internet, at the present time, is raising very important social, psychological, cultural, political, and spiritual questions.

The Noosphere, the Internet, and the Cyberpeace

Not long after WWI and at the beginning of the bloodiest century of history, Teilhard envisioned the capacity of communicating with everyone swiftly and efficiently. This would be a global consciousness – a realm of the mind he called "noosphere." Such a "reality" would, as he thought, provide a profound driving force for peace because it would be the next step in the evolution toward an ethical course that is more concerned with understanding, purposefulness, love, and higher quality of life.

Humanity is witnessing at the present time changes of unprecedented proportions. Nowhere is this more obvious than in the communications fields – "an explosion in communication,"[19] as Alfred Stikker wrote. Who

---

[18] PM, p. 313 -- I, p. 348.

[19] Allerd Stikker wrote: "Teilhard sees the present strongly increasing coherence in human society by an explosion in communication (both directly through travel and indirectly through books, radio, television – and what he didn't know at that time – the new acceleration through satellites and micro chips) as a distinct new step on the road to a higher level in the evolution of mankind. His classification into the geosphere (the earth), the biosphere (living things on earth) and the noosphere (the mental reservoir of mankind) leads him to the conception that the increasingly larger volume and quality of the noosphere – clearly undergoing a growth phase – will lead to a new dimension for mankind (supermankind) with entirely new

doesn't use now, and with addiction for many of us, all these electronic devices that connect us instantly with anyone, anywhere, and at any time? The ever-growing and expanding communications systems that make distances irrelevant, is making the world smaller and smaller. We are becoming a "global village" indeed. Consequently, nothing will ever be the same anymore. Something different has happened in human consciousness; "Beneath a change of age lies a change of thought,"[20] Teilhard has said.[21]

What are we supposed to do with this compelling information-age – accumulate endless, non sense trivialities, commercials, toxic viruses, and lessons on how to harm others, or create a web of wisdom that contributes greatly in finding better ways for making peace with ourselves, with others, and above all with God, and for making us better human beings?

Teilhard envisioned and posited a "noosphere" – a "cyberspace" – where a super-consciousness could emerge and expand day after day, and where we could realize our unity with everyone else, no matter who and where they are, and begin to behave accordingly. With its horizontal and wide power of connection, its ability to bring people together in new ways, and its effectiveness in communicating ideas of great concerns for the survival and development of humanity, the Internet might very well be

---

relationships and properties which are not predictable (just as in the past the creation of life, awareness and self-awareness also transpired as unpredictable)". See Alfred Stikker, "Interdisciplinary Integration and Dualism in Society" in Leo Zonneveld and Robert Muller, ed., *The Desire to Be Human*, "International Teilhard Compendium" Centenary volume (Netherlands: Mirananda Publishers b.v. Wassenaar, 1983), p. 182.

[20] PM, p. 215 – I, p. 238.

[21] Technology contributed greatly to this "change of thought." J. de Marneffe explained: "In an essay on 'The Place of Technology in a General Biology of Mankind' -1947 – Teilhard develops the thesis that general technology is not just a sum total of commercial enterprises or a kind of mechanical gravity. It is 'the sum of the procedures which are arranged thoughtfully to keep up among men the level of consciousness which corresponds to our level of aggregation and reunion'. Technology has thus a real biological function and this explains why Teilhard favours it. We are far from the 'uneasiness' before the technological world which affected a man even as optimistic as the existentialist philosopher Gabriel Marcel. With the growing population of Asia and its needs, technology is not something which we can afford to ignore. It is something which we must assume and exploit for our good." See J. de Marneffe s.j., "Teilhardian Thought as a Methodology for the Discernment of Socio-Cultural Options in an Evolutionary World" in Leo Zonneveld and Robert Muller, ed., *The Desire to Be Human*, "International Teilhard Compendium" Centenary volume (Netherlands: Mirananda Publishers b.v. Wassenaar, 1983), pp. 198-199.

leading to the realization of Teilhard's dream – the evolving collective consciousness.

Indeed, when a civilization adds new knowledge, new discoveries, new progress in any fields of human development, it has registered itself as a higher rung in the evolution of the human species. Humanity has evolved, and continues to evolve, through the cultures and civilizations that extend "the psychic zones of the world,"[22] as Teilhard put it, to more and more people. The noosphere becomes, then, an ever growing reservoir of an ever-growing human knowledge. It unifies all human experiences and becomes quite literally a collective human consciousness that Teilhard calls sometimes "super-consciousness."[23]

The World Wide Web (WWW) is certainly one of the most important and influential developments ever made in human history. It is a major tool for individual and social transformation. It can destroy our future. But it can also create sane conditions for a better life on earth, and for a more harmonious future. It is too bad that some people choose to use this tool for destruction, but it is great to see a good majority using it to build a new earth, as Teilhard would like to say. There is no doubt that the Internet is booming and remaking human culture. But is that good news or bad news after all? It certainly depends on how we look at it and how we use it. One should always remember that high tech is power and power cannot be neutral.

There is the danger that it will reduce us to virtual human beings – isolated, dehumanized, "machine-ized," and commercialized; the cyber-content constitutes an enormous pressure – a subtle dictatorship – to "be conformed to this world."[24] Also there is the great risk of depersonalizing by reducing the "I-Thou" relationship that Martin Buber was famous of using, to the "I-it" relationship that lacks openness, reciprocity, and any kind of interpersonal and interactive dimensions. On-line "realities"

---

[22] "... evolution is now, whether we like it or not, gaining the psychic zones of the world and transferring to the spiritual constructions of life not only the cosmic stuff but also the cosmic 'primacy' hitherto reserved by science to the tangled whirlwind of the ancient 'ether'." (PM, pp. 220-21 – I, p. 244).

[23] "We are faced with harmonised collectivity of consciousnesses equivalent to a sort of super-consciousness. The idea is that of the earth not only becoming covered by myriads of grains of thought, but becoming enclosed in a single thinking envelope so as to form, functionally, no more than a single vast grain of thought on the sidereal scale, the plurality of individual reflections grouping themselves together and reinforcing one another in the act of a single unanimous reflection." (PM, pp. 251-52 – I, p. 279).

[24] Romans 12:2.

involve false expectations, fantasies, lies, and deceit. They may enslave us while convincing us that this is the right way to more freedom, more equality, and more "democracy." The effects of the noosphere do not uproot evil. A perverted use of the Internet and any other tool of high tech is always possible, especially when one intends to use science to divide, or wishes to crash life altogether.

There is also the possibility for the Internet to help us to be more harmonized, reconciled, unified, and with a much better and peaceful future. The Internet helps us to perceive the interconnectedness of all things and to loosen the boundaries that traditionally divide cultures, languages, sciences, religions, nations, races, ethnic groups, and individuals. Whether we are aware of it or not, and whether our intentions are positive or negative, every time we log on, we become participants in, and contributors to, the creation of the global mind field.

Despite its negative sides, the Internet should be considered as one of the most promising roads to enlightenment, wisdom, development, harmony, and peace. There are cyber activists for any purpose imaginable. Hopefully, we will see more and more activists on the side of bettering the world, and less and less activists on the side of its destruction.

In any case, no one doubts that technologies are giving us different frames of mind, and the Internet is changing our understanding of our relationships with the world and with God. It has the potential to give the "Love your neighbor as yourself" new expressions and extensions by being a redemptive tool for carrying humankind to higher levels of consciousness. This is exactly what Teilhard intended when he kept insisting on the "noosphere" concept and its evolving process.

Moreover, Teilhard, we should perhaps say, found in the Bible a God who is more compatible with a world in evolution than the static, aloof, and far away old God of certain philosophers. Rather than seeing creation as a one-time event, some theologians think, as Teilhard does, that creation is a continuous process, and it is still going on; the creative power of God made humans co-creators as he intended them to be. In such a case, it wouldn't be out of the ordinary to consider any invention or achievement made by humans, the emergence of cyberspace and the digital world included, as part of the continuous creation of God. When men and women are creative, they do it not to replace God with other gods, but because they find God in their creativity; they use God's gifts for them to continue his creation.

Let us not forget that Teilhard was a mystic-priest first, then a scientist, a theologian, a philosopher, a psychologist, and a poet. This means that, like Julian of Norwich, Hildegard von Bingen, Master

Eckhart, or the other mystics, he testifies to divine immanence. No wonder he wrote *The Divine Milieu* that was a masterpiece of modern spirituality.[25] His God was an incarnated God. His God lived and breathed the life of the creation; he gave birth to, was born from, and continues to give birth to, the magnificent organism of the universe. Therefore, when Teilhard talks about evolution, it should not be taken as Darwin would have it – "the survival of the fittest" – but as an evolution that was planned, guided, and sustained by divine power and will. Teilhard wrote:

> Now we understand that this paradoxical movement is sustained by a prime mover ahead. The branch climbs, not supported by its base but suspended from the future. That is what rendered the movement not only irreversible but irresistible. From this point of view (which is that not only of simple antecedences, but of causality itself) evolution assumes its true figure for our mind and our heart. It is certainly not 'creative', as science for a brief moment believed; but it is the expression of creation, for our experience, in time and space.[26]

Then he added:

> And it is thus, in the end, that above the rediscovered greatness of man, above the revealed greatness of humanity, not violating but preserving the integrity of science, the face of God reappears in our modern universe.[27]

Clearly, no one can doubt that the present moment of our modern life is Teilhard's moment. The noosphere is here, the Internet is here, and we are using both.

Surely enough, we know that ill-intentioned people are using the "cyber" as cyberwarfare and cyberterrorism. What is still lacking is our determination and eagerness to use the "cyber" as cyberpeace. We can do that by using the Internet to create a highly evolved collective consciousness through sharing hopeful stories, peace-building movements and organizations, positive global kinds of cooperation, a state of mind that considers wars unnecessary and futile, common purposes for development and social improvements, and unlimited number of other possible ways. This was Teilhard's dream. Then we are "techno-logian

---

[25] See Jean Maalouf, *The Divine Milieu: A Spiritual Classic for Today and Tomorrow*, "Teilhard Studies Number 38." Autumn 1999, (American Teilhard Association for the Future of Man, Inc.).

[26] VP, p. 231 -- III, pp. 323-24.

[27] VP, p. 231 -- III, p. 324.

[s],"[28] as Paolo Soleri would say, and we "need to co-operate if [we] want to survive."[29]

After decades and centuries of short-sighted militarisms, blind chauvinisms, and biased nationalisms and colonialisms, it is time to count on the promise of the global consciousness and try it. It is the time for Teilhard's prophetic conclusion, "Driven by the forces of love, the fragments of the world seek each other so that the world may come into being."[30]

---

[28] Paolo Soleri wrote: "For the technocrat-technologist the true vocation could be found in the realization that matter is wanting of consciousness, sensitivity, and grace. The technologist must become a techno-logian, the theologian of reality." See Paolo Soleri, "Teilhard and the Esthetic" in *Teilhard and the Unity of Knowledge*, 'The Georgetown University Centennial Symposium', edited by Thomas M. King, S.J. & James F. Salmon, S.J. (New York/Ramsey: NJ.: Paulist Press, 1983), p. 79.
[29] Ursula King wrote: "Today, in a politically post-colonial world, all societies are economically, technically and scientifically closely interdependent and need to co-operate if they want to survive." See Ursula King, *Toward a New Mysticism: Teilhard de Chardin and Eastern Religions*, (New York: Seabury Press, 1980), p. 169.
[30] PM, pp. 264-65 – I, p. 294.

Part IV

The Future Has a Goal

Chapter Thirteen

The Future Has a Goal

When we read Teilhard de Chardin's works, we get the impression that we read the history of the universe from the future more than from the past. Here one cannot but think of what Aristotle called the final cause[1] -- for the sake of which something is made. In a sense, what drives history is the reason that gives sense and direction to history, and this reason comes from the fundamental purpose and goal of life in the first place. For Teilhard, this fundamental goal is what he called the Omega Point, the cosmic Christ, and "Super-Humanity, Super-Christ, Super-Charity."[2]

For many of us, life is actually a meaningless routine even though we usually don't want to admit it. It remains so until the day we ask ourselves why we are doing what we are doing. This is how Albert Camus described this situation in his book, *The Myth of Sisyphus*. He wrote:

> It happens that the stage sets collapse. Rising, streetcar, four hours in the office or the factory, meal, streetcar, four hour of work, meal, sleep, and Monday Tuesday Wednesday Thursday Friday and Saturday according to the same rhythm – this path is easily followed most of the time. But one day the "why" arises and everything begins in that weariness tinged with amazement.[3]

This "weariness" indicates a high level of existential uneasiness and discomfort, and requires an answer to the "why" that gives meaning to it

---

[1] Aristotle's Four Causes explain our world in terms of material, efficiency, form, and final result: 1. *Material cause* (out of which something is made: this table is made of wood). 2. *Efficient cause* (by which something is made: a carpenter made this table). 3. *Formal cause* (into which something is made: four legs and a flat top made this table a table). 4. *Final cause* (for the sake of which something is made: this table is made for eating or writing on).
[2] See SC, pp. 151-173 -- IX, pp. 193-217.
[3] Albert Camus, *The Myth of Sisyphus and Other Essays*, (New York: Random House, 1955), p. 10. See http://www.goodreads.com/quotes/687695-it-happens-that-the-stage-sets-collapse-rising-streetcar-four.

all. In fact, this was the task of religions and cultures throughout the centuries, and it still is their task and the task of every human being for that matter. Famously, Henry David Thoreau said something that would speak for many of us. He said: "I went to the woods because I wished to live deliberately, to confront only the essential facts of life, and see if I could not learn what it had to teach, and not, when I came to die, discover that I had not lived."[4]

It is the answer to the "What we are living for?" question that gives meaning to what we are doing in and with our lives.

At the personal level, do you think your purpose is to be a teacher, a writer, an attorney, a politician, a plumber, a good spouse? While these and many other roles are a marvelous contribution to society, they remain secondary to your fundamental purpose in life. The tasks we do in life are relevant in particular circumstances, but they do not reach the depth of meaning that will make our life worth living. St. Paul indicated the direction by saying, "Whether you eat or drink, or whatever you do, do everything for the glory of God"[5] and "We know that all things work together for good for those who love God, who are called according to his purpose."[6]

Before St. Paul, it was already written: "I know the plans I have for you, says the Lord, plans for your welfare and not for harm, to give you a future with hope."[7] No wonder why someone like Albert Einstein was so eager to know God's thoughts by saying, "I want to know God's thoughts; the rest are details."[8]

Men and women of different religions, cultures, and backgrounds throughout history tried hard to find an answer to the fundamental questions of life. Teilhard was one of them. But he had a very particular answer since he had a unique position to do so. Indeed, his responses to the questions came from the fact that he belonged to the "children of heaven"[9] since he was a Christian whose vocation was being a Jesuit priest; he was a "child of the earth"[10] since he had this feeling even when

---

[4] Henry David Thoreau, *Walden*, (Salt Lake City: Gibbs M. Smith, Inc., 1981), p. 82.
[5] 1 Corinthians 10:31.
[6] Romans 8:28.
[7] Jeremiah 29:11.
[8] See http://rescomp.stanford.edu/~cheshire/EinsteinQuotes.html
[9] Teilhard wrote: "By upbringing and intellectual training, I belong to the 'children of heaven' ; but by temperament, and by my professional studies, I am a 'child of the earth." (CE, p. 96 -- X, p. 117).
[10] Ibid.

he was still a child; and he had a scientist career since he was a paleontologist by choice. During his entire life, he sought a way to reconcile his Christian faith with the science of the earth, spirit and matter, and the within and without of things. His intention was to see "a universe in which the old earth-heaven conflict vanishes (or is correctly adjusted) in the new formula, 'To heaven through fulfillment of earth.'"[11] In this sense, the history of the universe becomes the history of our pilgrimage toward God. Consequently, to read the history of the universal reality is to read the divine reality in action, because spiritual realities and material realities are one reality and not two separate realities. Therefore, real history becomes the history of the salvation of humanity written with human vocabularies. No wonder if, like Teilhard, thinkers like Jean Daniélou and Emmanuel Mounier consider that we live in a universal holy history, or like Hans Von Balthasar who was convinced that there was no separation between the history of salvation and a human history of the profane.[12] In the words of Richard P. McBrien, we could state:

> Christ is both the bearer and the goal of the upward movement of the universe toward the divine. Christ is the Omega Point, the focus of union needed by the "noosphere" in order that the noosphere might achieve a creative breakthrough into a new and final state of complexity and convergence. All of history, therefore, is a movement toward Christ, and yet Christ is at the same time already present in the world. His presence gives all of reality a Christic dimension. The Church is that place where that Christification is explicitly understood and acknowledged. Insofar as the Church practices Christian charity, the Church injects the most active agent of hominization into the world. The world thereby becomes a commonwealth of persons united in selfless love.[13]

---

[11] SC, p. 220 -- IX, p. 289.
[12] Hans Von Balthasar wrote: "'La chute du mur de la séparation' signifie la suppression de la différence entre l'histoire du salut (littéralement 'historique') particulière et une histoire profane universelle : depuis le Christ, toute histoire est foncièrement 'sacrale,' mais elle est cela surtout par la présence comme attestation de l'Eglise du Christ au sein de l'histoire du monde tolale. » (Hans Von Balthasar, *Théologie de l'histoire*, traduit de l'allemand par R. Givord, (Paris : Le signe/Fayard, 1970), p. 168.
[13] Richard P. McBrien, *Catholicism* (Minneapolis, MN: Winston Press, Inc., 1981), pp. 487-488.

Reading History from the End

Paradoxically, history can be read from its end – the point of destination – and not only from its beginning, and on through the past. This is precisely what Teilhard did. It was very strange and curious to hear a geologist-paleontologist, who is supposed to be interested in the beginning of things, say: "The past is left behind."[14] Here he is reading history from the Omega Point. The Omega Point[15] is the divine reality to which everything converges and from which everything starts and acquires meaning. It is the source, the foundation, and the generator. Teilhard wrote: "The sun is rising *ahead*."[16] Also, it is only on this divine Point that all humans and all things are able to reach their fulfillment. Consequently, history has a direction, existence is justified, life has meaning, and nothing is absurd; every task we perform, no matter how small, becomes significant and "historic" because it is permeated by God. Christ will never finish being born again and again.[17] Attracting all things to him, this Christ is the guarantee of the final success.

This is the correct way for reading not only the vision of Teilhard, but also the history of the universe – from the future. Also, this is the eschatological theology and the theology of hope that has enormous practical consequences. Those who hope are revolutionary, for, with all certainty, they bring transformation to the world because, if this transformation does not happen, it would be, as Professor Emile Rideau says, "an insult to the all powerful and to the infinite goodness of Christ."[18] For "Christ is our hope," wrote Bernard Häring, C.Ss.R., "as the risen Lord; he is the new creation"[19] who makes "all things new."[20] Based

---

[14] VP, p. 187 -- III, p. 265.

[15] Teilhard explains that "Christ coincides (though this assertion will have to be examined more deeply) with what I earlier called Omega Point" (SC, p. 164 -- IX, p. 209).

[16] VP, p. 187 -- III, p. 264.

[17] See HM, p. 58 -- XIII, p. 70.

[18] Emile Rideau (Docteur Es-Lettres, Professeur à l'Ecole Sainte-Gneviève) wrote: "Il nous est impossible de nous représenter une défaite de la Rédemption dans l'œuvre de l'Eglise, une généralisation progressive de l'apostasie, un insuccès absolu du Christ lui-même. Cette pensée serait une injure à la toute- puissance et à l'infinie bonté du Christ. » (Emile Rideau, *Consécration : Le Christianism et l'activité humaine*, Lettre-préface de Paul Claudel, Desclée de Brouwer, 1946, p. 74).

[19] Bernard Häring, C.Ss.R., wrote: "Christ is our hope as the fulfillment of God's saving love, God's saving mercy and God's saving justice. He is our hope as the great sacrament, the great visible sign of God's fidelity and love for all men. Christ

on an eschatological horizon, reality cannot resist transformation; a revision of structures, laws, habits, rites, behaviors, ways of seeing and doing things will continuously take place because the Absolute always transcends the relative, and because "Those who hope in Christ," as Jürgen Moltmann put it, "can no longer put up with reality as it is, but begin to suffer under it, to contradict it."[21]

Because of this Christian hope, Teilhard cannot but be optimistic. Omega, through us, will transform our daily realities by purifying them from any idolatry. This is why Omega is the true subject – the true engine – of history.

Teilhard does not stop there; he goes a step further. He claims that the world is not only transformed but it is also "christified" and "divinized." This is, then, how he sees the march of history: Cosmogenesis – biogenesis – anthropogenesis – noogenesis – christogenesis. Christ is the foundation and the principle of history, for, as Teilhard wrote, "In the whole range of our experience, the only principle we can see which can give the sense of man its justification and its solidity, is a Christ to whom are attached both a concrete history and the attributes of divinity."[22] "At every moment," he continued, "Christ, and he alone, must be able to give a sense of direction and a guarantee to the growing expectations of the modern world. It is Christ who gives fullness and who consummates. It

---

is our hope as victor over all evil powers, over frustration, over sin, over solidarity in sinfulness and selfishness, over anguish and death. Christ is our hope as the risen Lord; he is the new creation. He is the final Word of God to man, the last and final prophet promised to those who believe in him and are truly his disciples." (Bernard Häring, C.Ss.R., *Hope Is the Remedy*, (Garden City, NY: Doubleday & Company, Inc., 1972), pp. 21-22.

[20] Revelation 21:5.

[21] Jürgen Moltmann wrote: "Faith, wherever it develops into hope, causes not rest but unrest, not patience but impatience. It does not calm the unquiet heart, but is itself this unquiet heart in man. Those who hope in Christ can no longer put up with reality as it is, but begin to suffer under it, to contradict it. Peace with God means conflict with the world, for the goad of the promised future stabs inexorably into the flesh of every unfulfilled present. If we had before our eyes only what we see, then we should cheerfully or reluctantly reconcile ourselves with things as they happen to be. That we do not reconcile ourselves, that there is no pleasant harmony between us and reality, is due to our unquenchable hope. This hope keeps man unreconciled, until the great day of the fulfillment of all the promise of God" (Jürgen Moltmann, *Theology of Hope,* (New York and Evanston: Harper & Row, Publishers, 1967), pp. 21-22.

[22] TF, p. 37 -- XI, p. 42.

will become ever more true that it is by that sign, *and by that sign alone*, that we shall recognize him."[23]

The Coming Transformation

With Christ, nothing will stay the same. By permeating deeply our lives and our world – the "Sacred Presence"[24] – Christ makes our lives and our world similar to him, and we become generators of reconciliation, love, and peace. God's grace makes us fashion the true history of a world that is made of both weeds and wheat. Because the Spirit always overcomes human limitations, in faith and hope, we will be able to structure not only the present but the future as well, and we will be capable of "building the earth."[25] In faith and hope, the final success is certain because the world would be "omegalized." Teilhard wrote:

> The truth is that if a man's *vision can extend* beyond the immense and the infinitesimal almost into the complex, a way of acting opens up for him which has the power to synthesize and transfigure every other form of activity: by that I mean the specific act of experiencing and advancing, in and around himself – through the whole expanse and the whole depth of the real – the unification of the universe upon its deep-seated centre, with the consciousness of that unification it acquires as a consequence: the total and totalizing act (if I may so call it, for I can find no other name) of *omegalization*.[26]

This is the mystery of the grand transformation that Teilhard called "Super-Humanity, Super-Christ, Super-Charity."[27] If evolution is the obvious

---

[23] TF, p. 37 -- XI, p. 43.
[24] Henri de Lubac explained: "Nevertheless, as Pere Teilhard never ceased to realize, if man is correctly to balance his activity he must henceforth clearly discern 'the already recognizable face' of him towards who, through all things, he is moving. The mystical attitude of *Le Miliey Divin* still makes itself felt. And the more the years go by, the more the man who seeks the truth recollects and looks into himself, questions himself about the Presence, studies the Presence more deeply, advances further into the 'Sacred Presence.'" Henri de Lubac, S.J., *The Religion of Teilhard de Chardin* (Garden City, N.Y: Image Books, a Division of Doubleday & Company, Inc., 1968), p. 255.
[25] Teilhard wrote: "The age of nations has passed. Now, unless we wish to perish we must shake off our old prejudices and build the earth" (HE, p. 37 -- VI, p. 46).
[26] AE, pp. 55-56 -- VII, pp. 62-63.
[27] See SC, pp. 151-173 -- IX, pp. 193-217. With regard to the "Super-Christ" that could bring doubt and confusion, Teilhard was quick to clarify by saying: "By Super-Christ, I most certainly do not mean *another* Christ, a second Christ

mechanism of this transformation, convergence is the process of the mechanism, for "everything that rises must converge,"[28] declares Teilhard, and for him the ultimate convergence is the Omega Point.

The fundamental purpose in life is the great magnet that attracts events and circumstances that make things happen the way they are supposed to happen.[29] After all, what really matters in life isn't where we finish? A personal life purpose as well as a community or humanity life purpose is the driven life energy that explains what life is about, what its meaning is, and how it can be fulfilled. It can also explain what makes our hearts sing, what rings a bell in our minds, and what keeps us going in life. When we know where we are heading and align ourselves with that goal, we create what we want, without falling victims to circumstances, difficulties, and even impasses.[30] Unstoppable will become our determination if that goal is something larger than ourselves, and especially, if that goal is Someone who is the "Super-Christ"[31] – "the Prince of peace."[32]

"A communion with God through earth"[33] is Teilhard's deepest longing and it is his way to reconciliation and peace. "Divine grace, in the end," wrote Beatrice Bruteau, "is revealed as the real guarantee of

---

different from and greater than the first. I mean *the same* Christ, the Christ of all time, revealing himself to us in a form and in dimensions, with an urgency and area of contact, that are enlarged and given new force." (SC, p. 164 -- IX, p. 208).

[28] FM, p. 199 -- V, p. 242.

[29] Ursula King remarked: "A future evolution is both necessary and unavoidable. Yet the determination of its course will depend on the planned use of our collective power of invention and reflection. We hold, so to speak, all the future in our own hands; it is our responsibility to decide which further direction the evolution of humankind will take. Thus the problem of *right human action* and the *ultimate quality of human thought and life* are of primary importance." Ursula King, *The Spirit of One Earth: Reflections on Teilhard de Chardin and Global Spirituality* (New York, N.Y.: Paragon House, 1989), p. 105.

[30] Thomas M. King observed: "The Idealism of Teilhard could be identified as an Idealism of the future: 'the universe transforms itself into an Idea.' The process is still taking place and only at the end will there be a unified world of ideas." Thomas M. King, *Teilhard's Mysticism of Knowing* (New York, N.Y.: The Seabury Press, 1981), p. 56. In this same book, Thomas M. King wrote: "Now Teilhard argues that the fundamental unity of the cosmos does not come from the common *root* of all things in matter—matter is total disunity—now the unity of the cosmos is seen to proceed from some *formae cosmicae* 'imposed on the Multiple by a breath from on high.' For these cosmic forms would further be united in a single all-embracing Form, the Form of Christ." (*Ibid*, p.10).

[31] SC, p. 164 -- IX, p. 208.

[32] Isaiah 9:6; see also Ephesians 2:13-18.

[33] WTW, p. 14 -- XII, p. 19.

evolution and consequently the sure ground of our hope and the liberator of our energy of action."[34]

---

[34] Beatrice Bruteau, *Evolution Toward Divinity: Teilhard de Chardin and the Hindu Traditions* (Wheaton, Ill: The Theosophical Publishing House, 1974), p. 196.

Chapter Fourteen

The Project of Personalization

There would be no future for the world without the development of the forces of love, liberty, and respect of every human person. In Teilhard's evolutionary perspective, a growing complexity would mean a growing consciousness of these forces. With them, peace should prevail on earth because, then, the understanding will be that the "I" does not exist without the "other." It is even more than that: the more "other" one becomes, the more the self becomes authentic, and the more authentic the self is, the more "other" it becomes.

The "team spirit"

Teilhard talks often about the "team spirit." He wrote:

> If we are to avoid the road of brute material force, there is no way out *ahead* except the road of comradeship and brotherhood – and that is as true of nations as it is of individuals; not jealous hostility, but friendly rivalry: not personal feeling, but the team spirit.[1]

The "team spirit" is critical for any development because of the "organic unity of the world." Teilhard affirms:

> From the point of view of creative union the law and ideal of all good (whether moral or physical) are expressed in a single rule (which is also a hope): 'in all things to work for, and accept, the organic unity of the world.'[2]

Also critical is "the impulse of a collective drive," as he writes: "In its evolution, mankind is making a fresh leap, under the impulse of a collective drive, towards a still-to-come maturation-point."[3]

---

[1] AE, p. 17 -- VII, p. 23.
[2] SC, p. 66 -- IX, p. 94.
[3] TF, p.149 -- XI, p. 164.

"We," as individuals, community, and humanity are a "project" – an ideal to achieve. We do not have our models necessarily and only in the past. While we should learn from history, we are not supposed to repeat it. The future should be the predominant force that provides the energy for building it. It is precisely because we have a sense of the future that we do things, invent things, write things, discuss things, and produce things. We are responsible co-creators. "We hold Earth's future in our hands,"[4] affirms Teilhard. We are responsible for humanity as a whole and responsible for the development of ourselves as individuals, and we must grow together with the entire universe toward, as Teilhard put it, "a *distinct Centre radiating at the core of a system of centres*; a grouping in which personalisation of the All and personalisations of the elements reach their maximum, simultaneously and without merging, under the influence of a supremely autonomous focus on union."[5]

Teilhard thinks that personal development can come through the realization of the potentialities and virtualities of total humanity. He also thinks that the realization of humanity as a whole can only come through the development of each individual in the community as well as each group in that community. Therefore, an individual ought to strive for his or her self-development in the first place. He or she has to create for the self the best conditions for personalization; personalization is essential to a sane humanity. One has to learn how to grow physically, psychologically, intellectually, and spiritually. One has to educate himself or herself to become a mature person. Personalization is not a static state we can reach; it is rather a movement. This is how Teilhard describes it:

> I conceive of a new movement which would effectuate the rallying together, no longer based on the three words liberty, equality, and brotherhood, but on *universalism*, *futurism* and *personalism*: after which one would adopt the political-economic form that would appear to be *technically* the best.[6]

---

[4] FM, p. 77 -- V, p. 98.
[5] PM, pp. 262-63 -- I, p. 292. In note we find this explanation: "It is for this central focus, necessarily autonomous, that we shall hence-forward reserve the expression 'Omega Point'."
[6] On 11 October 1936, Teilhard wrote to M. l'Abbé Gaudefroy: "Il me semble que toutes les vielles catégories (démocraties, communisme, fascisme) ne signifient plus rien et couvrent des poussées absolument hétérogènes. Je conçois un nouveau mouvement ... qui opèrerait le ralliement sur les trois suivants : non plus liberté, égalité, fraternité, mais *universalisme, futurisme, personnalisme* ; après quoi on adopterait la forme politico-économique qui paraîtrait *techniquement* la meilleure » (LI, p. 114).

Then he goes on insisting:

> *Futurism* (by which must be understood the existence of a boundless sphere of improvements and discoveries) *Universalism*, and *Personalism*: those are the three characteristics of the progress that leads us on, with the whole mass and the whole infallibility of the universe behind it. And these, in consequence, are three unshakeable axes upon which our faith in man's effort can and must rest with complete assurance. Futurism, Universalism, Personlism; the three pillars on which the future rests.[7]

Society and person, community and individual, or socialization and personalization must not exclude each other. They should not be rivals or mutually antagonistic. They are in a constitutional need of each other. They complete each other. A deep interaction is critical for both of them to exist and survive, otherwise we would have caricatured people without a future. For Teilhard, a true socialization must help the person to grow at all levels and stages of his or her development. This means that, at the deepest level, "I" and "you," "we" and "them," "mine" and "yours" or "theirs" are not separated by walls of enmity or indifference. They rather are in a constitutional interaction. This means, in Teilhard's language, that "The whole is not the antipodes but the very pole of the person. Totalisation and personalisation are two manifestations of a single movement."[8] Between the individual and society, self-affirmation and socialization, personalization and humanization, there is not only a dialectical movement, as many philosophers think, but a synthesis and a real affirmation of the person, as Teilhard affirms:

> … The differentiation born of union may act upon that which is most unique and incommunicable in the individual, namely his personality. Thus socialization, whose hour seems to have sounded for Mankind, does not by any means signify the ending of the Era of the Individual upon earth, but far more its beginning.[9]

Paradoxically speaking, a convergent socialization makes the individual more personalized, not less, and vice versa.

In fact, "individual" as such is an ambiguous abstraction. "Community" as such is also an ambiguous abstraction. These particular words are useful

---

[7] SC, p. 137 -- IX, p. 178.
[8] SC, p. 137 -- IX. p. 178. Teilhard added a note to this quotation saying, "This is obviously only the outline of theory that would call for much lengthier elaboration to be absolutely clear."
[9] FM, pp. 56-57 -- V, p. 75.

for studies and speculation. What exists in reality is a "community of individuals" and "individuals in a community." The individual and the collective exist at the same time, and if separated, both of them cease to exist. Therefore we exist "we-ly." Together we exist and together we die. Consequently, the more engaging my "I" is in the community, the more my "I" is affirmed and strengthened, and the more a community is strong and universal, the more the "I" gains in personalization and authenticity. The "other" is not someone who is in the way, a nuisance, an obstacle. The "other," for Teilhard, is a partner in the greater task of building the earth. Indeed, as he sees it, "By revealing to each one that a part of himself exists in all the rest, the sense of the earth is now bringing into sight a new principle of universal affection among the mass of living beings: the devoted liking of one element for another within a single world in progress."[10] Doesn't the best way to love ourselves consist in loving others?[11] Emmanuel Mounier offered the following insight: "... if the first condition of individualism is the centralization of the individual in himself, the first condition of personalism is his decentralization, in order to set him in the open perspectives of personal life."[12]

Indeed, there are forces in us which, were it not for the coexistence with others, would find no expression for their inherent power. The person can only be by being in interaction with others, for being a stranger to others would also mean being a stranger to the self – the true self. After all, to be is to love. We possess only that which we give, and that which

---

[10] HE, p. 35 -- VI, p. 44.

[11] Ursula King observed: "In Teilhard's view, it is essential to distinguish clearly between the universal and the personal, but also to relate them to each other and see them both in an evolutionary perspective. Only in the Christian understanding of love are all these elements brought together for, in Teilhard's view, no other religious faith in history has ever released 'a higher degree of warmth, a more intense dynamism of unification' than Christianity, especially the Christianity of our own day. The essential elements of Christian love find themselves prolonged in what he called 'a new mystical orientation,' linked to the 'love of evolution.' In the past, Christian love has not always found its full expression, since it has often been too 'other worldly.' Instead, a truly dynamic form of Christian love must be concerned with the effort of developing human beings beyond themselves. He therefore referred to 'a radical reinterpretation' and 'recasting' of the notion of Christian charity." See Ursula King, *Teilhard de Chardin and Eastern Religions: Spirituality and Mysticism in an Evolutionary World* (Mahwah, N.J.: Paulist Press, 2011), pp. 223-224.

[12] Emmanuel Mounier, *Personalism* (Notre Dame, Indiana: University of Notre Dame Press, trans. by Philip Mairet, first published in England in 1952 by Routledge & Kegan Paul Ltd.), p. 19.

we give is ourselves. The truth is that we can never escape the immense network of relationships that form our milieu and constitute the person we are. Whether we like it or not, existence is coexistence. Therefore, one would expect that Teilhard is going to reject all kinds of individualism because they are not consistent with the facts of human socialization. For him, there is no right for the individual to remain inactive in society and there is no right to a society to suppress the individual to the point of crashing his or her uniqueness. Personalization and socialization share in the fullness of life. Teilhard, wrote Benjamin T. Hourani, "frequently returns to the individual person to indicate how in union with others he becomes more rather than less."[13]

Toward a fuller-being

"To be more"[14] is the point, and it is a dynamic point. Teilhard wrote:

For the ancient philosophers, 'to be' was above all 'to know'. For modern philosophers, 'to be' is coming to be synonymous with 'to grow' and 'to become'. We are witnessing the entry, not only into physics but into metaphysics too, of a dynamism.[15]

We must always be in continuous transformation at all levels of our human journey. We are in the process of becoming and growing. All our "beliefs" and all our "definitions" are nothing but temporary steps. We always have to go further. We can never stop. We should never stop. If we do, we fall. Teilhard has this warning question: "And yet, if I stand still,

---

[13] See Benjamin T. Hourani, "Teilhard's Political Ecumene: Empire or Commonwealth" in Leo Zonneveld and Robert Muller, ed., *The Desire to Be Human*, "International Teilhard Compendium" Centenary volume (Netherlands: Mirananda Publishers b.v. Wassenaar, 1983), p. 216. Hourani wrote also in the same paragraph: "The current notions of individualism are rejected by Teilhard because they are not consistent with the facts of human socialization. It is the individual person's singularity that is important. Far from being fused into a cult of the All, in union, the individual centers of consciousness 'accentuate the depth and incommunicability of their egos'. The more 'other' they become in association, the more they find themselves as authentic selves.... Teilhard went so far as to claim that the individual 'has no right to remain inactive' since upon his development depended the 'perfection of all his fellows.'" (*Ibid*, pp. 216-217).
[14] Teilhard wrote: "Why do we ourselves seek and why do we invent? In order to *be better*; and above all, in order to *be more*, stronger and more conscious." (VP, p. 72 -- III, p. 103).
[15] SC, p. 174 -- IX, p. 221.

how can I fail to fall?"[16] We will fall into violence again if we stop at some "truth" that we have created for ourselves and has become our ideology and idol. There is nothing more violent than the "ideology-idol" that we take as the truth – the only truth. Only those people who are always beginners are peaceful, because they are humble and open. These learn, improve, and are closer to the Truth. Life is larger, by far, than the so-called "truths" of our narrow horizons. Teilhard talks about "the passion for fuller-being" that is beyond these things. He writes:

> What man is looking for now, and would die were he not to find it in things, is a *complete pabulum* to nourish in him the passion for fuller-being, in other words for evolution.[17]

The fulfillment of every person's vocation definitely presupposes two movements: a reaching out to others and a return to self. It is imperative to convince ourselves of, and to practice, this living oneness: union with others and unity within ourselves. "A human person," Romano Guardini reminds us, "is not solely an individual entity, not solely a private reality. Along with having autonomy, each human being exists in relation to other people."[18] We, as human beings, disintegrate if we lose ourselves in external affairs. Also we disintegrate if we focus our entire attention on the self as if the external affairs do not exist. No matter how we look at it, the normal conclusion of our reality on earth is this: existence is co-existence, and being is inter-being.

Therefore, true personalism is defined and enhanced by altruism not by individualism. It culminates when the individual finds his or her fulfillment outside himself or herself. An authentic being is always found in the context of other beings and never alone. Understood this way, there is no doubt that Teilhard made a great contribution to the development of the human person and to the concept of personalism. This was also the observation of André Ligneul who wrote:

> Teilhard made an inestimable contribution to personalism with his suggestion that man's future lies in the direction of a deliberately communitarian life. He sought to prove this, moreover, no longer in the name of a philosophy or of a theology, but in the name of the most certain data of paleontology and biology. So central was this insight to his thought,

---

[16] WTW, p. 229 -- XII, p. 340.
[17] AE, p. 280 -- VII, p. 290.
[18] See Robert A. Krieg, *Romano Guardini: Spiritual Writings* (Maryknoll, N.Y.: Orbis Books, 2005 – "Modern Spiritual Masters Series"), p. 52.

that for him, as for Mounier,[19] to speak of a "personalist and communitarian revolution" would be a pleonasm.[20]

Consequently, the goal of creation for Teilhard is not simply well-being (bien-être), but more-being (plus-être or "être plus") – more love, more justice, more beauty, more understanding, more goodness, more truth, and more peace. Furthermore, since Teilhard rejects the impersonal or infra-personal, he spiritualizes matter and the whole creation and he makes the universe a "home" whose summit is a personalized Omega; this is the summit of a personalized universe and the centering of the noosphere. He describes it – it is worth repeating this quotation – as "a *distinct Centre radiating at the core of a system of centres*; a grouping in which personalisation of the All and personalisations of the elements reach their maximum, simultaneously and without merging, under the influence of a supremely autonomous focus of union."[21]

---

[19] Emmanuel Mounier wrote, in this context, the following lines: "Personalism therefore includes among its leading ideas, the affirmation of the *unity of mankind*, both in space and time, which was foreshadowed by certain schools of thought in the latter days of antiquity and confirmed in the Judeo-Christian tradition. For the Christian there are neither citizens nor barbarians, neither bond nor free, neither Jew nor gentile, neither white, black or yellow, but only men created in the image of God and called to salvation in Christ…. Any man, however different, or even degraded, remains a man, for whom we ought to make a human way of life possible." See Emmanuel Mounier, *Personalism* (Notre Dame, Indiana: University of Notre Dame Press, trans. by Philip Mairet, first published in England in 1952 by Routledge & Kegan Paul Ltd.), p. 30.

[20] André Ligneul, *Teilhard and Personalism*, trans. by Paul Joseph Oligny, O.F.M. and Michael D. Meilach, O.F.M. (Glen Rock, N.J., New York, N.Y: Paulist Press Deus Books, 1968), pp. 27-28.

[21] PM, pp. 262-63 -- I, p. 292. In note we find this explanation: "It is for this central focus, necessarily autonomous, that we shall hence-forward reserve the expression 'Omega Point'." Emile Rideau offers the following explanation about the dynamic understanding of the person: "L'immense estime, en effet, de Teilhard pour la personne ne vient pas seulement de sa conception d'une histoire évolutive qui oriente la montée du monde vers la conscience, ni d'une réflexion sur la pensée ; elle jaillit surtout de la vocation surnaturelle de l'homme à Dieu, donc de sa recréation spirituelle comme 'image' du Christ. Ce personnalisme est doublement *dynamique*, car l'homme est pensé tout à la fois comme mouvement intérieur vers l'Absolu-Dieu et comme mouvement collectif et historique vers un Terme suprême, qui est le rassemblement des consciences dans l'amour." See Emile Rideau, S.J., *Teilhard Oui ou Non* (Paris : Librairie Fayard, 1967, 'Jalons'), p. 105.

But there is also the big Other. It is inconceivable to "be more" and live fully without being with and in God. Bede Griffiths describes this most profound connection with the divine as follows:

> ... in the Christian mystical understanding each person is unique. Each is a unique expression of God, a unique manifestation of the divine, and each is in all and all are in each. There is a total transparency. All are one in God and one in each other. But we are not lost in this oneness; we are found in our total being. "He who will lose his life shall find it." When we lose ourselves totally in that abyss of love, we find ourselves.[22]

If Teilhard has faith in, and exalts, the human person as such, he does not do it the way of "the Titans, of Prometheus, of Babel and of Faust,"[23] but he does it the Christ way. "Correctly interpreted," wrote Teilhard, "faith in Man can and indeed must cast us at the feet and into the arms of One who is greater than ourselves."[24] The human person, then, is not the rival of God. The human person is the image of God. Therefore, the human person is unthinkable without God and a God who does not respect the liberty and responsibility of the person is not the God of the unconditional love one can trust. This is how Teilhard talks about the two faiths:

> ... the two faiths confronting one another (faith in God and faith in man) are not in opposition to one another: on the contrary, they represent the two essential components of a complete humano-Christian mysticism. There can be no truly live Christian faith if it does not reach and raise up, in its ascending movement, the totality of mankind's spiritual dynamism (the totality of the 'anima naturaliter Christina'.) Nor is faith in man psychologically possible if the evolutionary future of the world does not meet, in the transcendent, some focal point of irreversible personalisation. In short, it is impossible to rise Above without moving Ahead, or to progress Ahead without steering towards the Above.[25]

Perhaps more than anyone else, Teilhard thought that believing in the human being is also believing in God, and believing in God is believing in

---

[22] Bede Griffiths, *A New Vision of Reality: Western Science, Eastern Mysticism and Christian Faith* (Springfield, IL: Templegate Publishers, 1989, 1990), p. 253.
[23] FM, p. 195 -- V, p. 238.
[24] FM, p. 195 -- V, p. 238.
[25] SC, p. 203 -- IX, p. 261.

the human person.[26] The project of personalization cannot be understood without understanding the Above-Ahead movement.

---

[26] Gérard-Henry Baudry affirmed: « Plus qu'aucun autre en notre temps, Teilhard a cru en l'homme du même mouvement qu'il a cru en Dieu. Le dynamisme de sa foi en l'homme le conduisait à la foi en Dieu, et dans sa foi en Dieu, il trouvait des raison surnaturelles de croire encore plus en l'homme. Car en Dieu il avait la révélation du Christ, et dans la foi au Christ la merveilleuse synthèse qui rend intégralement possible et la foi en l'homme et la foi en Dieu, ainsi qu'un universel amour. » See Gérard-Henry Baudry, *Ce que croyait Teilhard* (France: Mame, 1971), p. 84. The structural definition of the person that is based on the ultimate relation to God was explicitly mentioned by many spiritual authors. One of these authors is Romano Guardini who remarkably wrote: "Man is not so constructed as to be complete in himself and, in addition, capable of entering into relations with God or not as he sees fit; his very essence consists in his relation to God. The only kind of man that exists is man-in-relation-to-God; and what he understands by that relationship, how seriously he takes it, and what he does about it are the determining factors of his character. This is so, and no philosopher, politician, poet, or psychologist can change it." Then Guardini continued: "It is dangerous to ignore realities, for they have a way of avenging themselves. When instincts are suppressed or conflicts kept alive, neuroses set in. God is the Reality on whom all other realities, including the human, are founded. When existence fails to give Him His due, existence sickens." See Romano Guardini, *The End of the Modern World* (Wilmington, Delaware: ISI Books – Intercollegiate Studies Institute, 1998), p. 218.

CHAPTER FIFTEEN

ON HUMAN RIGHTS

At the time of the adoption of the 1948 Universal Declaration of the Human Rights by the United Nations, Teilhard de Chardin offered his UNESCO solicited observations on the subject in a short note entitled, "Some Reflections on the Rights of Man."[1] In that note he wrote that in 1789[2] "the Rights of Man were primarily an expression of the individual will to autonomy."[3] In 1948, however, Teilhard saw a different spirit at work when he observed that "Whether we wish it or not, Mankind is becoming collectivized, totalized under the influence of psychic and spiritual forces on a planetary scale. Out of this has arisen, in the heart of every man, the present-day conflict between the individual, ever more conscious of his individual worth, and social affiliations which become ever more demanding."[4]

Teilhard saw a problem in the fragmentation of an excessive individualism. That is why he advocated the development of the individual only in association with others. Men and women cannot be fully "human"

---

[1] FM, pp. 201-203 -- V, pp. 245-249.
[2] The 1789 date was the date of the French Revolution and the French Declaration of the Rights of Man and of the Citizen. Teilhard was critical of this Declaration. He wrote: *"Liberty, Equality, Fraternity.* It was in 1789 that this famous slogan electrified the western world: but events have shown, its meaning was far from clear to the minds of those it inspired. Liberty – to do *anything?* Equality – in *all* respects? Fraternity – based on *what* common bonds?... Even today the magical words are much more *felt* than understood. But does not their undeniable, if vague, attraction take on a clearer aspect if we consider them, as I suggest, from a biological standpoint?" (FM, pp. 250-51 – V, p. 312); in another occasion, he wrote from Peking to a friend on August 5, 1941: "I have no confidence in reforms, however timely, that are built upon a foundation of cowardice. I think I cried a year ago when I read the famous slogan, 'Work, family, country!' It is not with prudence that you make people move, but with a little passion. Where are our fathers of '89! Actually I feel as if for the moment I no longer have a country. But there is still the Earth" (LTF, p. 100 – *Accomplir l'homme,* p. 122).
[3] FM, p, 201 -- V, p. 247.
[4] FM., p. 201 -- V, p. 247.

unless they are "socialized," "totalized," and "humanized." The collective and the individual are not, and should not, be antagonistic. A dialectical force brings them together; it is not an external coercive force, but an internal harmonization. For this to be done, Teilhard proclaimed three fundamental principles that should be "guaranteed in any new Charter of Humanity."[5] They are:

> The absolute duty of the individual to develop his own personality.
>
> The relative right of the individual to be placed in circumstances as favourable as possible to his personal development.
>
> The absolute right of the individual, within the social organism, not to be deformed by external coercion but inwardly super-organised by persuasion, that is to say, in conformity with his personal endowments and aspirations.[6]

Accordingly, the Declaration should not be the result of exceeding isolationism. It should rather be the consequence of greater awareness of Humanity and the fruit of ever-growing humanization in the very process of what Teilhard called cosmogenesis. Therefore, in order to have a successful theory for the Human Rights, a dialectical necessary interaction between the individual and society is required, and also required a dialectical interaction between rights and duties. When Teilhard talked about personalization and about socialization, he implied the very idea of the Human Rights that evolved greatly over time and will continue to evolve.

The fact that, by virtue of his or her humanity, every human being is entitled to certain human rights, is relatively new. It took World War II to provide a certain global conscience and gather people from different traditions, nationalities, and cultures to come together with certain principles on which they can all agree. However, the very roots of the human rights idea go very far back in time. Indeed, throughout much of history, people acquired rights, responsibilities, duties, and caring toward the self and others through their membership in a group – a family, tribe, religion, class, community, state, continent, or regional coalitions and United Nations.

History tells us that Cyrus the Great, the king of ancient Persia, freed the slaves of Babylon after he conquered that city in 539 B.C.; this is known today as the Cyrus Cylinder. After Babylon, the idea of certain

---

[5]FM, p. 203 – V, p. 249.
[6]FM, p. 203 – V, p. 249.

forms of human rights started to spread to India, Greece, and Rome. The fact that people tended to follow certain unwritten laws in the course of life started to appear, and the concept of "natural law" arose. The Greeks, for example saw a distinction between "nature" *(physis, φύσις)* and "law" *(nomos, νόμος)*. What the law commanded varied from place to place according to customs, conventions, and traditions. But what was "by nature" should be the same everywhere and for everyone. Aristotle (384-322 BC) was more explicit on this than Plato and Socrates when he argued that there was a universal law – the law of nature that is common for everyone – beside the particular law that could be different for each people.[7] St. Thomas Aquinas (1225-1274), who provided perhaps the most comprehensive understanding of the different forms of law,[8] believed that the eternal law of God is conveyed to human beings in part through revelations and in part through reason. What could be discerned of the eternal law through reason is natural law. St. Thomas Aquinas, as well as many other saints and theologians in Christianity, insisted on the concept of the human being as the image of God, and made this anthropology of image and likeness the cornerstone of ethical considerations.

Moreover, it is important in this context to reserve a special place for the "Golden Rule" that is a common denominator among the different religions, transcends the various cultures and traditions, and is supposed to be honored by everyone, anywhere, anytime.

Although the world's religions differ in their individual beliefs and in their traditions and practices, the golden rule stands out in all of them. It is universal, precise, and simple. It is the law of ethical reciprocity. In essence, it recommends treating others as one wishes to be treated by others. This is, for example, how these religions express it. In Brahmanism we read: *"This is the sum of Dharma [duty]: Do naught unto others which would cause you pain if done to you."*[9] In Buddhism we read: *"Hurt not others in ways that you yourself would find hurtful."*[10] In Christianity we read: *"In everything do to others as you would have them do to you,"*[11] and *"You shall Love your neighbor as yourself."*[12] In Confucianism we

---

[7] See Aristotle, *Rhetoric*, bk. I, ch. 13, 1373b 2-8.
[8] See St. Thomas Aquinas, Summa Theologiæ: A Concise Translation, Ed. By Timothy McDermott, "Christian Classics" (Notre Dame, IN: Ave Maria Press, 1989), pp. 276-307.
[9] Mahabharata, 5:1517.
[10] Udana-Varga 5:18.
[11] Matthew 7:12 ; see also Luke 6:31.
[12] Matthew19:19; Mark 12:31; Luke 10:27; Romans 13:9; Galatians 5:14; James 2:8.

read: *"Do not do to others what you do not want them to do to you."*[13] In Hinduism we read: *"This is the sum of duty: do not do to others what would cause pain if done to you."*[14] In Islam we read: *"None of you [truly] believes until he wishes for his brother what he wishes for himself."*[15] In Jainism we read: *"A man should wander about treating all creatures as he himself would be treated."*[16] In Judaism we read: *"...you shall love your neighbor as yourself,"*[17] and *"What is hateful to you, do not to your fellow man. This is the law: all the rest is commentary."*[18] In Sufism we read: *"The basis of Sufism is consideration of the hearts and feelings of others. If you haven't the will to gladden someone's heart, then at least beware lest you hurt someone's heart, for on our path, no sin exists but this."*[19] In Taoism we read: *"Regard your neighbor's gain as your own gain, and your neighbor's loss as your own loss,"*[20] and *"The sage has no interest of his own, but takes the interests of the people as his own. He is kind to the kind; he is also kind to the unkind: for Virtue is kind. He is faithful to the faithful; he is also faithful to the unfaithful: for Virtue is faithful."*[21] In Zoroastrianism we read: *"That nature alone is good which refrains from doing unto another whatsoever is not good for itself,"*[22] and *"Whatever is disagreeable to yourself do not do unto others."*[23]

If this golden rule is one of the common and favorite themes in nearly every religion, why in the world do we keep hearing that religion is the number one cause of conflicts and wars? The golden rule was and is one of the most powerful, consistent, moral standards throughout history. The problem is not in religion; it is in the deformed interpretation of what religion is all about. No matter how we spin things around, deep in our souls we know that true religion is, after and above all, about love because love is the very definition of God, as St. John revealed,[24] and love, in human affairs, must be the philosopher's stone[25] that has the power to turn

---

[13] Analects 15:23.
[14] Mahabharata 5:1517.
[15] Fortieth Hadith of an-Nawawi, 13.
[16] Sutrakritanga 1.11.33.
[17] Leviticus 19:18.
[18] Talmud, Shabbat 31a.
[19] Dr. Javad Nurbakhsh, Master of the Nimatullahi Sufi Order.
[20] T'ai Shang Kan Ying P'ien.
[21] Tao The Ching, Chapter 49.
[22] Dadistan-i-dinik 94:5.
[23] Shayast-na-Shayast 13:29.
[24] 1 John 4:16.
[25] The philosopher's stone is commonly defined this way: "Philosopher's stone, in Western *alchemy*, an unknown substance, also called "the tincture" or "the

everything into gold. In one way or another, Teilhard never missed any opportunity to affirm this reality. Here are a few examples: "Driven by the forces of love, the fragments of the world seek each other so that the world may come to being"[26]; "Love in all its subtleties is nothing more, and nothing less, than the more or less direct trace marked on the heart of the element by the psychical convergence of the universe upon itself"[27]; "Love is the most universal, the most tremendous and the most mysterious of the cosmic forces"[28]; "The most telling and profound way of describing the evolution of the universe would undoubtedly be to trace the evolution of love"[29]; "'Love one another'... the *only* imaginable principle of the earth's future equilibrium ... the only true peace"[30]; "Love one another or you perish."[31]

Other important documents related to the Human Rights were: the Magna Carta or "Great Charter," signed by the king of England in 1215, the Petition of Right of 1628, the US Constitution of 1787, the French Declaration of the Rights of Man and of the Citizen of 1789, the US Bill of Rights of 1791, the First Geneva Convention of 1864, the United Nations Charter of 1945, and the Universal Declaration of Human Rights of 1948. Believing totally in the inherent rights of all human beings, the Declaration unequivocally proclaims in its preamble and its first article:

> *Whereas* recognition of the inherent dignity and of the equal and inalienable rights of all members of the human family is the foundation of freedom, justice and peace in the world,
> *Whereas* disregard and contempt for human rights have resulted in barbarous acts which have outraged the conscience of mankind, and the advent of a world in which human beings shall enjoy freedom of speech and belief and freedom from fear and want has been proclaimed as the highest aspiration of the common people…

---

powder," sought by alchemists for its supposed ability to transform base metals into precious ones, especially gold and silver. Alchemists also believed that an *elixir* of life could be derived from it. Inasmuch as alchemy was concerned with the perfection of the human *soul*, the philosopher's stone was thought to cure illnesses, prolong life, and bring about spiritual revitalization." (http://www.britannica.com/topic/philosophers-stone)

[26] PM, pp. 264-65 -- I, p. 294.
[27] PM, p. 265 -- I, p. 294.
[28] HE, p. 32 -- VI, p. 40.
[29] HE, p. 33 -- VI, p. 41.
[30] AE, p. 20 -- VII, p. 26.
[31] HE, p. 153 -- VI, p. 189.

> All human beings are born free and equal in dignity and rights. They are endowed with reason and conscience and should act towards one another in a spirit of brotherhood.[32]

Then came the Earth Charter, whose text was approved at the UNESCO headquarters in Paris in March 2000, and was finalized and launched June 29, 2000, in a ceremony at the Peace Palace, in The Hague. "The Earth Charter," as it was defined, "is an ethical framework for building a just, sustainable, and peaceful global society in the 21st century. It seeks to inspire in all people a new sense of global interdependence and shared responsibility for the well-being of the whole human family, the greater community of life, and future generations. It is a vision of hope and a call to action."[33]

It is striking to notice how similar the language used in this Charter of the year 2000 is to the language used by Teilhard several decades earlier. Maybe the words themselves are not the same because Teilhard has his own vocabulary, but the reality behind the words is more or less the same to the point that one has the impression that one could be reading Teilhard when in fact one is reading the Charter. In the Charter we read for example:

> We stand at a critical moment in Earth's history, a time when humanity must choose its future. As the world becomes increasingly interdependent and fragile, the future at once holds great peril and great promise. To move forward we must recognize that in the midst of a magnificent diversity of cultures and life forms we are one human family and one Earth community with a common destiny. We must join together to bring forth a sustainable global society founded on respect for nature, universal human rights, economic justice, and a culture of peace. Towards this end, it is imperative that we, the peoples of Earth, declare our responsibility to one another, to the greater community of life, and to future generations.

Humanity is part of a vast evolving universe.

> To realize these aspirations, we must decide to live with a sense of universal responsibility, identifying ourselves with the whole Earth community as well as our local communities. We are at once citizens of different nations and of one world in which the local and global are linked. Everyone shares responsibility for the present and future well-being of the human family and the larger living world. The spirit of human solidarity and kinship with all life is strengthened when we live with reverence for

---

[32] See http://www.un.org/en/universal-declaration-human-rights/index.html
[33] http://earthcharter.org/discover/the-earth-charter/

the mystery of being, gratitude for the gift of life, and humility regarding the human place in nature.

Ensure that communities at all levels guarantee human rights and fundamental freedoms and provide everyone an opportunity to realize his or her full potential.

Recognize that peace is the wholeness created by right relationships with oneself, other persons, other cultures, other life, Earth, and the larger whole of which all are a part.

… This requires a change of mind and heart. It requires a new sense of global interdependence and universal responsibility. We must imaginatively develop and apply the vision of a sustainable way of life locally, nationally, regionally, and globally. Our cultural diversity is a precious heritage and different cultures will find their own distinctive ways to realize the vision. We must deepen and expand the global dialogue that generated the Earth Charter, for we have much to learn from the ongoing collaborative search for truth and wisdom.

Life often involves tensions between important values. This can mean difficult choices. However, we must find ways to harmonize diversity with unity, the exercise of freedom with the common good, short-term objectives with long-term goals. Every individual, family, organization, and community has a vital role to play. The arts, sciences, religions, educational institutions, media, businesses, nongovernmental organizations, and governments are all called to offer creative leadership. The partnership of government, civil society, and business is essential for effective governance.

Let ours be a time remembered for the awakening of a new reverence for life, the firm resolve to achieve sustainability, the quickening of the struggle for justice and peace, and the joyful celebration of life.[34]

One could have read these principles, wishes, and hopes throughout Teilhard's writings from 1916 to 1955. In a more specific way, let us mention especially the following essays that Teilhard wrote:

* "Cosmic Life,"[35] written in 1916
* "Nostalgia for the Front,"[36] written in 1917
* "Creative Union,"[37] written in 1917

---

[34] See The Earth Charter, http://earthcharter.org/discover/the-earth-charter/
[35] WTW, pp. 13-71 – XII, pp. 17-82.
[36] HM, pp. 167-181 – XII, pp. 225-241.

- "The Soul of the World,"[38] written in 1918
- "The Universal Element,"[39] written in 1919
- "The Spirit of the Earth,"[40] written in 1931
- "Sketch of a Personalistic Universe,"[41] written in 1936
- "The Salvation of Mankind. Thoughts on the Present Crisis,"[42] written in 1936
- "Human Energy,"[43] written in 1937
- "The Grand Option,"[44] written in 1939
- "Some Reflections on Progress,"[45] written in 1941
- "Super-Humanity, Super-Christ, Super-Charity. Some New Dimensions for the Future,"[46] written in 1943
- "A Great Event Foreshadowed: The Planetization of Mankind,"[47] written in 1945
- "Faith in Peace,"[48] written in 1947
- "Faith in Man,"[49] written in 1947
- "Some Reflections on the Rights of Man,"[50] written in 1947
- "The Essence of the Democratic Idea,"[51] written in 1949
- "How May We Conceive and Hope That Human Unanimization Will Be Realised on Earth?"[52] Written in 1950
- "From the Pre-Human to the Ultra-Human: the Phases of a Living Planet,"[53] written in 1950
- "Evolution of the Idea of Evolution,"[54] written in 1950
- "The Evolution of Responsibility in the World,"[55] written in 1950

---

[37] WTW, pp. 151-176 – XII, pp. 193-224.
[38] WTW, pp. 177-190 -- XII, pp. 243-259.
[39] WTW, pp. 289-302 -- XII, pp. 429-445.
[40] HE, pp. 19-47 -- VI, pp. 25-57.
[41] HE, pp. 53-92 -- VI, pp. 69-114.
[42] SC, pp. 128-150 -- IX, pp. 169-191.
[43] HE, pp. 113-162 -- VI, pp. 143-198.
[44] FM, pp. 39-63 -- V, pp. 57-81.
[45] FM, pp. 64-84 -- V, pp. 85-106.
[46] SC, pp. 151-173 -- IX, pp. 191-218.
[47] FM, pp. 129-144 -- V, pp.159-175.
[48] FM, pp. 154-160 -- V, pp. 191-197.
[49] FM, pp. 192-200 -- V, pp. 235-243.
[50] FM, pp. 201-203 -- V, pp. 247-249.
[51] FM, pp. 248-254 -- V, pp. 309-315.
[52] FM, pp. 295-302 -- V, pp.367-374.
[53] FM, pp. 303-311 – V, pp. 377-385.
[54] VP, pp. 245-247 -- III, pp. 347-349.
[55] AE, pp. 205-214 -- VII, pp. 213-221.

- * "The Zest for Living,"[56] written in 1950
- * "The Convergence of the Universe,"[57] written in 1951
- * "The Transformation and Continuation in Man of the Mechanism of Evolution,"[58] written in 1951
- * "Hominization and Speciation: The Present Discomforts of Anthropology,"[59] written in 1952
- * "The Energy of Evolution,"[60] written in 1953
- * "The Christic,"[61] written in 1955

The Earth Charter seems to be one good expression of what Teilhard calls "The Spirit of the Earth," "The Convergence of the Universe," and "Creative Union" that allow the emergence of a mind and consciousness that make a better world for all.

In the end, where does the idea of the human rights come from? Religions, traditions, and different individuals may or may not be always explicit about them, but it is undeniable that there are universal standards that apply to all humankind throughout all time. These universal principles that transcend time, culture, and government were, are, and continue to be discoverable by all of us, and form the basis of a "Human Rights" society. Teilhard would call this process, by using his own terminology, "personalization," "socialization," "planetization," "humanization," "cosmogenesis," or "Christogenesis."

Teilhard's writings express great hope regarding the future. This hope springs from his religious faith, from his faith in "Super-Humanity, Super-Christ, Super-Charity," from his "Faith in Man," and from his "Faith in Peace." He wants us to always see the future with both faith and reason, heart and head, passion and wisdom, and mystical intuition and science.

---

[56] AE, pp. 229-243 -- VII, pp. 239-251.
[57] AE, pp. 281-296 -- VII, pp. 295-309.
[58] AE, pp. 297-309 -- VII, pp. 313-323.
[59] VP, pp. 256-267 -- III, pp. 365-379.
[60] AE, pp. 359-372 -- VII, pp. 381-393.
[61] HM, pp. 80-102 -- XIII, pp. 93-117.

Chapter Sixteen

Hope:
The Ultimate Reality

Does hope make sense after the century of WWI, WWII, Hiroshima, and Auschwitz? Does the millennium of September 11, the Arab Spring, the reign of terror, and the destruction of nations inspire any hope? What does hope mean when we seem to have been starting a "Third World War fought piecemeal,"[1] as Pope Francis said? The facts show that it is more reasonable to conclude that hope is rather an illusion and its reality cannot be justified. The dramatic, even explosive, existential situation to which we have grown accustomed to, in addition to the rapid deterioration of values that suggests the possibility of self-destruction and the tragedy of de-humanization and total annihilation cannot be more obvious. In such a context, the line of Friedrich Nietzsche that says, "In reality [hope] is the worst of all evils, because it prolongs the torments of Man,"[2] seems closer to the truth indeed.

Yet, we continue to hope, and we cannot live without it. Moreover, hope acquires a foundational quality for someone like Teilhard de Chardin, because it is fundamental for our very survival. What is meant by hope here is not these little hopes and wishes that change according to time, place, and circumstances, but our foundational and fundamental hope that is related to salvation and eternal life, as well as to the final state of being of the whole world.

By affirming and insisting on the fact that the convergence of the cosmos is inevitable, Teilhard is convinced that the progress in nature, and in humanity in particular, is an evolving reality that is organic, irreversible, foreseeable, and infallible. For him, such a reality is not a theoretical or a virtual reality; it is based upon a "serious scientific proof,"[3]

---

[1] See https://zenit.org/articles/pope-francis-a-pope-who-sees-a-wwiii-and-pleas-for-it-to-stop/
[2] http://www.lexido.com/EBOOK_TEXTS/HUMAN_ALL_TOO_HUMAN_BOOK_ONE_.aspx?S=71
[3] PH, p. 307 -- I, p. 341. See also AE, pp. 321-22 -- VII, pp. 335-36.

and upon the fact that the human being "*must reach the goal*, not necessarily, doubtless, but infallibly."[4] The human being will reach that goal not through hopes (espoirs) but by true hope (esperance)[5] and universal love. Teilhard wrote:

> To go on putting our hopes in a social order obtained by external violence would simply mean to abandon all hope of carrying the spirit of the earth to its limits.
> Now human energy, being the expression of a movement as irresistible and infallible as the universe itself, cannot possibly be prevented by any obstacle from freely reaching the natural goal of its evolution.
> Therefore, despite all checks and all improbabilities, we are inevitably approaching a new age, in which the world will throw off its chains and at last give itself up to the power of its affinities.
> Either we must doubt the value of everything around us, or we must utterly believe in the possibility, and I should now add in the inevitable consequences, of universal love.[6]

Teilhard's radical optimism in the future[7] is based on his evolutionary theory of the universe and humanity that is following the ascending path of love. It is also, and especially, based on the divine Omega Point that is, by its transcendence and immanence, transforming and attracting everything and everyone to its glory and peace. When faced with the end

---

[4] PH, p. 276 -- I, p. 307.
[5] The original French text says: "Continuer à mettre nos espoirs dans un ordre social obtenu par violence externe équivaudrait simplement pour nous à abandonner toute espérance de porter à ses limites l'Esprit de la Terre. » (VI, p. 190)
[6] HE, p. 153 -- VI, p. 190.
[7] For Kathleen Duffy, "Teilhard was adamant that faith in the future is a fundamental condition for survival (F, 84). 'Nothing is more dangerous for the future of the world… than… resignation and false realism' (F, 154)." See Kathleen Duffy, SSJ, Teilhard's Mysticism: Seeing the Inner Face of Evolution (Maryknoll, N.Y.: Orbis Books, 2014), p. 107. This is also what James W. Skehan saw: "Teilhard had an optimistic outlook on life and the prospect that the work of Christ in the world would turn out successfully in spite of the obviously sinful and even depraved state of affairs in the world. His optimism was born of a deep-rooted faith in the efficacy of the Incarnation in the lives, sufferings, depths, and resurrection of those who share their humanity with Jesus." See James W. Skehan, SJ, *Praying with Teilhard de Chardin* (Winona, MN: Saint Mary's Press, 2001 "Companions for the Journey"), pp. 109-110.

of history, hope is to be founded upon a trust in the Other,[8] who will not forsake us, much more than upon a trust in the human beings who can make bad choices that include their own self-destruction. This is why it is important to say that our destination point has an enormous impact on the decision that each and every one of us makes in regard to his or her participation or nonparticipation in the culture of war or peace. Our conflicts and solutions are, whether we know it or not, theological conflicts and have theological solutions. No wonder Teilhard put so much faith and hope in that divine Omega Point in spite, or perhaps because of, the phenomenon of the death experience. He wrote, for example:

> The radical defect in all forms of belief in progress, as they are expressed in positivist credos, is that they do not definitely eliminate death. What is the use of detecting a focus of any sort in the van of evolution if that focus can and must one day disintegrate? To satisfy the ultimate requirements of our action, Omega must be independent of the collapse of the forces with which evolution is woven.[9]

Only through our faith and hope do we know for certain that death for the individual, or for the species, is not absolute and sure; its true meaning is the passage to a new life through Christ.

Teilhard knew that the fundamental purpose that we choose will influence how we see the world, how we see our life in it, and how we participate in government, politics, public morality, and the transformation of culture. In such a context, the "not yet" does not belong to some utopian

---

[8] In this context, it would be worthwhile to quote a paragraph written by Romano Guardini. It says: "To believe means to be certain that God is acting since the beginning of creation until its end through the unfolding of all historical periods. To believe means doing what is demanded by the situation at the present moment and collaborating in the progress of God's actions toward the goal that God intends, namely, the second coming of Jesus Christ and the victory of God's kingdom. So we do well to break through the surface of a pure system of doctrines and to acknowledge that God is doing something even today, even here, even also with me. I must place myself in this convergence of things, and I must join in it, act in it, and fight for it. It is in this convergence that the meaning of 'hope' will become significant and clear to me. That is, hope means having the confidence that Christ's good news will be realized despite everything that brings about the resistance of disbelief and disobedience and despite the apparent impossibility of the realization of the good news. Hope means trusting that the rebirth to new life will surely come about in me and in creation." See Robert A. Krieg, *Romano Guardini: Spiritual Writings* (Maryknoll, N.Y.: Orbis Books, 2005 – "Modern Spiritual Masters Series"), p. 111.

[9] PM, p. 270 -- I, p. 300.

wishes; it becomes a "realistic" hope that invites individual and societal changes. "Hope alone," Jürgen Moltmann wrote insightfully, "is to be called 'realistic,' because it alone takes seriously the possibilities with which all reality is fraught. It does not take things as they happen to stand or to lie, but as progressing, moving things with possibilities of change."[10] This phenomenon cannot be called other than active hope because the object hoped for is at the same time the source of inspiration and the dynamic motivation for action.

The "Not Yet" Reality

Since we are not born to be satisfied, it should not surprise us if we keep looking for what we are not, and for what we don't have, with the hope that a little more of this or a little more of that will do it. But we find sooner than later that even this "more" is not enough. That is the tragedy of our human condition, and also its beauty; it makes us hope for the Infinite. The truth is that this is precisely this Infinite that really defines us and defines the world we live in. We are finite beings as all things are finite, but we reject the idea that death could be the horizon of our existence; we long for the Infinite. "You have made us for yourself, [O Lord]," wrote St. Augustine, "and our hearts are restless until they can find peace in you."[11] We live in hope. Henri Nouwen explains this hope very well. He wrote in his book, *With Open Hands*:

> When we live with hope we do not get tangled up with concerns for how our wishes will be fulfilled. So, too, our prayers are not directed toward the gift, but toward the one who gives it. Our prayers might still contain just as many desires, but ultimately it is not a question of having a wish come true but of expressing an unlimited faith in the giver of all good things. You wish that… but you hope for…. For the prayer of hope, it is essential that there are no guarantees asked, no conditions posed, and no proofs demanded, only that you expect everything from the other without binding him in any way. Hope is based on the premise that the other gives only what is good. Hope includes an openness by which you wait for the other

---

[10] Jürgen Moltmann, *Theology of Hope*, (New York and Evanston: Harper & Row, Publishers, 1967), p. 25.
[11] *The Confessions of St. Augustine,* trans. Rex Warner (New York, NY: The New American Library of World Literature, Inc., 1963), Book I, p. 17.

to make his loving promise come true, even though you never know when, where or how this might happen.[12]

Only the Infinite – God – can be the sure ground for a real hope. This is why we can dare to stay open to whatever happens. God is in charge.

Needless to say that there is always tension between the "already here" and the "not yet." A "not yet" horizon that becomes an "already here" is only a step toward another horizon. This tells about the very nature of our being, which is to be constantly on a pilgrimage. We are constantly on a journey – on the way. "If I stand still, how can I fail to fall?"[13] asked Teilhard. Settling down, except for a moment of rest, would end the search, the progress, the journey, and life. Hope, with its powerful ability to transcend the present and its obvious limitations, opens the door to other possibilities and other realities. The possible has no fixed frontiers. The "not yet" is the unrealized potential within every one of us and within our world. When the "not yet" horizon becomes "already here," another "not yet" horizon appears. In the first Letter of John we read: "We are God's children now [already here]; what we will be has not yet been revealed [not yet]."[14]

Thus, my real "I," that is continuously expanding, no longer coincides with my social "I," that is defined by the role I am playing in my community. The content of the "not yet" must come from a different order. We realize that it is the divine consciousness – "the mind of Christ"[15]—that gives real meaning to our lives. Hope transforms us by giving meaning to our lives. Hope never disappoints us. For Charles Péguy:

> Remarkable virtue of hope, strange mystery, she's not a virtue like the others, she is a virtue against the others…. And she stands up to them. To all the virtues. To all the mysteries…. When they go down she goes up, (she is the one who's right)…. It's she who causes this reversal…. (Who would have believed that such power, that supreme power had been given

---

[12] Henri J. M. Nouwen, *With Open Hands*, (New York, NY: Ballantine Books/Epiphany Edition, 1985 – edition published by arrangement with Ave Maria Press), p. 46.
[13] WTW, p. 229 -- XII, p. 340.
[14] 1 John 3:2.
[15] 1 Corinthians 2:16.

to this little child Hope).... She is the only one who does not fool us.... She is the only one who does not disappoint us.[16]

Why is it that this little child does not disappoint us? Why is it that this kind of hope is not just part of good wishes and does not belong to utopians dreams? That is because hope is a dynamic aspect of God's life within us. God's will for us is to hope for better conditions, a healing, a new life, a new community, even a new humanity. God is our hope. Our hope is God in us and through us. There is no bigger hope than this hope. The world belongs to whoever offers it the greater hope, and no one can give greater hope to the world than the fountain of all hope, Jesus Christ – "CHRIST-THE-EVOLVER."[17] "It... towards Christ, in fact, that we turn our eyes," wrote Teilhard, "when, however approximate our concept of it may be, we look ahead towards a higher pole of humanisation and personalisation."[18]

God has a divine plan for every one of us and for the world.[19] Hope, because of its direct connection with the very source of all life, will help us live God's plan for us and for the world. It makes us believe that it is possible to improve our situation and create a better future for us and for the whole world. True hope never disappoints us.

Brother Lawrence of the Resurrection wrote: "Everything is possible for one who believes, still more for one who hopes, even more for one who loves, and most of all for one who practices and perseveres in these three virtues."[20] This quotation inspired the following prayer:

> Without you, O God, I cannot do anything, but with you I can do everything. You are the Lord of the future. You hold the future – my

---

[16] Charles Péguy, *The Portal of the Mystery of Hope*, trans. David Louis Schindler, Jr., (Grand Rapids, Michigan: William B. Eerdmans Publishing Company, 1996), pp. 80, 118.
[17] CE, p. 147 -- X, p. 172.
[18] SC, p. 165 -- IX, p. 219.
[19] André Dupleix wrote in this context: "For Teilhard, all the hopes and expectations of Christianity for the future are fulfilled by God through absolute faithfulness in him. The future is viewed with great optimism, as the world continues to evolve and grow toward God. It is through 'panamorization,' that is, transforming the world's structures by our love, that Christianity will retain its pivotal place in the world." See André Dupleix, *15 days of Prayer with Pierre Teilhard de Chardin,* trans. by Victoria Hébert and Denis Sabourin (Liguori, Missouri: Liguori Publications, 1999), p. 93.
[20] Brother Lawrence of the Resurrection, *The Practice of the Presence of God*, trans. Salvatore Sciurba, OCD, (Washington, D.C.: ICS Publications, 1994), p. 35.

future, the future of my family and country, and the future of the world. I put all my hope in you. You are my future because you are in my present.[21]

Eschatological[22] Mission

Beside the particular calling that every one of us has in and for our own community, every one of us is supposed also to have a more fundamental calling for the future of the world.[23] One can no longer identify with his or her role in society. One is part of the whole and cannot be other than a self-expanding individual who has a future and needs to invest in it. Jürgen Moltmann explained:

> The expectation of the promised future of the kingdom of God which is coming to man and the world to set them right and create life, makes us ready to expend ourselves unrestrainedly and unreservedly in love and in the work of the reconciliation of the world with God and his future. The

---

[21] Jean Maalouf, *Practicing the Presence of the Living God: A Retreat with Brother Lawrence of the Resurrection*, (Washington, D.C.: ICS Publications, 2011), p. 78.

[22] "Eschatology," wrote Robert Faricy, "studies the polar tension between things-as-they-are and things-as-they-ought-to-be, between the present and the ultimate future. The religious thought of Pierre Teilhard de Chardin is fundamentally eschatological. Teilhard de Chardin's theology is future-oriented, worked out with the framework of a worldview that understands the importance of progress, of history, of building towards the future. As a result of this future-directedness, the central Christian mystery in Teilhard's writings is the *Parousia*, the second coming of Jesus Christ. For Teilhard, who thought in terms of growth and evolution, endings – terminal states of growth – are more important than beginnings. Naturally enough, the evolution of the world, the second coming of Christ, has a dominating position in the whole structure of his theology. It might be said that Teilhard sees the world and its progress from a projected point in the future. That point is the Parousia, the end of the world, the second coming of Christ." See Robert Faricy, S.J., *The Spirituality of Teilhard de Chardin* (Minneapolis, Minnesota: Winston Press, 1981), pp. 47-48.

[23] Robert Faricy and Lucy Rooney remarked: "The spirituality of Teilhard de Chardin is for people living in the world today, a world conscious that it is headed into a future that it sees as uncertain and even threatening, at a collective level and sometimes at a personal level. The central mystery of Teilhard's spirituality is the ultimate future: the Second Coming of Jesus Christ, the Parousia. The central virtue of his spirituality is the virtue that helps us to move into the future, the virtue of hope." See Robert Faricy, S.J. & Lucy Rooney, S.N.D.de N., *Knowing Jesus in the World: Prayer with Teilhard de Chardin* (Santa Barbara, CA: Queenship Publishing Company, 1996), p. 65.

social institutions, roles and functions are means on the way to this self-expending. They have therefore to be shaped creatively by love, in order that men may live together in them more justly, more humanely, more peacefully, and in mutual recognition of their human dignity and freedom.[24]

Then, he added:

> This world is not the heaven of self-realization, as it was said to be in Idealism. This world is not the hell of self-estrangement, as it is said to be in romanticist and existentialist writing. The world is not yet finished, but is understood as engaged in a history. It is therefore the world of possibilities, the world in which we can serve the future, promised truth and righteousness and peace.... The glory of self-realization and the misery of self-estrangement alike arise from hopelessness in a world of lost horizons. To disclose to it the horizon of the future of the crucified Christ is the task of the Christian Church.[25]

God promises and calls. God proves his divinity daily; he makes possible what seems impossible; he gives us the mission to keep history moving; he grants us the eschatological hope of finding our salvation in him; he provides meaning to our life; he offers assistance for the journey; he marks the point of our destination; he invites us to share with him what he is; he "[entrusts] the message of reconciliation to us,"[26] as St. Paul wrote, leading us in "a new creation."[27]

Even if Teilhard championed the idea of a scientific evolution that leads to the "noosphere" phase with the help of technology and its interconnection devices as part of the process, he did not see that this process is the ultimate decider for building the earth. If he thought this way, as some people believed he did, the entire system would have been a utopian system, as these same people thought it was. But no! Teilhard did not stop there; he went much further by introducing the role of the heart for the success of the system. "It is not a *tête-à-tête* or a *corps-à-corps* that we need," he wrote, "it is a heart-to-heart."[28] He also, and especially, recognized, and insisted on, the most important and critical role of

---

[24] Jürgen Moltmann, *Theology of Hope*, (New York and Evanston: Harper & Row, Publishers, 1967), pp. 337-38.
[25] Jürgen Moltmann, *Theology of Hope*, (New York and Evanston: Harper & Row, Publishers, 1967), p. 338.
[26] 2 Corinthians 5:19.
[27] 2 Corinthians 5:17.
[28] FM, p. 78 -- V, p. 99.

"CHRIST-THE-EVOLVER,"[29] as the very engine for the entire process.[30] This makes all the difference in the world indeed. In this sense, Hope cannot be an accumulation of little hopes – good wishes, illusions, fantasies, utopian dreams. No! Hope is the ultimate reality. "Teilhard himself," wrote Ursula Kind, "was carried by a deep-rooted optimism, by an act of hope and faith in the future. It is not only survival that people seek; it is not only to live on and live well; it is to live a qualitatively better, higher life. Humanity seeks a superlife, a superconsciousness."[31]

We are not finished beings; we are "project"beings. Our world is not a finished world; our world is a "project"-world. We are in the making, in *via*, on the way. We keep making progress in spite of our many setbacks, falls, and mistakes. But this is when we need hope in a special way because hope does the work. Hope – the "CHRIST-THE-EVOLVER" – the Omega Point – is the ultimate reality. "Hope," wrote Romano Guardini, "means trusting that the rebirth to new life will surely come about in me and in creation."[32]

---

[29] CE, p. 147 -- X, p. 172.

[30] Teilhard counted much on St. Paul. He certainly had present in mind words like these: "We walk by faith, not by sight" (2 Corinthians 5:7) and "For it is the God who said, 'Let light shine out of darkness,' who has shone in our hearts to give the light of the knowledge of the glory of God in the face of Jesus Christ. But we have this treasure in clay jars, so that it may be made clear that this extraordinary power belongs to God and does not come from us" (2 Corinthians 4:6-7) and many others. Bishop Robert Barron offered the following insight: "As Christians, our primary orientation is not given by reason; it's given by faith. And this has nothing to do with irrationality or credulity. It has to do with appreciation of God and the movement of God.... Sometimes it is exceedingly hard to see what God is doing. But we trust. It might happen slowly and in the face of overwhelming contrary evidence, but God is always acting. From the smallest beginnings can come the accomplishment of God's purpose.... God is working, though we can't see it with our eyes and our ordinary categories." (Bishop Robert Barron's Lent Reflections 2016, Lent Day 25. See http://www.wordonfire.org/).

[31] Ursula King, *The Spirit of One Earth: Reflections on Teilhard de Chardin and Global Spirituality* (New York, N.Y.: Paragon House, 1989), p. 170.

[32] Robert A. Krieg, *Romano Guardini: Spiritual Writings* (Maryknoll, N.Y.: Orbis Books, 2005 – "Modern Spiritual Masters Series"), p. 111.

Part V

Call to Action

Chapter Seventeen

"To See or to Perish"[1]

When we open our eyes and see with our physical eyes, we usually see appearances. When we close our physical eyes and see with our mind, heart, and soul, we usually see what lies under the appearances. We see the connection, the whole, the universal, and what matters most – the essence of reality.

We see what we want to see after all; the world is not better or worse than we want it to be. We may see the same things over and over again, but each time we may see them differently. The truth is that we seldom see things as they are; we see them as we are. That is why, when we change our mind, our priorities, our values, and our references, we see different realities altogether.

What does this mean, existentially?

It means that we are not just observers of a so-called reality, or its photographers, or its recorders. We are active participants, artists, co-creators, or destroyers. When we watch the evening news, what do we really watch? We don't really watch the facts of the event; we watch rather how the reporter conveyed the facts. It is really an interpretation, if not a translation, of the facts.

We can be co-creators as well. For the sake of more clarity, let us try this little exercise: "see" God, really and existentially, everywhere: in the sun, the stars, the flowers, the doves, the fire, the water, the desert, the woods, the mustard seed, the faces of every man and woman, and in your own circumstances. Do you still see all these the same way? When you realize that God is the loving force of the whole, you immediately see how interrelated, interconnected, and interdependent we all are. At this very moment, the walls of polarizations, limits, frontiers, restrictions, prejudices, and narrow-mindedness collapse. Whether we know it or not, the way we live our life has been influenced, controlled, and conditioned by our personal philosophy – our dominant way of thinking. If the world is a reflection of what we see, what we see makes our world as well; *what* we

---

[1] PM, p. 31 -- I, p. 25.

see is *how* we see it. It has been said that "The way you look at things is the most powerful force in shaping your life. In a vital sense, perception is reality,"[2] and "It is a startling truth that how you see and what you see determine how and who you will be."[3] Didn't Michelangelo see the statue of David in the marble first?

This is the way it is. Every time we close our eyes to see the reality with our mind, heart, and soul, we open our eyes to see things transformed. Our outlook on life has changed in such a way that now we see a world without limited horizons. Our vision is now universal, and the scope of our consciousness has become open to the infinite.

The consequences of this operation are enormous. As soon as we begin to recognize the essential under the appearances and what is important over what is secondary, we will start to see our consciousness extended into the "universal realities." As early as 1927, Teilhard talked about these realities. He wrote:

> Humanity was sleeping – it is still sleeping – imprisoned in the narrow joys of its little closed loves. A tremendous spiritual power is slumbering in the depths of our multitude, which will manifest itself only when we have learned to *break down the barriers* of our egoisms and, by a fundamental recasting our outlook, raise ourselves up to the habitual and practical vision of universal realities.[4]

Then, ten years later, he also wrote: "If we wish to discern the phenomenon of spirit in its entirety, we must first educate our eyes to perceiving collective realities."[5]

If for Hamlet, "To be or not to be"[6] was the question, for Teilhard, it seems fair to say, the question was, "To see or not to see." To the best of my knowledge, nobody has insisted on the importance of *seeing*[7] more than Teilhard. He spoke about it many, many times. He wrote, for example: "In order to see, as we know, we have to do more than open our

---

[2] John O'Donohue, *Anam Cara: A Book of Celtic Wisdom*, (New York, NY: HarperCollins Publisher Inc. – Harper Perennial – 1998, 2004), p. 105.
[3] Ibid., p. 62.
[4] DM, p. 146 -- IV, p. 186.
[5] HE, p. 95 -- VI, p. 119.
[6] William Shakespeare, *Hamlet* (Act III, Scene 1).
[7] Ursula King affirmed: "[Teilhard] assigns a central place to 'seeing.' This applies to both the visual perception of the many phenomena that constitute the outer world as well as the development of an inner vision." See Ursula King, *Teilhard de Chardin and Eastern Religions: Spirituality and Mysticism in an Evolutionary World* (Mahwah, N.J.: Paulist Press, 2011), p. 3.

eyes."[8] He talked about education of the eyes.[9] He considered that an "effort at perspective is indispensable."[10] His book, *The Divine Milieu*, was introduced as a way "to teach how to see God everywhere, to see him in all that is most hidden, most solid, and most ultimate in the world."[11] His essay, "My Fundamental Vision,"[12] which is the translation of the French essay "Comment je vois"[13] (literally: "How I See"), is preceded by the words: "It seems to me that a whole life-time of continual hard work would be as nothing to me, if only I could, just for one moment, give a true picture of what I see."[14] The first sentence of the Foreword of his book, *The Phenomenon of Man*, that was one of the most important books of the twentieth century, was: "This work may be summed up as an attempt *to see* and *to make others see*...."[15] Then he wrote the following striking declaration:

> *Seeing*. We might say that the whole of life lies in that verb – if not ultimately, at least essentially. Fuller being is closer union: such is the kernel and conclusion of this book. But let us emphasize the point: union increases only through an increase in consciousness, that is to say in vision. And that, doubtless, is why the history of the living world can be summarized as the elaboration of ever more perfect eyes within a cosmos in which there is always something more to be seen.... *To see or to perish* is the very condition laid upon everything that makes up the universe, by reason of the mysterious gift of existence.[16]

Why is that so? Why is seeing so important? What does "to see" mean, in the first place, and what is there to see?

"To see"

"To see" means to get knowledge and impressions through the eyes. It also means to understand, to learn, to discover, to have more and more information, to witness, to experience, to guess, and to plan. Moreover, it means to be aware, to have insight, to be enlightened, and "The more one

---

[8] AE, p. 24 -- VII, p. 30.
[9] See DM, p. 46 -- IV, p. 25; AE, p. 24 -- VII, p. 30; AE, p. 295 -- VII, p. 308.
[10] PM, p. 91 -- I, p. 94.
[11] DM, p. 46 -- IV, p. 25.
[12] TF, pp. 163-208.
[13] XI, pp. 177-223.
[14] TF, p. 164 -- XI, p. 181.
[15] PM, p. 31 -- I, p. 25.
[16] PM, p. 31 -- I, p. 25.

looks," as Teilhard said, "the more one sees. And the more one sees, the better one knows where to look."[17] That is why, as Teilhard also said, "In order to see, as we know, we have to do more than simply open our eyes. In addition, our observation must, as it proceeds, be reinforced by a certain number of auxiliary ways of seeing."[18]

To see!

To see that there is something much larger than what the physical eyes can see. Helen Keller describes this well by saying, "Worse than being blind would be to be able to see but not have a vision," for "Where there is no vision, the people perish."[19] Probably there is more truth in saying "believing is seeing" than in the truism "seeing is believing" because what we believe or disbelieve controls a good deal of what we will perceive and do in life.

To see that everything is linked to everything; that anything belongs to the cosmos and that everything is interdependent with everything else; that the part is in the whole and the whole is in the part; that we co-create each other, we heal each other, and we heal our community, our earth, and the universe; that the best is still to come.

To see that the cosmos is in constant movement; that the movement is in progress, from the lower level to the higher level, and from the simple to the complex; that this movement is not smooth but in continuous struggle with unending ups and downs.

To see that there is an orientation, a direction, and a meaning for the universe; that there is an open road ahead; that there is limitless progress for everything; that progress is continuously growing and developing through sciences, art, poetry, music, spiritual practices, and all kinds of other sources of knowledge.

To see that the progress is not a product or a conclusion, but a force; that "it [progress] is the consciousness of all that is and all that can be."[20] To learn to see means "to develop a *homogeneous* and *coherent* perspective of our general extended experience of man. A *whole* which unfolds."[21]

To see that the planet earth is starting a new phase with the globalization of humanity; that consciousness and "personnalisation" are intensifying; that humankind is heading toward unity; that unity is not

---

[17] PM, pp. 280-81 -- I, p. 312.
[18] AE, p. 24 -- VII, p. 30.
[19] Proverbs 29:18 (KJV).
[20] FM, p. 20 -- V, p. 31.
[21] PM, p. 35 -- I, p. 29.

uniformity; that unity does not imply having the same ideas, the similar points of views, and the identical ways of doing things.

To see that unity is a complete interdependence of the immense varieties of cultures, civilizations, societies, histories, and ethnicities; that, because we organically "interbe,"[22] we will survive together or we will die together; that even that they lost their humanness in war, the human beings ironically gain more ground in regard to unification, and they also learned what is essential and what is not.[23]

To see that, when one sees far enough, one sees unity and, further, one sees God. Teilhard was very clear on this point and very explicit. In the introduction of his book, *The Divine Milieu*, he wrote:

> This little book does not more than recapitulate the eternal lesson of the Church in the words of a man who, because he believes himself to feel deeply in tune with his own times, has sought to teach how to see God everywhere, to see him in all that is most hidden, most solid, and most ultimate in the world. These pages put forward no more than a practical attitude – or, more exactly perhaps, a way of teaching how to see.[24]

To see that, when we want to see the truth, we need educated and trained[25] – healthy – eyes. Otherwise we will live in darkness. The Gospel says: "The eye is the lamp of the body. So, if your eye is healthy, your whole body will be full of light; but if your eye is unhealthy, your whole body will be full of darkness. If then the light in you is darkness, how great is the darkness!"[26]

To see that, while retaining confidence in reason, logic and syllogism, we know how to transcend the ordinary way of thinking and think vertically by going down, down, down – the further we can go in our consciousness to the center of our soul. There we can find our true selves and others in God. There we can find all in God and God in all. Peace might be right there. It is there. Ursula King offers this condensed insight:

> "Seeing" in the Teilhardian sense is a process that implies "seeing more" and also "seeing differently," looking at the world from a different

---

[22] A word used often by Thick Nhat Hanh. See for example his book, *Peace Is Every Step: The Path of Mindfulness in Everyday Life*, edited by Arnold Kotler. New York: Bantam Books, 1991, pp. 96, 127-130.
[23] Cf. Jean Maalouf, *Le mystère du mal dans l'oeuvre de Teilhard de Chardin*, Cerf, 1986, pp. 22-32.
[24] DM, p. 46 -- IV, p. 25.
[25] See DM, p. 46 -- IV, p. 25; AE, p. 24 -- VII, p. 30; AE, p. 295 -- VII, p. 308.
[26] Matthew 6:22-23.

perspective in order to attain a larger vision, a new consciousness, a fuller life. To "see all things," especially to see all things in God, as is part of the Ignatian tradition to which Teilhard belongs, can no longer be taken as a straightforward descriptive statement. The mention of "all things" means so much more today than in the past.... [27]

The mystical eye

The mystical eye is different from the ordinary eye. While the ordinary eye is content with what it sees at the surface, the mystical eye sees underneath the surface; it sees the realities of the mind, heart, soul, and the divine. This is what matters most. It is, as Teilhard put it, the "true mystical science, that really matters.... Obviously, many primitive intuitions have been corrupted and blunted by civilisations and speculation.... However, mysticism remains the great science and the great art, the only power capable of synthesizing the riches accumulated by other forms of human activities."[28] Concepts may obscure the vision by their heaviness and complexity to the point that they may even blind the eye. The mystical eye is unobstructed, unclogged, and unobligated.

To see with a mystical eye and to be a revolutionary are not opposite at all. In fact, they can be best allies. No wonder why most mystics in human history were not only tolerated or simply rejected by society, they were also condemned, persecuted, and sometimes executed, and that is because they can never be supporters of the establishment and the status quo.

A real mysticism and a real revolution deal with a radical change. Both of them face the human condition as it is, and both of them want to grasp the secret of a sick society. Both of them are concerned with freeing their fellow human beings from their alienations, fears, and paralysis. Both of them call to arms to fight the petty fantasies of the egos and, by their far reaching vision, create an atmosphere of harmony and reconciliation. Both of them, by digging deep into the very core of things and touching the human hearts, aim to change things around. Both of them know well that no radical change in society will be possible unless there is a change of heart first.

To see means to discern, understand, and develop a worldview from a different angle; it is not the natural seeing of the common physical eye, but a seeing of an altogether different order. For Teilhard,

---

[27] Ursula King, *Christ in All Things: Exploring Spirituality with Teilhard de Chardin* (Maryknoll, NY: Orbis Books, 1997), pp. 14-15.
[28] LT, pp. 86-7 -- *Lettres de voyage*, pp. 46-7.

The perception of the divine omnipresence is essentially a seeing, a taste, that is to say a sort of intuition bearing upon certain superior qualities in things. It cannot, therefore, be attained directly by any process or reasoning, nor by any human artifice. It is a gift, like life itself, of which it is undoubtedly the supreme experimental perfection.[29]

Therefore, and as Ursula King said, "In other words, seeing is not simply a human activity but something we are endowed with, something given to us like an innate treasure from which we can draw immeasurable benefits."[30] Nothing will stay the same when we see things from the perspective of God – the "mind of Christ."[31] A shift in consciousness would have taken place, and it is this new consciousness that will run the "show."

To see means to re-construct the world and co-create reality according to one's own mystical perception, in the image and likeness of one's already transformed heart.[32] Reality will be as perfect and peaceful as the quality of our seeing is. "Our future is in our own hands,"[33] Teilhard affirms. Therefore, as he also says, "A new way of seeing, combined with a new way of acting – that is what we need."[34] Consequently, all these categories – conservative, liberal, right, left, fascist, communist… which label and rule our lives, should be put to rest in the history books, and new patterns of human relationships should be created in the direction of the human and the forward.

To see does not only mean to survive, but to ascend into a higher state of existence in unity with an immense variety of interdependent cultures, activities, and civilizations. Peace, then, may move forward by using essentially the human beings' psychic powers which can be maximized by contemplation. Contemplation has the potential to increase the psychic temperature of the noosphere (the thinking envelope of the earth), by

---

[29] DM, p. 131 -- IV, p. 163.
[30] Ursula King, *Teilhard de Chardin and Eastern Religions: Spirituality and Mysticism in an Evolutionary World* (Mahwah, N.J.: Paulist Press, 2011), p. 12.
[31] 1 Corinthians 2:16.
[32] Thomas M. King wrote: "What we 'see' effects our ability to act. If we see that we and the evolutionary process are going nowhere—then revolt is more than our option; it is our duty. If we see life to be consumed by entropy and humanity reduced to naught, then why should we continue to struggle? And a human revolt would effect evolution as a whole." See Thomas M. King, S.J., *Teilhard de Chardin* (Wilmington, Delaware: Michael Glazier, Inc., 1988, 'The Way of the Christian Mystics'), p. 108.
[33] WTW, p. 285 -- XII, p. 425.
[34] AE, p. 295 -- VII, p. 308.

nurturing the most profoundly human, and by quickening an increased consciousness.

To see means to change the way we think, the way we imagine, the way we perceive things. It means that we have to change our angle and mode of vision, our attitude, and our approach to life. It means that we have to change.

To see deep, clear, big, forward, upward, and far, very far is the way not only to survive, but also to real peace.

"To see or to perish."[35]

---

[35] PM, p. 31 -- I, p. 25.

Chapter Eighteen

Rediscovering the Fire

Our world is on fire, and the fire seems to be out of control. The fires of violence, aggression, greed, hate, lust, chauvinism, racism, prejudice, and selfishness are sweeping the world. We are constantly under the gun, with the gun, for the gun, and we sometimes run our affairs by the gun, individually, nationally, and internationally.

Peace!

Everyone wants peace, but everyone is thinking war, preparing for war, or is already at war. The United Nations can hardly cope with gathering storms in different parts of the world – in the Middle East, Africa, the Far East, and many other places. It has been like this for a long time. We may put an end to one war to immediately initiate another one. That is the pattern. No wonder Dag Hammarskjöld, who was the Secretary General of the United Nations (1953-61), told Billy Graham at a meeting in his office in New York: "I see no hope for permanent world peace. We have tried so hard and we have failed so miserably." Then he added: "Unless the world has a spiritual rebirth within the next few years, civilization is doomed."[1]

About the time when Dag Hammarskjöld said what he said, Teilhard de Chardin was ending his long career of writing (he died in 1955). Teilhard pointed to this "spiritual rebirth" so many times. But, in a remarkable way, he condensed his thoughts with these lines:

> The day will come when, after harnessing the ether, the winds, the tides, gravitation, we shall harness for God the energies of love. And, on that day, for the second time in the history of the world, man will have discovered fire.[2]

---

[1] Billy Graham, *World Aflame*, (Garden City, NY: Doubleday & Company. 1965), p. 1.
[2] TF, pp. 86-7 -- XI, p. 92.

Teilhard wrote these lines in 1934. But even before this date, he already in 1917 talked about the ultimate form of love in union with God. He wrote at that time:

> It is not by making themselves more material, relying solely on physical contacts, but by making themselves more spiritual in the embrace of God, that things draw closer to each other and, following their invincible natural bent, end by becoming, all of them together, one.[3]

Also, he used the fire-theme several times before 1934. In 1917, he wrote, for example, "... And now the Fire is with us: it has come down, as though upon a burnt-offering."[4] In 1919, he described his vocation as that of someone "whom the Lord had drawn to follow the road of fire."[5] In 1923, he wrote, "Fire, the source of being.... Once again the Fire has penetrated the earth."[6] "Christ. His Heart. A Fire: a fire with the power to penetrate all things – and which was now gradually spreading unchecked.... Let your universal Presence spring forth in a blaze that is at once Diaphany and Fire. O ever-greater Christ!"[7]

What could have been the connection, in Teilhard's mind, between Fire and Love? How can one extinguish the earthly fire with the heavenly fire?

Love as cosmic energy

"Love one another," for Teilhard is not merely a moral order.[8] It is the sap that vitalizes and invigorates everything. It is the energy that holds things together. He wrote:

> Nevertheless there can be no doubt that it is something in the way of love that is adumbrated and grows as a result of the mutual affinity which

---

[3] WTW, p. 143 -- XII, p. 186.
[4] WTW, p. 144 -- XII, p. 186.
[5] HM, p. 74 -- XIII, p. 88.
[6] HM, pp. 121, 123 -- XIII, pp. 143, 145.
[7] HM, pp. 47, 58 -- XIII, pp. 58, 70.
[8] In the context of Teilhard's reasoning, Paul Chauchard offered the following insight: "To love one's neighbor as oneself is not enough for human nature. God is not the most distant, but the most near. Man needs an ideal; the most human ideal is a personal ideal with which a personal relationship is possible. The superior level of man's amortization is the prayer relationship to the God of love." See Paul Chauchard, *Teilhard de Chardin on Love and Suffering*, trans. Marie Chêne (Glen Rock, N.J.: A Deus Books Edition of the Paulist Presss, 1966), p. 36.

causes the particles to adhere to one another and maintains their unity during their convergent advance.[9]

'Love one another, recognising in the heart of each of you the same God who is being born.' Those words, first spoken two thousand years ago, now begin to reveal themselves as the essential structural law of what we call progress and evolution. They enter the scientific field of cosmic energy and its necessary laws.[10]

Love is a cosmic attraction – "the most universal, the most tremendous and the most mysterious of the cosmic forces"[11] that directs to the universal synthesis. For "Love in all its subtleties is nothing more, and nothing less, than the more or less direct trace marked on the heart of the element by the psychical convergence of the universe upon itself,"[12] and this is how "Driven by the forces of love, the fragments of the world seek each other so that the world may come to being."[13] Love is nothing but "the energy proper to cosmogenesis."[14] "Love," commented Sister Maria Gratia Martin, "is the ultimate energy, the spiritualized form of that radial or axial energy that has been the single basic drive operating in the complexity/consciousness pattern of cosmogenesis right from the beginning."[15]

Love is also an impetus for more creativity that strives for greater consciousness. It is an ascending force of evolution and a momentum for a being that is always progressing. It is the basic motivation that leads to action. "Only love," Teilhard says, "has the power to move being."[16] This is why "The most telling and profound way of describing the evolution of the universe would undoubtedly be to trace the evolution of love,"[17] and this is also why the precept "love one another" is "the *only* imaginable, principle of the earth's future equilibrium."[18] That would be the path to peace. Teilhard continues:

---

[9] AE, p. 119 -- VII, p. 125.
[10] FM, pp. 78-9 -- V, p. 100.
[11] HE, p. 32 -- VI, p. 40.
[12] PM, p. 265 -- I, p. 294.
[13] PM, pp. 264-65 -- I, p. 294.
[14] AE, p. 119 -- VII, p. 126.
[15] Sister Maria Gratia Martin, I.H.M., *The Spirituality of Teilhard de Chardin* (New York, NY: Newman Press, 1968), pp. 24-25.
[16] WTW, p. 200 -- XII, p. 289.
[17] HE, p. 33 -- VI, p. 41.
[18] AE, p. 20 -- VII, p. 26.

If we did so decide, what awaits us would be the true victory and the only true peace. In its own heart, force would be constrained to disarm, because we should at last have laid our hands on a stronger weapon with which to replace it.[19]

So, the way to go is to replace the earthly fire (weapon of the earth) with the heavenly fire (weapon of the Spirit).

How this could happen?

Relationships among people develop along with general biological and universal evolution.[20] In fact, beyond the traditional and convenient relationships, humanity more and more seeks groupings by a higher quality of connections. Human beings look forward to coming together because of intellectual and especially spiritual affinities. A grain of internal motivation is more effective than mountains of external coercion. "It is not with prudence that we make people move," affirms Teilhard, "but with a little passion."[21] With the knowledge of sciences, we understand the truth. With the knowledge of love, we live the truth. We are involved in it. We are converted by it. We are transformed by it. We are transfigured by it. "Love is a sacred reserve of energy; it is like the blood of spiritual evolution."[22] The miracle of love!

To be in love with God, others, and the universe is the mystical experience[23] with the ultimate truth that will undoubtedly produce practical

---

[19] AE, p. 20 -- VII, p. 26.

[20] Paul Chauchard commented: "The biological evolution continuing through history, having as norm and meaning a rise which is more union, more coherence, more convergence, necessarily demands a source of attraction which is more love. This source of attraction, which is above and ahead, has the power of amortization only if it is real, if it be not merely a false god who comes but the true God outside of time who has been, is and shall be, world without end. In amortizing the world, in amortizing society, man is on the march toward the God of love, that Omega point of supreme convergence, a view which Teilhard proposes to us in harmony with Christian eschatology." See Paul Chauchard, *Teilhard de Chardin on Love and Suffering*, trans. Marie Chêne (Glen Rock, N.J.: A Deus Books Edition of the Paulist Presss, 1966), pp. 36-37.

[21] LTF, p. 100 -- *Accomplir l'homme*, p. 122.

[22] HE, p. 34 -- VI, p. 42.

[23] Ursula King commented: "The love of God and the love of the world are inextricably combined, having as their central focus the universal and cosmic Christ. Thus, the essay ['The Heart of Matter'] culminates in a 'Prayer to the ever greater Christ' which is remarkable for its mystical depth and beauty of expression. It is a continuation of all that is most central to Christianity, and reminds one of the hymn of the fourth century Christian writer Prudentius who describes Christ as

peace ramifications other sources of knowledge do not necessarily produce. We might use the forces of intellect, persuasion, argument, common interest, convenience, international law, and more. We may sign treaties and contracts. But these are not love. They may work for a while and they may provide a temporary peace and then they will put us against each other again. But when love meets truth, a sense of wholeness is created and the ecstatic feeling of union is experienced. Here, there is nothing but peace.

However, peace is not a passive state of satisfaction and contentment. Peace is a job to do, a mission to carry out, a book to write, a new path to a higher ground to find, a policy to apply, a philosophy to inspire, an ethical principle to live by, a hand to shake, a neighbor to help – an earth to build.

Peace is like happiness. When one grasps it, it disappears. Not because it is evasive, but because it is fluid like a river that is continuously in progress. It is a by-product. We are on the right track when we are on the road, looking for more consciousness and more liberty. Peace is nothing but a "unanimity in search and conquest, sustained among us by the universal resolve to raise ourselves upwards, all straining shoulder to shoulder, towards even greater heights of consciousness and freedom."[24]

Love stirs mysterious forces. It is the explanation of all that grow within and without. It is a growing peace. It is growth. It is the dynamic state of the higher consciousness. It is peace.

Love is peace

"'Love one another'... the only true peace."[25]

The reality is that it is only at the deepest level of the human heart that conflicts can come to an end. All our intellectual concepts and constructions and systems and "wisdoms" remain ineffective in serving

---

    Of the Father's heart begotten
    Ere the world from chaos rose,
    He is Alpha: from the fountain
    All that is and has been flows;
    He is Omega, of all things
    Yet to come the mystic Close
    Evermore and evermore.

See Ursula King, *Toward a New Mysticism: Teilhard de Chardin and Eastern Religions,* (New York: Seabury Press, 1980), p. 33.

[24] FM, p. 159 -- V, p. 196.

[25] AE, p. 20 -- VII, p. 26.

the cause of peace so long as our hearts entertain feelings of hate and repugnance. No wonder Teilhard insists so much on the "Love one another" because it "is the *only* imaginable, principle of the earth's future equilibrium."[26]

Our world is consuming itself by its un-satiable and never fulfilled thirst for physical energy and material things. We must shift to a higher form of energy – the energy of love – if the earth is to survive as a viable planet. This energy gives life, controls the other forms of energy, and effects the change needed.

Therefore, it is unrealistic to leave love aside when we talk about peace and about the ways we can use to build the earth. On the contrary, we must admit that, by introducing it inside, it is the natural milieu where evolution is taking place. Consequently, love is not simply a "passion" in the sense understood by psychologists and moralists. Love physically builds the universe. With its specific manifestations, it appears then as the supreme realism. It is so because it is above all the supreme energy that possesses a cosmic dimension and is a creative force in the evolutionary process itself. Love is God in action – the transforming Fire.

Love is an involvement in God's activity. Creativity, compassion, development, integration of all human values, and participation in all the aspects of life are parts of God's "work" of creating the world. This is so because God is the source and origin,[27] and the goal and destiny of everything – the Alpha at the beginning and the Omega[28] at the end – and

---

[26] AE, p. 20 -- VII, p. 26.

[27] William D. Dinges and Ilia Delio, OSF, wrote: "[Teilhard] believed in love as the personal energy of evolution: 'Love is the most universal, the most tremendous and the most mysterious of the cosmic forces' (HE, 32). Divine love is evolutionary—it changes, grows, complexifies—and this growth and complexification is the basis of unity. What Teilhard tried to show is that evolution in all its materiality is not only the universe coming to be but it is God who is coming to be. Thus he states, 'God is entirely self-sufficient; and yet the universe contributes something that is vitally necessary to God' (CE, 177). Evolution, he claimed, requires a divine source located not in the past or 'up above' in a timeless present but 'up ahead' in the future." See William D. Dinges and Ilia Delio, OSF, "Teilhard de Chardin and the New Spirituality" in Ilia Delio, ed., *From Teilhard to Omega: Co-creating an Unfinished Universe* (Maryknoll, N.Y.: Orbis Books, 2015), p.177.

[28] Robert Faricy offered the following comment: "Teilhard fills out his general analysis of human love by pointing out the necessity of some existing autonomous centre that would be structurally and functionally capable of inspiring and releasing within mankind the necessary forces of love. Only a kind of 'super-love' can synthesize all the earthly loves. Without a really existing and personal centre

it is God who created us to be creative in an unfinished world. Our purpose as human beings would be, as Teilhard sees it in his evolutionary vision, to be aware of this divine source and to learn to utilize it to build the earth and bring peace to humanity. "Love alone," wrote Ursula King, "is capable of creating one earth, one human community."[29]

The Spirit of God – the Fire of Love – will help us cement our brains and our hearts. The fire of love that will replace the fire of war will make us all evolve toward a lasting peace. Then, and if we really want to know human history, we should and we will read the history of love instead of the history of wars. Teilhard suggests that "The most telling and profound way of describing the evolution of the universe would undoubtedly be to trace the evolution of love."[30]

Again, the "Love one another" is not only a principle of moral perfection, it should be a survival principle as well. "Love one another or you perish."[31]

What is the force that causes the universe to evolve to ever higher states of complexity and consciousness that make humanity more unified and more peaceful? What is that "thing" that motivates humans to strive for making their impossible dreams come true? The physical and material forms of energy undoubtedly play their role. So do the mental forms of energy such as information and knowledge. But more important are the energies of love – love of God for humanity, love of humanity for God, and love of neighbor and creation. Love has the capacity to do the work. It changes minds and hearts. It points to a new way of "seeing." It "gives significance to everything around us."[32] It unifies.[33] It "builds up."[34] It

---

of universal coherence, there can be no true union of mankind; this personal centre of love must be Someone who draws mankind towards himself." See Robert Faricy, S.J., *The Spirituality of Teilhard de Chardin* (Minneapolis, Minnesota: Winston Press, 1981), p. 26.

[29] Ursula King wrote: "The most powerful energy to transform our world, the energy most needed today, is the spirit of love. Love alone is capable of creating one earth, one human community. Love is *the* spirit of one earth, the life-giving, transforming dynamic at the heart of the noosphere. Teilhard understood this sphere as a thought-love-energy-network, a cosmic web of complex interaction and attraction that weaves new ways of being and sharing." See Ursula King, *The Spirit of One Earth: Reflections on Teilhard de Chardin and Global Spirituality* (New York, N.Y.: Paragon House, 1989), p. 176.

[30] HE, p. 33 -- VI, p. 41.

[31] HE, p. 153 -- VI, p. 189.

[32] Pierre Teilhard de Chardin, *Building the Earth* (Wilkes-Barre, PA: Dimension Books, Inc., 1965), p. 46.

transforms. "Love," wrote Ilia Delio, "draws together even in the face of resistance. If energy is the fire of life, then love is the energy of all life. Evolution rests on the power of love because what ignites the core of being is ultimately unitive and transformative."[35] Love gives new life.

A new humanity will certainly dawn when the fire of love fuels the engines of the world.

The best way to finish this chapter is to quote a few lines of a letter that Albert Einstein left to his daughter. This letter demonstrates how much these two geniuses, Einstein and Teilhard, were very often on the same wave length. Einstein wrote:

> There is an extremely powerful force that, so far, science has not found a formal explanation to. It is a force that includes and governs all others, and is even behind any phenomenon operating in the universe and has not yet been identified by us. This force is LOVE.... This force explains everything and gives meaning to life.... If instead of E=mc2, we accept that the energy to heal the world can be obtained through love multiplied by the speed of light squared, we arrive at the conclusion that love is the most powerful force there is, because it has no limits.... If we want our species to survive, if we are to find meaning in life, if we want to save the world and every sentient being that inhabits it, love is the one and only answer. Perhaps we are not yet ready to make a bomb of love, a device powerful enough to entirely destroy the hate, selfishness and greed that

---

[33] Ursula King wrote: "The external forces of unification that press in upon us in the field of economics, politics, and world communications are by themselves not enough to create one world. The most powerful energy in bringing about a greater unity of mankind is the energy of love. Teilhard used to say that we must summon and harness the powers of love – the powers of an all-transforming spiritual energy – as we have harnessed the powers of wind and water, of atoms and genes, in order to build a future worth living, a future which will extend rather than diminish our capacity of being human." See Ursula King, *The Spirit of One Earth: Reflections on Teilhard de Chardin and Global Spirituality* (New York, N.Y.: Paragon House, 1989), p. 24.

[34] Ursula King remarked: "The greatest deficiency of the socializing forces at present is their use of force and coercion. Love alone can lead to the deepest affinity and integration among people. Teilhard reckoned with love as a form of energy as important in the universe as the energy of matter. The energy of love unifies and builds up; it integrates and synthesizes different elements into a higher unity – it creates unanimization, as Teilhard says." See Ursula King, *The Spirit of One Earth: Reflections on Teilhard de Chardin and Global Spirituality* (New York, N.Y.: Paragon House, 1989), p. 55.

[35] See Ilia Delio, OSF, *The Unbearable Wholeness of Being: God, Evolution, and the Power of Love* (Maryknoll, N.Y.: Orbis Books, 2015), p. 55.

devastate the planet. However, each individual carries within them a small but powerful generator of love whose energy is waiting to be released....[36]

---

[36] See https://wearelightbeings.wordpress.com/2015/04/15/a-letter-from-albert-einstein-to-his-daughter-about-the-universal-force-which-is-love/

CHAPTER NINETEEN

CALL TO ACTION

Teilhard's vision of the universe and how the universe operates is full of hope. How could it be otherwise since the whole of creation is permeated by the active presence of God, its original creator, its continuing evolver, and its final aim! The path is the matter evolving into life and inner consciousness, and the human life and the inner consciousness into personal and universal "com-union" with Christ – the Omega point of evolving creation. God then is eternally transforming and redeeming all that exists because "God saw everything that he had made, and indeed, it was very good"[1] and because "God so loved the world."[2] This is what Christianity is offering to the world. Dr. Eugene Wahl wrote insightfully: "Christianity has come to see that the fundamental calling of being human is to be the Incarnation now. The Christ-event happened once, and continues happening. Every moment is full of the continual Christ-event in this way. This is a fundamental underpinning of Christianity as living religion."[3] This is also the realization of the importance of the Christian engagement as well as others' engagement, for that matter. We should have no fear for doing that because, as Teilhard put it, "Our faith imposes on us the right and the duty to throw ourselves into the things of the earth."[4] Sister Catherine R. O'Connor, C.S.J, appropriately commented:

> The sense of the sacredness of the earth and of man's rootedness in it could be, in conjunction with ritual and sacrament, a rich source of nourishment for the human spirit. Teilhard's particular thrust in the area of the importance of human action and passion in making 'contact' with God

---

[1] Genesis 1:31.
[2] John 3:16.
[3] Rev. Dr. Eugene Wahl, "On the Implications of Ecology for Incarnation: Triangle Theology." See http://www.env-steward.com/reflect/cme/triangle.htm
[4] MD, p. 14 -- IV, p. 61.

through the earth would add a new dimension to an approach to Christianity that still tends to be merely legal and moral.[5]

There is, especially in Teilhard's book *The Divine Milieu*, an authentic conception of Christian life, which consists not in a passive resignation, nor in a fearful withdrawal, nor in a mimic conformation to the world, but in an active conformation to Christ, by living in and transforming the world. Thus, every individual is supposed to unfold his or her true self in what God wants him or her to be and do. That is his or her unique way to the God who has planted within us the seeds of our destiny.

We matter. Everyone of us matters. What we think matters. What we do matters. The way we do what we do matters. Every moment matters. Every thing matters. Dr. Wahl suggested:

> There is no way for any living creature to be isolated from other creatures and from the inanimate world. Life as we know it means that we are in a flow of energy and materials – into us as creatures and out from us as creatures – and that the inanimate world is very much part of the flow.... There is no way for Jesus to become incarnate, to become flesh, without being *fully engaged* in this web of flows.... In this way, the fish that Jesus ate, the grain that he consumed, the water he drank, the air that he breathed and exhaled, all of these interactions mean that the entire environment in which he lived is necessarily brought into the Incarnation.... We are the Body of Christ, and the rest of Creation, we now must say, is the *Rest of the Body of Christ*.[6]

We are the Body of Christ and everything in this Body matters, every action matters, and every way of living matters. We are, and every "other" is, the embodiment of Christ. How we treat others, as well as how we treat ourselves, should be done the way we treat Christ.[7] This should be the solid base of our action in the world because "In him we live and move and have our being,"[8] as St. Paul put it, and who also said that "For from him and through him and to him are all things."[9]

---

[5] Sister Catherine R. O'Connor, C.S.J., *Woman and Cosmos: The Feminine in the Thought of Teilhard de Chardin*, (Englewood Cliffs, N.J.: Prentice-Hall, Inc., 1971), p. 150.
[6] Rev. Dr. Eugene Wahl, "On the Implications of Ecology for Incarnation: Triangle Theology." See http://www.env-steward.com/reflect/cme/triangle.htm
[7] See Matthew 25:40, 45.
[8] Acts 17:28.
[9] Romans 11:36.

St. Paul's vision of Christ is what Teilhard had in mind when he talked about the Omega Christ who is holding all creation in all its dimensions and complexity together, and also when he used the terms "divine milieu" to describe how the whole of creation is supposed to be as the tabernacle of God among us. No wonder if we hear St. Paul talking about this continuing Incarnation in him, proclaiming, "It is no longer I who live, but it is Christ who lives in me."[10] No wonder if Teilhard talked about [Christification][11] and about "Super-Humanity, Super-Christ, Super-Charity."[12] No wonder if his faith in Christ – the ultimate goal of the world's history – became the source of inspiration and the greatest incentive for our attitude and work in this temporary plane for building the future. No wonder if he enthusiastically wrote:

> Nothing is more certain, dogmatically, than that human action can be sanctified. 'Whatever you do,' says St. Paul, 'do it in the name of our Lord Jesus Christ.'... The actions of life, of which Paul is speaking here, should not, as everyone knows, be understood solely in the sense of religious and devotional 'works' (prayers, fastings, almsgivings). It is the whole of human life, down to its most 'natural' zones, which, the Church teaches, can be sanctified. 'Whether you eat or whether you drink,' St. Paul says. The whole history of the Church is there to attest it.... Each one of our works, by its more or less remote or direct effect upon the spiritual world, helps to make perfect Christ in his mystical totality.[13]

Therefore, not a single activity of ours happens outside the divine milieu. Our activities are supposed to be merging with God's activity. "Action," wrote André Dupleix, "is an adhesion, and adhesion to God."[14] Teilhard describes it this way: "To begin with, in action I adhere to the creative power of God; I coincide with it. I become not only its instrument but its living extension."[15] Then, nothing is profane, nothing is trivial, and nothing is meaningless. We can be reading a book, walking the dog,

---

[10] Galatians 2:20.
[11] See HM, p. 47 -- XIII, p. 58 ; AE, p. 263 -- VII, p. 272.
[12] SC, p. 151 -- IX, p. 193.
[13] DM, pp. 50-51, 62 -- IV, pp. 32-33, 50-51. (See also DM, pp. 66-67 -- IV, pp. 57-58).
[14] André Dupleix, *15 days of Prayer with Pierre Teilhard de Chardin,* trans. by Victoria Hébert and Denis Sabourin (Liguori, Missouri: Liguori Publications, 1999), p. 41.
[15] MD, p. 62 -- IV, p. 51.

cooking,[16] washing dishes, planning a picnic, shopping for groceries, playing racquetball, telling jokes with a friend, planting a smile on someone's face, and whatever we happen to be doing. That particular action and "with each one of our *works*," said Teilhard, "we labour (…) to build the Pleroma; that is to say, we bring to Christ a little fulfillment,"[17] and "God is inexhaustible attainable in the *totality* of our action."[18] Then comes Teilhard's recommendation:

> Try, with God's help, to perceive the connection – even physical and natural – which binds your labour with the building of the kingdom of heaven; try to realise that heaven itself smiles upon you and, through your works, draws you to itself; then as you leave church for the noisy streets, you will remain with only one feeling, that of continuing to immerse yourself in God.[19]

For Teilhard, the Christians more than anyone else have the mission to advance God's kingdom in every domain of humankind, for their faith imposes on them "the right and the duty to throw [themselves] into the things of the earth,"[20] and their endeavor should go as far as to "test every barrier, try every path, plumb every abyss…. God wills it, who willed that he should have need of it."[21]

---

[16] It was attributed to St. Teresa of Avila of saying, "The Lord walks among the pots and pans." Translation in Teilhard's terms: "By virtue of the Creation and, still more, of the Incarnation, *nothing* here below *is profane* for those who know how to see" (DM, p. 66 -- IV, p. 56).
[17] DM, p. 62 -- IV, p. 50.
[18] DM, p. 63 -- IV, p. 53.
[19] DM, p. 66 -- IV, p. 56.
[20] MD, p. 69 -- IV, p. 61.
[21] MD, p. 70 -- IV, pp. 61-62. Also, in a letter of September 8, 1916, Teilhard wrote: "To grow and to fulfil oneself to the utmost – that is the law immanent in being. I do not believe that in allowing us glimpses of a more divine life God has excused us from pursuing, even on its natural plane, the work of creation. It would, I think, be 'tempting God' to let the world go its own way without trying to master it and understand it more fully. We must do all we can to lessen death and suffering. We must develop the significance of revealed dogma through a more searching criticism of truth. I should even go so far as to say that religious faith can be justified only in a mankind that constantly exercises such a leverage on the unknown that every divinity other than our adored Lord would appear if, *per impossible*, it still remains hidden from us… It would be so grave an objection to the truth of the Church to be able to reproach it with making men lazy!" (MM, pp. 126-27 -- *Genèse*, pp. 161-62).

Robert L. Faricy interpreted very well Teilhard's explanation and importance of the Christian work. He wrote:

> If it is true that what we do contributes to the building up of the world, that the tangible, material results of man's effort are important in moving the world closer to the fullness of the Pleroma, then it follows that the Christian should act with the utmost seriousness so that the world comes always a little closer to the fullness of Christ. More than any non-Christian, the Christian should promote human endeavor in all its forms, and especially that human effort that directly increases the general consciousness of mankind. The Christian should move in the direction of human progress audaciously and with Christian hope. The same point of view on the Christian's duty to develop himself and to build the world is found in *The Divine Milieu*....[22]

With such a vision, perhaps we can start to "see," as Teilhard did, a new and different path to peace and true human values for our world in this twenty-first century. The cosmic Christ horizon that permeates every personal, societal, national, and international activities should make all the difference in the world. Only the "Christ consciousness" will silence the wars – internal and external – and will transform the energies of conflicts into energies of reconciliation and love. Then, will emerge spontaneously and imperatively for the world ahead appropriate actions such as new patterns of human relations, new patterns of rights, new patterns of regulations, new patterns of structures, and new patterns of political directions that are beyond Left or Right and toward the Human and the Divine. The Christ consciousness[23] that inspires and guides our actions will close the gap between "what is" and "what might be." David Grumett wrote:

> An action is something in which God is involved, acting in us by making us do in reality what we most deeply will. Action is a reflective movement of soul and body. In *The Divine Milieu*, Teilhard affirms:
> 'It requires no less than the pull of what we call the Absolute—no less than you yourself—to set in motion the frail liberty which you have

---

[22] Robert L. Faricy, S.J., *Teilhard de Chardin's Theology of the Christian in the World*, (New York: Sheed and Ward, 1967), p. 178.
[23] The Christ consciousness counts also on Jesus Christ's words: "If in my name you ask me for anything, I will do it" (John 14:!4); "For mortals it is impossible, but for God all things are possible" (Matthew 19:26; Mark 10:27); "All things can be done for the one who believes" (Mark 9:23); "Apart from me you can do nothing" (John 15:5). St. Paul also wrote: "I can do all things through him who strengthens me" (Philippians 4:13).

given us. And that being so, everything which diminishes my explicit faith in the heavenly value of the results of my effort, diminishes irremediably my power to act' (DM, 13).'[24]

Action suggests participation. Participation suggests unity and unification. Again David Grumett observed: "Teilhard has a passion for unity; no part of the world is entirely separate from any other or can be understood or described in isolation from the rest. In a holistic world, each part of the world needs to be viewed with reference to the larger reality in which it participates."[25]

Teilhard's understanding of participation has mystic-prophetic-political dimensions; it is a contemplation in action.[26] This means that one does not have to dissociate between what is divine and what is human.[27] A

---

[24] See David Grumett, "Metaphysics, Morality, and Politics" in Ilia Delio, ed., *From Teilhard to Omega: Co-creating an Unfinished Universe* (Maryknoll, N.Y.: Orbis Books, 2015), p.116.

[25] See David Grumett, "Metaphysics, Morality, and Politics" in Ilia Delio, ed., *From Teilhard to Omega: Co-creating an Unfinished Universe* (Maryknoll, N.Y.: Orbis Books, 2015), p.121.

[26] Segundo Galilea wrote in the context: "Authentic Christian contemplation, passing through the desert, transforms contemplatives into prophets and heroes of commitment and militants into mystics. Christianity achieves the synthesis of the politician and the mystic, the militant and the contemplative, and abolishes the false antithesis between the religious-contemplative and the militantly committed. Authentic contemplation, through the encounter with the absolute of God, leads to the absolute of one's neighbor." See Segundo Galilea, "Liberation as an Encounter with Politics and Contemplation" in Richard Woods, O.P., *Understanding Mysticism* (Garden City, N.Y.: Image Books, A Division of Doubleday & Company, Inc., 1980), p. 536.

[27] Reflecting about Teilhard's vision, Pierre Smulders offered the following comment: "Le monde lui-même s'en trouve consacré. Les racines profondes qui relient l'homme au monde, 'le goût sacré de l'être', deviennent saintes. La volonté d'être soi-même, de se développer et de se réaliser en tant qu'homme jusqu'aux extrêmes limites de ses possibilités, la grande poussée vitale de l'homme et de l'humanité, tout cela n'est autre chose que l'écho de la parole créatrice de Dieu. Croire a l''active présence' de Dieu signifie donc, si notre foi ne doit demeurer purement verbale, faire droit a l'appel qui retentit du fond de notre être. L'homme *doit* vouloir vivre et vouloir travailler, vouloir monter vers une réalisation plus entière de son être humain. C'est un devoir sacré, parce que c'est la volonté de Dieu, incarnée dans la nature même du monde et de l'humanité…. Le manque de volonté de vie, le découragement et le relâchement devant les tâches grandioses que lui impose le monde, sont pour l'homme une faute grave. Il refuse en effet d'obéir a la parole de Dieu qui retentit des profondeurs du monde et de son être

contemplative attitude is seen as decisive, eschatological, and effecting a sociopolitical transformation aiming for unity, harmony, and peace. In their most profound meanings and roles, a theologian is supposed to be a politician, and a politician is supposed to be a theologian. The mystic, then, like Teilhard, is a political theologian. When this is the case, life should be called infallible because God is active there: "God is at work within life," wrote Teilhard. "He helps it, raises it up, gives it the impulse that drives it along.... I can feel God, touch Him, 'live' Him in the deep biological current that runs through my soul and carries it with it."[28] He also wrote: "I am convinced that *fidelity* to Life is the only and the highest form of *sainteté*."[29]

The kind of mysticism that Teilhard belongs to leads into the world rather than out of it. No one can reach the summit of the transformative evolution on their own, in separation from others. Unity and peace are a societal effort. A common human effort is needed.[30] Commenting on Teilhard's spirituality, Sister Maria Gratia Martin wrote:

> All work... is for Thought; we labor collectively, fulfilling a variety of necessary but insufficient functions, so that together we may know—and ultimately, so that knowing we may come together in love and fullness of vision.... No degree of progress in the perfecting of man individually and collectively, however, will of itself ensure the successful outcome of noogenesis; nor would that progress even be possible, were it not accompanied by a correlative growth of unanimization, that is, of the personal union of mankind in love. This fact... points to the necessity of an increasingly collective dimension of any research that is to meet the progressive demands of noogenesis.[31]

---

propre. » See Pierre Smulders, *La vision de Teilhard de Chardin : essai de réflexion théologique* (Paris : Desclée de Brouwer, 1965), p. 223.

[28] WW, p. 61 -- XII, p. 70.

[29] LTF, p. 199 -- *Accomplir l'homme*, p. 242.

[30] Beatrice Bruteau remarked: "The root of Teilhard's rejection of oriental philosophical and religious thought can be found in his judgment that these systems would not justify and inspire work for the progress of the world. Pierre Leroy tells us that Teilhard had a great intolerance for anything that suggested 'disgust with life, contempt for the works of man, fear of the human effort.' Following the oriental path, Teilhard believed, we could be lulled to sleep in 'the cradle of nirvana,' having obtained 'a sort of abstraction of God... by loosening the effort of differentiation whereby we engage the cosmic phenomenon.'" See Beatrice Bruteau, *Evolution Toward Divinity: Teilhard de Chardin and the Hindu Traditions* (Wheaton, Ill: The Theosophical Publishing House, 1974), p. 3.

[31] See Sister Maria Gratia Martin, I.H.M., *The Spirituality of Teilhard de Chardin* (New York, NY: Newman Press, 1968), pp. 13, 20.

All in all, the efforts of all of us must cooperate together toward the fulfillment of the world in Christ. Teilhard explains:

> It is through the collaboration which he stimulates in us that Christ, starting from *all* created things, is consummated and attains his plenitude. ... We may, perhaps, imagine that the creation was finished long ago. But that would be quite wrong. It continues still more magnificently, and at the highest levels of the world.... And we serve to complete it, even by the humblest work of our hands. That is, ultimately, the meaning and value of our acts. Owing to the interrelation between matter, soul and Christ, we bring part of the being which he desires back to God *in whatever we do.* With each one of our works, we labour—in individual separation, but no less really—to build the Pleroma; that is to say, we bring to Christ a little fulfillment.[32]

This suggests that every work – no matter what it is – has the potential of being holy and unifying. Cooperating consciously to build the Pleroma is not only an act of worship and adoration, but it is also a unifying way to center on God the whole of our lives. It means, as Teilhard put it, "to devote oneself body and soul to the creative act, associating oneself with that act in order to fulfil the world by hard work and intellectual exploration."[33] Once our eyes are opened and we will "see" that we are truly collaborating to achieve an end[34] we desire together, then, overwhelmed by the joy of mystical co-creation, we cannot fail to realize how close we are to each other.

---

[32] DM, p. 62 -- IV, p. 50.
[33] CE, p. 92 -- X, p. 111.
[34] Gérard-Henry Baudry offered the following comment: "Toute action exige un but, une fin. Que dire de l'Action humaine prise dans sa totalité, c'est-à-dire de l'action non seulement individuelle, mais de l'Humanité entière, sinon qu'elle exige un Fin absolue ? L'Action humaine a une dimension d'éternité ; elle est implicitement recherche de plus-être et pas seulement de bien-être or de mieux-être. Elle vise à créer une œuvre de valeur absolue et permanente. 'Agir, c'est créer, et créer, c'est pour toujours' (VI, 175, 1937). Sans ce but moteur, l'action humaine n'aurait plus de sens et le monde serait absurde. » See Gérard-Henry Baudry, *Ce que croyait Teilhard* (France : Mame, 1971), p. 73.

Chapter Twenty

Process Peace

Of course, there is plenty of evidence against the possibility of peace. In fact, evil seems to grow along with civilization. "Divisions, hostility, wars exist," reminds François Euvé. "But despite all these hostiles forces, Teilhard sees a unification process as irreversible."[1]

Are we going to forget that we are always in the human condition, that we can never escape the laws of the struggle for life – the struggle of *becoming*? Peace is not a state to be attained. On the contrary, peace has to be *in the process* – a process peace. It is a momentum to build, day after day, year after year, and generation after generation. It is a continuous transformation.

What we can now detect, in spite of all appearances, is that the human species, instead of diverging, is converging into races, ethnic groups, nations, regional, national, and international organizations and coalitions. These converging organisms are still like mustard seeds and still like a promise of green leaves, fruits, and fresh air. Needless to say that not all these organisms are contributing to building the earth. In fact, some of them are destroying it. Nevertheless, they are gathering and converging, and this is the only point considered in this chapter.

What is actually going on in humanity at the present time? Don't we feel a deep aspiration for unity and, in spite of the appearances, don't we have signs of a growing togetherness in many aspects of our life? This is what Teilhard saw:

> A wind of revolt is passing through our minds, it is true. But, born of the same growths of conscience, another breeze is blowing through the human masses; one that draws us all by a sort of living affinity towards the splendid realization of some foreseen unity. Disputed, suspect and often scorned, unitary aspirations in politics, in thought, in mysticism, arise

---

[1]François Euvé, SJ, "Humanity Reveals the World" in Ilia Delio, ed., *From Teilhard to Omega: Co-creating an Unfinished Universe* (Maryknoll, N.Y.: Orbis Books, 2015), p. 71.

everywhere around us; and because the subject is not what is material and plural but what is spiritual and common to all in each one of us, no force of routine or egoism seems capable of arresting them; irresistibly they infiltrate and gradually dissolve old forms and false barriers.[2]

These "unitary aspirations" are not just something to wish for; they are actually at work in the world. They are producing a more organized and unified humanity.[3]

Let us take a quick look at how humanity is growing closer and more unified. The earth seems to become smaller and smaller because of the many forces at work. Here are some of them.

Tightening

There are many types of tightening at all levels of our life.

a) *Demographic tightening*: There is a very rapid increase in the earth's population. It is like an explosion. Based on current growth trends, the world population of humans will continue to grow. In 1900, it was 1.6 billion. In 1979, it was 4.2 billion. In 2000, it was 6 billion. In 2015, it was 7.3 billion. In 2030, it is projected to be 8.5 billion. In 2050, it is projected to be 9.7 billion. In 2100, it is projected to be 11.2 billion.[4] This increase in the population will

---

[2] VP, p. 78 -- III, pp. 110-11.

[3] Ursula King has a revealing interpretation for the "Trust life." She wrote: "Even in our times, so full of uncertainty and change, human beings still come into the world with a fundamental, underlying trust in life. It is an innate trust which in German is spoken of as *Ur-Vertrauen*—an elemental, primary, foundational trust that underlies all life and growth, a basic fundamental faith in the goodness of life, and in the world as our home. It is important to build on this primary trust, expand and consolidate it rather than become disenchanted and destroy it. 'Trust life,' Teilhard used to say; 'life is never mistaken.' This primary trust, this sense of being carried, affirmed, and supported, is so different from the *Ur-Angst* or existential anxiety that modern philosophers speak about. From a religious point of view, this trust is linked to a deep belief in being held and enfolded by something greater, of being cared for and protected by God's presence and loving care." See Ursula King, "The Zest for Life: A Contemporary Exploration of a Generative Theme in Teilhard's Work" in Ilia Delio, ed., *From Teilhard to Omega: Co-creating an Unfinshed Universe* (Maryknoll, N.Y.: Orbis Books, 2015), p. 192.

[4] The World Population Prospects of the United Nations (Revision 2015) says: "According to the results of the *2015 Revision*, the world population reached 7.3 billion as of mid-2015, implying that the world has added approximately one

lead to more agglomerations, more complexities, more gatherings together, and less and less empty spaces.
b) *Technical tightening*: "Communication" is, here, the key word. The means we use to transmit messages and to reach out to others are now greatly improved. The means of transportation by land, sea, and air are available to anyone. The media – radio, television, video, fax, telephone, Internet, and all other electronic devices – invade our public and private lives in a big way. The machine is shortening the distance by making us closer than ever to the one we would have never be able to communicate with and get to know.
c) *Economic tightening*: Demographic tightening and technological tightening have their repercussions on the economy. This seems obvious. We have, for example, to think about how to feed the billions of people on this earth. Also, the machine tends more and more to replace the reality called "independence" by the other reality called "inter-dependence" – inter-dependence between people, nations, races, continents, and cultures. Economic problems, as well as any other problems, now have their global solutions. One can no longer say of people who die of hunger, insecurity, or violence that this is only their problem.
d) *Political tightening*: It is becoming impossible to live alone, by oneself, and in total isolation, and this at any level of our human journey. No state can survive for a long time if it tries to isolate itself from the rest of the world. Instead, we are witnessing the growing and increasing cooperation between countries.
e) *Psychological and sociological tightening*: Uniformity seems to be, in spite of the apparent diversity, growing in our world. The tendency to be in one's own time by belonging to certain ways of thinking and living, pushes us to imitate what is going on in the biggest cities of the world. We long to follow certain customs and rules, the latest fashion, and the most recent idols' news. We even imitate the diversity. We would like to be different and affirm ourselves, but we seem to prefer the sentiment of belonging

---

billion people in the span of the last twelve years. Sixty per cent of the global population lives in Asia (4.4 billion), 16 per cent in Africa (1.2 billion), 10 per cent in Europe (738 million), 9 per cent in Latin America and the Caribbean (634 million), and the remaining 5 per cent in Northern America (358 million) and Oceania (39 million). China (1.4 billion) and India (1.3 billion) remain the two largest countries of the world, both with more than 1 billion people, representing 19 and 18 per cent of the world's population respectively".

because we feel lost if we are not followers, or if we don't have followers.

f) *Spiritual tightening*: Yes, there is a proliferation of spiritual traditions, denominations, and rites. But, there is also a clear tendency to ecumenism. It is not a question of creating some kind of religion that can accommodate and satisfy everyone, but a bringing together different experiences and different pieces of knowledge as a gift to others to enrich each other. It is not a fusion. It is a unification. Teilhard talked about "A tendency towards unification is everywhere manifest, and especially in the different branches of religion."[5]

Many examples can illustrate Teilhard's statement. One striking event happened on October 27, 1986. For the first time in history, leaders of twelve different religions came together to pray for world peace at Assisi in Italy. They didn't discuss anything. They simply showed that reconciliation and peace are possible in prayer and in the mystical way, which they are, indeed.

If tightening has its risks and dangers, it also has its advantages and benefits. In fact, all these kinds of tightening help people to think globally, give them the opportunity to share their common bond, and together find solutions for their common problems. From now on, every point on earth is close to every other point. The truth is that, in spite of some remaining isolationist, separatist, and dualist ideologies, the general trend in the human fields of serious thoughts is towards openness and unification. We are no longer strangers to each other. My heritage, yours, and theirs belong to humanity. The old world, the world of "blocs" will give way to interdependence and to a "human front,"[6] as Teilhard saw it. More and more, people are aware of their planetary dimension and their international responsibility. They feel more "earthwise." A new civilization is starting. Teilhard affirms: "Economically and spiritually speaking, the age of *civilisations* has ended, and that of *one civilisation* is beginning."[7]

Institutions without frontiers

In the heart of each man and woman, there is the sense of universalism – a need for universality. To describe this phenomenon,

---

[5] FM, pp. 196-97 -- V, p. 240.
[6] SC, p. 145 -- IX, p. 187.
[7] AM, p. 158 -- II, p. 218.

Teilhard used words like "socialization," "totalization," "planetization," "universalization," "synthesis".... Such words do not represent a static state of being, but a movement, a becoming, and an evolving state of being. Let us take a look at how humanity is moving toward this new reality. We do not need to enumerate all the international organizations and how they work. Many special books have covered this matter. But a few examples would be enough to show how humanity is moving toward unity.

a) *United Nations (UN)*
   * The General Assembly (the main deliberative assembly);
   * The Security Council (decides certain resolutions for peace and security);
   * The Economic and Social Council (assists in promoting international economic and social cooperation and development);
   * The Secretariat (provides studies, information, and facilities needed by the UN);
   * The International Court of Justice (the primary judicial organ).

The UN also includes various Funds, Programs, and specialized agencies. For example:
   o Food and Agriculture Organization
   o International Labour Organization
   o International Civil Aviation Organization
   o International Maritime Organization
   o International Refugee Organization
   o Joint United Nations Programme on HIV/AIDS
   o United Nations Atomic Energy Commission
   o United Nations Capital Development Fund
   o United Nations Children's Fund (UNICEF)
   o United Nations Development Programme
   o United Nations Educational, Scientific and Cultural Organization (UNESCO)
   o United Nations Environment Programme
   o United Nations Human Settlements Programme
   o United Nations Industrial Development Organization
   o United Nations Office for Disaster Risk Reduction (UNISDR)
   o United Nations Office on Drugs and Crime
   o Universal Postal Union
   o World Health Organization (WHO)
   o World Intellectual Property Organization
   o World Food Programme

- World Meteorological Organization
- World Tourism Organization
- International Rescue Committee (IRC)
  And many others.

b) *Trans-Atlantic Organizations such as:*
- North Atlantic Treaty Organization (NATO)
- Organization for Security and Co-operation in Europe (OSCE)
- South Atlantic Peace and Cooperation Zone (ZPCAS)

c) *The international non- governmental organizations (INGOs)*

The non-governmental organizations are voluntary groups of individuals or organizations that are formed to provide services or to advocate a particular public policy. These organizations usually address human concerns such as human rights, environment protection, disaster relief, development assistance, peace, etc. Their activities can be local, national, or international. It is not easy to know how many NGOs there are; they are many thousands and they keep growing. Despite their difficulties – and this depends on the cause they are working for – they continue to play an important role in developing global norms and rules on a wide range of national and international issues. A few of them have been awarded the Nobel Prize for peace.

d) *Other movements that transcend the frontiers of any single country:*

There are also many movements and institutions that transcend frontiers – physical, intellectual, religious… -- and are not INGOs. For example, the peace movements throughout the world, Ecumenism of Christian Churches, University for Peace in Costa Rica, women's liberation, meetings of the countries that speak the same language, the Islamic conferences, the synod of bishops from all over the world, the scientific research led by scholars of different countries, and many others. Here, it is interesting to see how Teilhard reacted to the Geo-physical Year. He wrote in a letter dated December 12, 1954:

> I was more than interested yesterday to read in *Time* a long article on the scheme – this time really international (Russia is co-operating) – for a Geo-physical Year in 1957, to develop a fuller scientific 'awareness' of the globe. As an effort for the spiritual unification of man, it is still terribly superficial, but it is the first step, a finger at least, you might say, on the gear-lever of unification; and I am deeply moved by this great concerted

movement in which for the first time in millions of years, a unanimous gesture – unanimous in orientation – will reach out to the end of the earth: Year 1 of the Noosphere.[8]

Here are examples of some social movements:

- Animal rights movement
- Anti-Apartheid movement
- Anti-consumerism
- Anti-nuclear movement
- Anti-war movement
- Anti-globalization movement
- Charismatic movement
- Civil rights movement
- Conservation movement
- Counter-culture movement
- Counter-terrorism movement
- Ecology movement
- Ecofeminism
- Environmental movement
- Feminist movement
- Ku Klux Klan
- Labor movement
- Non-violence movement
- Right to life
- Women's liberation movement
- Cursillo movement
- L'Arche Communities
- Light-Life movement
- Focolare movement
- Living in spirituality movement
- Union of European Guides and Scouts

Add to all these the unlimited number of professional associations and associations created to continue and perpetuate the ideas and works of individuals who made a difference in the understanding and development

---

[8] LT, pp. 355-56 -- *Lettres de voyage*, p. 360.

of the human condition. "Humanity now," wrote Ursula King, "bears full responsibility for its own future."[9]

Organizations, associations, and movements are put together for a common goal and they usually have a mission statement that inspires their members. It is ironic that these organizations that meant to work for a common good cause, may sometimes work for evil. The point here is to show that they gather regardless of the fact that their gathering is for a good cause or not. This kind of feeling that we belong to a larger self than ourselves gives impetus to planetization and to a sense of belonging to a more unified world.

The need for universalism in each human heart, which seeks to be embodied in organizations, associations, and movements is, at its very core, a recognition of belonging to the human family, our awareness of the sense of being human, and potentially a step forward toward world peace. Consequently, history, instead of recording wars and names of individuals who made wars, should from now on rather record the steps of convergence, improvement, growth, universalism, and the common spirit of all humanity. Now we can start to "see" that the true heroes of humanity are not those who declare wars and destroy, but those who make peace a reality and build.

---

[9] The entire paragraph that Ursula King wrote is worth quoting here. She wrote: "The education and general orientation of people toward the future is vital for the course and eventual outcome of the future. Humanity now bears full responsibility for its own future. This is an immense challenge which can only be met if we thoroughly prepare ourselves for this task. The kind of future we will get will depend to a large extent on the quality of people who shape it. Teilhard emphasized the need for a *homo progressivus*, a progressive, future-oriented and future-affirming being with wide, open awareness – a person who has the energy of thought to recognize the problems of the future and find their solutions, and the energy of action to put them into practice." See Ursula King, *The Spirit of One Earth: Reflections on Teilhard de Chardin and Global Spirituality* (New York, N.Y.: Paragon House, 1989), p. 37. Also about the responsibility for the future, Edward Vacek wrote: "'Whatever it takes to get to the future' is Teilhard's maxim. Teilhard's emphasis on the future has the salutary feature of making us responsible for the future (AE, 210-13; FM, 18). It refutes the cynicism of 'Why should I do something for posterity? What has posterity ever done for me?' In his holistic view, we are responsible for the future…. Our responsibility for evolution requires more than passing on a world no worse than the one we have inherited. Rather a morality of movement requires that we improve the world." (Edward Vacek, SJ, "An Evolving Christian Morality: Eppur si muove" in Ilia Delio, ed., *From Teilhard to Omega: Co-creating an Unfinshed Universe* (Maryknoll, N.Y.: Orbis Books, 2015), p. 162.

What Beatrice Bruteau wrote at the end of her book, *Evolution toward Divinity*, seems also very appropriate to end this chapter with. She wrote:

> If we have any advantage in vision—having learned a great deal from Teilhard himself—we may dare to protect and fulfill his beautifully constructed model of a world in process by adjusting one of his tenets: The axis of evolution, in the long perspective, does not run through the West, but is, like the lines of specific descent, a sheaf of axes, running through humanity as a whole, knitting together the rich heritages of all cultures in the mighty convergence which Teilhard glimpsed. We, the people of the future, can no longer think of ourselves as heirs only of this culture or that, belonging to one or another corner of our tiny globe. Each of us is the heir of all that humanity has ever produced in diversity and splendor of life, knowledge, art, and wisdom. Only as we bring all of this, our human wealth, into an intense but differentiated union, will we be able to live beyond, to survive, our present phase of development and continue our evolution toward divinity.[10]

---

[10] Beatrice Bruteau, *Evolution Toward Divinity: Teilhard de Chardin and the Hindu Traditions* (Wheaton, Ill: The Theosophical Publishing House, 1974), pp. 255-256.

Part VI

On the March

Chapter Twenty-One

Toward a Curriculum for Peace

If we make an extended survey and ask the largest number of people possible the question, "Do you think a curriculum in education should include a training for peace, or rather a preparation for war?" what do you think the answer would be?

So naïve and simple as such a question looks, the answer is neither simple nor obvious. Very often we know what is right, but somehow, something will make us do what is not right.

What does "to educate" mean, in the first place, and why the right education is the most important "revolution" for procuring human development and securing peaceful societies?

"To educate"

To educate" carries different meanings. It can mean to provide schooling, to provide formal instruction, or to provide with information. It can also mean to develop the whole person – mentally, morally, aesthetically, and spiritually. Moreover, it can mean to train for a profession, a career, or acquiring skills. Furthermore, it can mean to practice the art of persuasion for believing, thinking, and acting in a desired way. In any case, this means to help a "seed" to grow, and this takes place through a number of ways such as: family, school, work, church, and the right social environment.

However, this cannot be done unless we have a vision, an idea about where we are going, and a program that tells how to get there. All depends on that vision – what one is looking for and what one wants to achieve.

In a closed system, the important thing is to learn to adapt to the type of society in which one finds himself or herself. By conforming to this society's set of values and way of life, one finds himself or herself at peace with those who have the same ideals and values, and at the same time, he or she may feel distrust, fear, and "preventive aggressiveness" towards those who believe otherwise.

In such a context, a "well-educated" person would help develop in the group a certain biased peace by bringing reconciliation and rapprochement among the members of the group while engendering a conflict outside the group.

The closed systems, defined by their particular ideologies, set of beliefs, and organizations, were for a long time the systems that provided the good education. They seemed to have had clear ideas, the right knowledge, and the correct answers for every imaginable question. Libraries of books were there to convey their guidance from generation to generation. Here education would be that "stock" of the different types of knowledge that a student receives from a teacher, a master, a person of wisdom, or an erudite. Truth, then, was clear and "universal" and must be denied to all those who believe otherwise. Don't our history books prove this? Don't the history books of wars prove it? Don't the history books of colonialism, civilizations, cultures, "religions," and ideological ways of governing prove it? Don't the headlines of our daily newspapers and magazines prove it? Every day, again and again, we read about false democracies, pretentious collectivisms, and anarchies that are manifested in all kinds of violence, aggressive competitions, frauds, and lies. Every day, again and again, we read about those who choose the path to success at any price including the elimination of the one who thinks differently. Every day, again and again, we read about fundamentalism and fanaticism in religions in ideologies, and/or in our normal daily activities and relationships with others.

Although the ancestral "wisdom" and way of thinking of the closed systems are still here in our time and still have their merits, another approach to life seems to be emerging. There is a growing suspicion about the "our truths," a certain doubt about the exclusiveness of "our civilization," and a tendency to recognize the other systems that are different from ours. A trend towards openness is taking place – a certain universal consensus, a sense of belonging to a bigger reality, as "citizen of the world." "Hence the need of a new sense of responsibility."[1]

---

[1] J. de Marneffe commented: « Teilhard sees that the world aimed at order, first, at a physico-chemical level; then it achieved a symbiosis among the living; finally, it seeks harmony on the level of human freedoms. In the mind of Plato and Aristotle and in much of the Western tradition, the sense of responsibility was often considered under its juridical aspect, as an extrinsic requirement. In the evolutive perspective of Teilhard, responsibility becomes organic. One may compromise or get away with responsibility in a juridical set up. But the 'Organic', if we violate it, we pay for it. Hence the need of a new sense of responsibility." See J. de Marneffe, S.J., "Teilhardian Thought as a Methodology for Discernment of Socio-cultural

To feel that we belong to a unified world and to feel that frontiers – geopolitical and/or emotional-intellectual-spiritual frontiers – are only transient would give us a very different perspective on life, on things, and how to conduct our works. It may also have, at the same time, the advantage to pave the way to a lasting peace. This is exactly what Teilhard de Chardin felt.

Teilhard had his vision of the great convergence of everyone and everything in what he called the Omega Point, and he thought that the world should be prepared to meet such a challenge. How? By a new education that leads to a dynamic peace. This education is based on new principles (planetization, personalization, mystical unification…), new morality,[2] and new ways of thinking that promote higher consciousness. Teilhard advocates the "fidelity to Life [which] is the only and the highest form of *sainteté*."[3] Teilhard invites us "to be more."[4]

"To be more"

Teilhard reminds us that people have a duty to grow, to mature, to know more, to pass from childhood to adulthood, and to reach a higher level of consciousness – a consciousness that is a fuller being, at a personal level as well as at a social level.

"*To be more is in the first place to know more*,"[5] wrote Teilhard. To have faith in progress stimulates in us, according to Teilhard, the desire to know more. The aim of knowing more, though, should not be just to satisfy a personal curiosity or for a mere scientific result. The real purpose of digging deeper and deeper is to reach a higher level of consciousness and to become more universal – to be. Teilhard says: "No longer only to know out of curiosity, to know for knowing's sake, but to know out of faith in a universal development which was becoming conscious of itself in the human spirit, to know in order to create, to know in order to be,"[6] and "To know more in order to be capable of more, in order to be more."[7]

Options in an Evolutionary World" in Leo Zonneveld and Robert Muller, ed., *The Desire to Be Human*, "International Teilhard Compendium" Centenary volume (Netherlands: Mirananda Publishers b.v. Wassenaar, 1983), p. 200.

[2] See Jean Maalouf, *Le mystère du mal dans l'œuvre de Teilhard de Chardin*, Cerf (Thèses/Cerf, France), 1986, pp. 337-352.

[3] LTF, p. 199 -- *Accomplir l'homme*, p. 242.

[4] FM, p. 20 -- V, p. 31.

[5] FM, p. 20 -- V, p. 31.

[6] HE, p. 171 -- VI, p. 212.

[7] HE, p. 164 -- VI, p. 205.

Here, paradoxically and ironically, Teilhard is not afraid to consider the atomic bomb as progress in knowledge and social bond in the sense that it had produced another dose for universalism. He explained this phenomenon by saying:

> The atomic age is not the age of destruction but of union in research. For all their military trappings, the recent explosions at Bikini herald the birth into the world of a Mankind both inwardly and outwardly pacified. They proclaim the coming of the *Spirit of the Earth.*[8]

It is obvious that Teilhard was not so naïve as to approve the atrocity of the bomb or of any violence and war. No, no. We should never think this way either. His deep intention and convictions were to tell us that every discovery or invention in science may constitute a step forward in the evolution of humankind. But one day, as Teilhard sees it, will come "a world in which giant telescopes and atom smashers would absorb more money and excite more spontaneous admiration than all the bombs and cannons put together."[9]

The phenomenon of war is not going to stay forever with the human species. That is because the ever-growing thirst for knowledge and discovery is going to move the human effort away from war toward more research and more progress. Prophetically and solemnly, Teilhard declares:

> A decisive hour will strike for man, when the spirit of discovery absorbs the whole vital force contained in the spirit of war. A supreme phase of history in which the whole power of fleets and armies will be transformed, to reinforce that other power which the machine will have rendered idle. Then an irresistible tide of free energies will advance into the most progressive tracts of the noosphere.[10]

Therefore, "'Peace' cannot mean anything but a *higher process of conquest.*"[11]

Moreover, "To be more" is not only "to know more," for just "to know" does not give wings. The whole thing becomes so alive when we see it evolving, growing, and becoming. "To be more" is "to grow" and "to become." Teilhard says: "For the ancient philosophers, 'to be' was above all 'to know'. For modern philosophers, 'to be' is coming to be

---

[8] FM, p. 152 -- V, p. 186.
[9] PM, p. 280 -- I, p. 311.
[10] HE, p. 136 -- VI, p. 170.
[11] LTF, p. 146 -- *Accomplir l'homme*, p. 176.

synonymous with 'to grow' and 'to become.' We are witnessing the entry, not only into physics but into metaphysics, too, of a dynamism."[12]

It is obvious that we are not born ourselves; we become ourselves. Becoming is a lifetime program, effort, and discipline. Our body grows. Our mind grows. Our consciousness grows. So does humanity. Teilhard wrote: "Why do we ourselves seek and why do we invent? In order to *be better*; and, above all, in order to *be more*, stronger and more conscious."[13] Becoming is a progress, and progress is "the consciousness of all that is and all that can be,"[14] said Teilhard. In this sense, we should be loyal, not to received ideas and limitations,[15] but to life itself – and life is evolving.[16] That is why becoming requires detachment – detachment from our old ways of thinking and behaving. This kind of detachment is difficult for us, but we should have the courage to do it, because if we don't, the result could be disastrous; it could take the form of retardation, infantilism, neurosis, chauvinism, narcissism, intolerance, and war again and again.

Becoming may be a journey into an unknown territory, but it is a sure one. Infantilism could be a "secure" territory, but it could provoke the worst of catastrophes. Survival depends on a radical change of the human

---

[12] SC, p. 174 -- IX, p. 221.
[13] VP, p. 72 -- III, p. 103.
[14] FM, p. 20 -- V, p. 31.
[15] Emmanuel Mounier criticized the inadequate kind of education for our times with these words: "The education that is provided in these days is almost the worst possible preparation for such a culture. The universities distribute formal knowledge which predisposes men to ideological dogmatism or, by reaction, to sterile irony. The spiritual educators, too often, base moral edification upon scrupulousness and moral casuistry instead of the cultivation of decision. The whole climate of education needs to be changed if we no longer want to see, on the plane of action, intellectuals who set an example of blindness and men of conscience who inculcate cowardice." See Emmanuel Mounier, *Personalism* (Notre Dame, Indiana: University of Notre Dame Press, trans. by Philip Mairet, first published in England in 1952 by Routledge & Kegan Paul Ltd.), p. 94.
[16] Kathleen Duffy wrote: « For Teilhard, education has an evolutionary function— to develop our common memory and to ensure the noosphere's continuity. Evolution is no longer simply about the transmission of genetic information. Information of all types can now be gathered, organized, stored, and transmitted so that it is available on a global scale and for future generations. Information must also be 'furthered in a reflective form and in its social dimensions' (F, 36) through the transmission of a common body of knowledge that must be reworked and improved upon continually. 'A passionate faith in the purpose and splendor of human aspirations… must be the flame that illumines…teaching' (F, 37) if it is to achieve its task." See Kathleen Duffy, SSJ, *Teilhard's Mysticism: Seeing the Inner Face of Evolution* (Maryknoll, N.Y.: Orbis Books, 2014), p. 100.

consciousness and the human heart – a change in the human self. Teilhard did not hesitate a second to write in 1940:

> What I am afraid of is that the Allies do not seem to understand that no end and no peace – a real peace, I mean – can be expected except from a complete readjustment. The trouble is that the readjustment should include an intellectual and moral change in the men themselves.[17]

"To be more" is "to know more," "to become more," and above all "to unite more." "Fuller being is closer union,"[18] insists Teilhard.

Teilhard does not see humanity as being in a static universe, but in an evolving one. In our world, today, our capacity to extend and share everything has increased enormously. Mass media and technical communications are only part and means of this large sharing. Those who "see" in their hearts that life is good and that peace is a way of life are linked up together. They take steps to join with others. They share hope together. They work to improve themselves in every way possible. They share common goals. They share deeper love and union. Teilhard wrote: "The more intimate the union effected between more diverse elements… the more perfect and conscious the being that emerged,"[19] and again "Fuller being is closer union."[20]

Teilhard is looking far, far ahead. At the end of what he can see, he is "seeing" a world intimately united with God in all its phases of development, and we are called to make our contribution to this development by the gift of co-creating or "sur-creating."

"To sur-create"[21]

We are called to co-create – Teilhard used the word "sur-create" – both ourselves and the world. It would be ridiculous to think that a "co-creation" or "re-creation" or "sur-creation" is some kind of an usurpation of the power of God, or a coup to God's sovereignty. No. On the contrary, to co-create or to re-create or to sur-create is a recognition that we are created in God's image and that God has given us the power to create. If we reject this power by freezing ourselves in laziness and immobilism, we won't be at peace, neither with ourselves nor with others. To be in the

---

[17] LTF, p. 142 -- *Accomplir l'homme*, p. 171.
[18] PM, p. 31 -- I, p. 25.
[19] WTW, p. 155 -- XII, p. 201.
[20] PM, p. 31 -- I, p. 25.
[21] DM, p. 154 -- IV, p. 201.

image of God must mean to be creative, fully alive, imaginative, willing to suffer birth anew, to see God in everyone, and to recognize in the depths of our consciousness "the rise, which nothing can stop, of a sort of Other who could be even more I than I am myself."[22] To be in the image of God is to divinize all humanity and all the universe:

> To divinize does not mean to destroy, but to sur-create. We shall never know all that the Incarnation still expects of the world's potentialities. We shall never put enough hope in the growing unity of mankind.[23]

During his lifetime, Teilhard kept asking himself this question: "Is life an open road or a blind alley?"[24] All his writings show that an open road is the only possible answer. An open road means embracing an evolutionary universe, not a mechanistic one. Ilia Delio wrote:

> The starting point for educational reform is awakening to the fact that we no longer live in a mechanistic universe. Ours is an evolutionary universe. Mechanisms can operate efficiently, but as close systems they cannot evolve. Despite the fact that evolution has been known for over a hundred years, we continue to educate according to a mechanized course of study. One chooses a major and then breaks it down into parts, consuming large amounts of information all along the way. Do we ever ask: What forms the whole, the universe of study? How is human identity formed in relation to the cosmos through study? The integral relationship between living and loving has become irrelevant to the mastery of discipline in modern education. We no longer educate to love.[25]

    History has meaning because of the direction that is ahead of us and where we are going. History becomes the description of the path that is leading to the summit to be reached. God, the Alpha and the Omega and the principle and base of the movement, is found at the beginning, during, and especially at the end of the journey. That is why, in order to grow properly, our sight should be oriented ahead, along the open road, toward the infinite, until we reach the divine destination and destiny. There is no doubt that such growth is a source of power that activates the human behavior. The more we move along that "open road," the more peace will be incarnated because every human face is a human face of the divine.

---

[22] HM, p. 82 -- XII, p. 96.
[23] MD, p. 154 -- IV, p. 201.
[24] HU, p. 107 -- *Hymne de l'Univers*, p. 171.
[25] Ilia Delio, OSF, *The Unbearable Wholeness of Being: God, Evolution, and the Power of Love* (Maryknoll, N.Y.: Orbis Books, 2013), pp. 145-146.

Then, we find ourselves in love with the One above all, through all, and in all, so that we may all be one. Consequently, conflicts, greed, hatreds, divisions, violence, wars... would vanish by themselves. What external coercions are not able to accomplish, the internal motivation of the divine growth will certainly be able to accomplish because we would have, then, the optimum environment for human potential to continue to grow and flourish. In such an environment, the right attitudes, institutions, and structures will appropriately be created to sustain peaceful societies with "more complex union," as Františka Jirousová observed when she said:

> Teilhard's use of the word progress is often misunderstood as meaning that evolution is moving forward steadily in the 'right' direction. Rather Teilhard considers progress as a steady increase in the power of relationship depending on the degree of complexity. What these relationships will be used for is not determined beforehand; instead, they become increasingly more powerful in the sense of their ability to create more complex union.[26]

We will not find solutions for our problems of unhappiness, violence, and wars in increasing our medical doses, installing more security detectors, and writing more peace treaties, even though all these things can help. It would be smarter, more "revolutionary," and by far more effective, if we could let the divine growth operate in us and through us.

---

[26] Františka Jirousová, *Teilhard de Chardin's Theory of Spiritual Evolution* (American Teilhard Association, "Teilhard Studies" Number 70, Spring 2015), p. 11.

CHAPTER TWENTY-TWO

TOWARD A NEW RELIGIOUS ORDER

Do we really know where we are heading? On the surface, we seem to be going toward a secularized society, and we brag about the separation between Church and State thinking that religion is the main reason for going to war. In fact, a proliferation of religious trends fill many aspects of our society. Beside the great religions whose members are by the billions, we see the growth of new religious persuasions, spiritual movements, ecumenical services, different sects, and all kinds of New Age memberships. After several decades of research, David B. Barret concluded that "We have identified 9,900 distinct and separate religions in the world, increasing by two or three religions every day."[1] The plain truth is that secularization is counterbalanced by de-secularization that takes many forms whose most recognizable one is fundamentalism.

What does such a situation tell us about war and peace? Does a society without God bring more wars or more peace? Is God a God of war or a God of peace? Are religions causes of conflicts or factors of peace? How did Teilhard de Chardin deal with these questions and what were his answers?

Religion Does Not Seek War

It is not religion that seeks war, but the deformed interpretation of religion that stirs up violence, and that is the problem. This is a huge problem because, as Blaise Pascal put it, "Men never do evil so completely and cheerfully as when they do it from religious conviction."

Violence happens not because of religion, but in spite of it.

History taught us that religious people have failed their own religion so many times. They did not live up to their duties and ideals. The weaknesses of the human condition were often the reason, but more often it is no other than hypocrisy that was behind it all.

---

[1] Quoted by Jorge N. Ferrer, "The Future of World Religion: Four Scenarios, One Dream," in *Tikkun*, winter 2012, p. 14.

Who is really to blame – religion or those who use religion to mobilize ordinary people to go to war, God or those who hijack and use the name of God to subdue others to conform to their own agendas and purposes? Who should take responsibility for committed crimes – God or those who used God to justify almost any cruelty, from burning heretics, stoning adulterers, beheading any "other," and crucifying Jesus himself? Who to accuse – the religious or the hypocrites?

Atheists, seculars, and all those who, for personal reasons, do not like religion because it tells them what they are supposed to be doing, put forward the argument that religion is to blame for wars in the world. They give proofs to their claim by the examples of the Crusades, the Inquisition, and similar facts that happened in history. On this part of history, they are right and no one can deny these facts; religion, unfortunately, can certainly provide an advantageous cover for the evil-hearted. But this is a myopic and pick-and-choose reading of history. This is not the whole story.

The truth is that while the members of the different religions have engaged in violence, it is not true, however, to conclude that the "religious" wars were the majority among the wars in history. Some historians are proposing the number of 250,000 as the number of deaths in the name of religious zeal. A quarter of a million is horrific, indeed. But this is nothing in comparison with what the non religious wars have killed. Pol Pot of Cambodia killed 3 million. Stalin of the Soviet Union killed as many as 20 million. Mao Tse-Tung of China killed over 50 million. 150 million people were killed as a result of the 20th century wars, and none of these wars was attributable to religion. The attackers of the Jewish people were the irreligious Nazis. Even if we are confronted with particular conflicts, as is the case more recently with Taliban, Al-Qaeda, ISIS, and many other groups where religion is claimed to be the cause, a deeper research will find, more often than not, other hidden reasons such as: political liberation, rejection of foreign policies, nationalism, political ambition, control of territory and resources, and the like. Also, even when religion is alleged as the cause for violence, the real cause is elsewhere; it is for materialistic and "after-death" rewards that those terrorists, mercenaries, and suicide bombers engage in acts of violence.

Moreover, even when it appears like a war of religion, it really is not. There are always political and all kinds of self-interest reasons behind every war. Medieval and Renaissance wars were mainly about control and wealth. Most modern wars, including the Napoleonic Campaign, the French Revolution, the American Revolution, the Russia Revolution, the American Civil War, World War I, World War II, and the conflicts in Korea, Vietnam, Iraq, Palestine, Syria, and other places were and are not religious in nature. Even the war in Ireland and the rise of militant Islam in the 20th and 21st centuries are made primarily for political, nationalistic, and ethnic reasons, and not for religious reasons, in spite of the fact that they appear like "religious" wars. If religion is "bad," the lack of it or the misinterpretation of it is much, much worse.

Also, who would know what God is going to do when the members of every religious group pray for victory over those who are not members? Does God take a side? Is God interested in seeing all these people killing each other?

Furthermore, putting the blame on religion for violence and war shows little understanding of the human condition itself. From an anthropologic point of view, it would be wrong to see that criminal acts are the product of religion when the very root of such acts is our sinful and weak humanity. The reason there is violence, war, murder, rape, and other crimes is because there is a battle raging in every human soul, heart, and mind. As humans, we are at war against our best interests. We struggle to do what is right when we find ourselves inclined to do what is wrong. Can we see ourselves completely free of greed, excessive love of power and money, and overwhelming desire for prestige and pride? When can we stop, once and for all, a rapist from being a rapist, a thief from being a thief, and a liar from being a liar? Can we imagine a kind of "surgical" procedure that will uproot all these things from our human nature?

Religion is different from its members. Religion is not to be blamed for violence and war. The so-called "religious" people are to be blamed because they did not understand their religion – and this is bad enough – or they understood it and they did the opposite of what they understood – and this is much worse. Religion does not prescribe to commit crimes. Yet, people commit them in the name of religion or in spite of what religion says. For Pope Francis, "to use the name of God to justify [the path of violence] is blasphemy."[2] He also said: "Together, we must say no to hatred, to revenge and to violence, particularly that violence which is perpetrated in the name of a religion or of God himself. God is peace, *salam*."[3]

---

[2] In his Angelus Address, (Rome, November 15, 2015), Pope Francis said: "I want to vigorously reaffirm that the path of violence and hate does not resolve the problems of humanity. And that to use the name of God to justify this path is blasphemy."

[3] In his address to that Muslim Community in Bangui's Grand Mosque on November 30, 2015, Pope Francis said: "Christians and Muslims are brothers and sisters. We must therefore consider ourselves and conduct ourselves as such. We are well aware that the recent events and acts of violence which have shaken your

Real religion does not cause wars; it ends wars. Authentic religious people are not violent people; they are peacemakers.

Teilhard de Chardin was one of these peacemakers. How so?

Teilhard's Concept of Religion

Since Teilhard was a priest and member of the Jesuit Order, there is no wonder that his understanding of religion[4] was originated from a Christian and Catholic point of view. In his essay, "The Introduction to the Christian Life," he stated that

> a threefold faith is necessary, and sufficient, as a foundation for the Christian position:
> 1. Faith in the (personalizing) personality of God, the focus of the world.
> 2. Faith in the divinity of the historic Christ (not only prophet and perfect man, but also object of love and worship).
> 3. Faith in the reality of the Church *phylum*, in which and around which Christ continues to develop, in the world, his total personality.[5]

Such a statement indicates the intimate relation between God and the universe, as Teilhard saw it. His concept of the cosmic Christ is the "embodiment" of this relation. God is present in the world through the mystery of Christ – the historical Jesus and the universal Christ. This is not a static presence, but a dynamic one, active, and evolving toward the fulfillment of the universe in what Teilhard calls the Omega Point.

---

country were not grounded in properly religious motives. Those who claim to believe in God must also be men and women of peace. Christians, Muslims and members of the traditional religions have lived together in peace for many years. They ought, therefore, to remain united in working for an end to every act which, from whatever side, disfigures the Face of God and whose ultimate aim is to defend particular interests by any and all means, to the detriment of the common good. Together, we must say no to hatred, to revenge and to violence, particularly that violence which is perpetrated in the name of a religion or of God himself. God is peace, *salam*."

[4] Henri de Lubac, SJ, de l'Institut, wrote a remarkable book on the subject, called *La Pensée Religieuse du Père Teilhard de Chardin* (Mayenne, France: Aubier/Montaigne, 1962) ; translated into English under the title, *The Religion of Teilhard de Chardin*, by René Hague (Garden City, NY: Image Books, a Division of Doubleday & Company, 1968), ©1967 William Collins Sons & Co., Ltd., London and Desclée Co. Inc., New York.

[5] CE, pp. 151-52 -- X, p. 180.

Teilhard identifies this Omega of evolution with the Christ of revelation by affirming that "Christ is identical with Omega,"[6] and he goes on to base his claim on Johannine and Pauline texts, and he said: "I cannot quote them all here, but they come down to these two essential affirmations: 'In eo omnia constant' [in him all things hold together] (Col. 1:17), and 'Ipse est qui replete omnia' [he is the one who fills all things] (Col. 2:10, cf. Eph. 4:9), from which it follows that 'Omnia in omnibus Christus' [Chirst is all in all] (Col. 3:11) – the very definition of omega."[7]

When Teilhard identifies Christ and Omega, he is describing at the same time the intimate relation between the divine, the physical universe, and the human endeavor. He is seeing the presence of God acting throughout the universe. He is also seeing all human action as energy that can lead to Omega. This means that his concept of religion cannot be limited to the institutional religion, but it encompasses the secular as well.

Teilhard agrees with the secularists who focus on human effort, material values, and finite goals. However, while affirming the value of this world, he clearly and uncompromisingly sees the transcendent embodied within the world – a truth the secularists reject. His affirmation of God's immanence in the universe is so strong that some Christian theologians went as far as criticizing him for being pantheistic when he was not what they thought he was. Rather, he was finding himself in harmony with major strands of the Christian tradition – with St. Paul, for example, and the theophanic universe of the Greek Fathers and the Franciscan awareness.

Many examples show how much Teilhard was convinced of the presence of the divine in the physical world. One of the most well known texts would be his "Hymn to Matter"[8] in which he says, "I acclaim you [matter] as the divine *milieu*, charged with creative power, as the ocean stirred by the Spirit, as the clay moulded and infused with life by the incarnate Word."[9] Another salient text would be:

> All around us, to right and left, in front and behind, above and below, we have only had to go a little beyond the frontier of sensible appearances in order to see the divine welling up and showing through. But it is not only close to us, in front of us, that the divine presence has revealed itself. It has sprung up so universally, and we find ourselves so surrounded and

---

[6] SC, p. 54 -- IX, p. 82.
[7] SC, p. 54 -- IX, p. 82.
[8] HU, pp. 68-71 -- XIII, pp. 89-91.
[9] HU, p. 70 -- XIII, p. 90.

> transfixed by it, that there is no room left to fall down and adore it, even within ourselves.
>
> By means of all created things, without exception, the divine assails us, penetrates us and moulds us. We imagine it as distant and inaccessible, whereas in fact we live steeped in its burning layers.[10]

Still another text would be when Teilhard sees "A Christ who is no longer master of the world solely because he has been *proclaimed* to be such, but because he animates the whole range of things from top to bottom."[11] Teilhard also saw that "Religion and science are the two conjugated faces or phases of one and the same complete act of knowledge – the only one which can embrace the past and future of evolution so as to contemplate, measure and fulfill them."[12] Furthermore, his entire book, *The Divine Milieu*, could be considered as an indisputable example of the presence of God in the universe, especially when he talks directly about diaphany and epiphany. In this book, we find lines, as an example, like the following:

> If we may slightly alter a hallowed expression, we could say that the great mystery of Christianity is not exactly the appearance, but the transparence, of God in the universe. *Yes, Lord, not only the ray that strikes the surface, but the ray that penetrates, not only your Epiphany, Jesus, but your diaphany.*[13]

This universal Christ, therefore, is animating and energizing everything, and that includes physical things and every human effort. This means that every human person, whether a member of a religious community or not, should be dedicated to authentic secular concerns that are no longer "secular," since they are part of the co-creating power given to us by God in order to build the earth and bring humans to their fulfillment in the Cosmic Christ. In a sense, every endeavor should be a "religious" step forward in reaching a higher consciousness that adds another level in the noosphere.

Religion should then, according to Teilhard, energize and activate human creativity in finding better ways for the development of society, the peacemaking, the respect of our total environment, and the building of the earth. In such a context, it should not surprise anyone if we see Teilhard sketching the profile of the saint for modern times. The saint, according to him, is not the one who withdraws from the world to practice methods of

---

[10] DM, p. 112 -- IV, pp. 133-34.
[11] CE, p. 89 -- X, p. 108.
[12] PM, p. 285 -- I, p. 317.
[13] DM, p. 131 -- IV, p. 162.

severe asceticism, but the one who is engaging in the world in order to activate all the energies of the earth directing them to the fulfillment of the total cosmic process. Teilhard wrote:

> The saint, the Christian saint, as we now understand him and look for him, will not be the man who is the most successful in escaping from matter and mastering it completely; he will be the man who seeks to make all his powers – gold, love, or freedom – transcend themselves and co-operate in the consummation of Christ, and who so realizes for us the ideal of the faithful servant of evolution.[14]

Teilhard was talking about Christianity and the Christian saint, but how about the other religions? What do they offer?

The Convergence of Religions

The French writer and statesman André Malraux predicted in the middle of the 20th century that "The 21st century will be religious [spiritual] or it will not be at all."[15] Although this prediction remains as enigmatic as ever because of the highly technological and materialistic world we find ourselves immersed in, there are real signs of spiritual and religious awakening all around us. On the one hand, we see real interest in spirituality that is emerging from Western traditions as well as from Eastern traditions. On the other hand, we also see an excessive ideological "religiosity" that has little to do with the general welfare of humanity.

Moreover, we see an interfaith[16] honest dialogue between the different great religions of the world that is trying to find ways for living peacefully

---

[14] CE, p. 170 -- X, pp. 198-99.
[15] André Malraux (1901-1976) said: "Le vingt-et-unième siècle sera religieux ou ne sera pas. » Probably what he meant was that religion will be the measure of humanity in the 21st century. This declaration was coming from someone who had for sometime communist convictions. However, during the Nazi occupation, he found himself one of the leaders of the French Resistance. General Charles De Gaulle rewarded him with the first ever post of Minister for Culture. See https://www.quora.com/The-21st-century-will-be-spiritual-or-will-not-be-What-do-you-think-about-this-enigmatic-prophesy-Andre-Malraux-1901-1976.
[16] The prefix *inter* suggests an openness to others, an eagerness to communicate with them, and a readiness to exchange wisdom and knowledge, and it creates new bonds that affect our togetherness. "Inter," wrote Wayne Teasdale, "conveys a sense of responsibility to humankind as a whole, and to all living beings, to contribute to a larger understanding of spirituality in our time and in times to come. It is an important aspect of what the Dalai Lama calls our universal

together, if not striving to be completely unified. We also see very "religious" people who are criminalizing all those who believe differently to the point of trying to eliminate them if they don't convert to their way of thinking. In both cases, this is a significant religious phenomenon. In one case, people are growing toward peace by living a religious conviction. In the other case, people are killed by living another "religious" conviction. Are religions called to eliminate each other or rather to contribute in bringing more growth and peace to humanity? Are they a reason for divergence or rather the best reason for convergence?

What did Teilhard say on such a thorny issue? He said:

> In the great river of mankind, the three currents (Eastern, human and Christian) are still at cross-purposes. Nevertheless there are sure indications which make it clear that they are coming to run together.... A general convergence of religions upon a universal Christ who fundamentally satisfies them all: that seems to me the only possible conversion of the world, and the only form in which a religion of the future can be conceived.[17]

Such a statement seems naïve and impossible to conceive unless we consider the convergence of religions from the standpoint of Teilhard's theory of the evolution of consciousness. Professor Ewert H. Cousins explains this point thoroughly while using the very words of Teilhard. In a concise and compact way that is worth repeating here, he said:

> According to Teilhard, consciousness emerges out of a process that has its roots in the geosphere and the biosphere. Throughout the process a single dynamic is at work, which he articulates as the law of "complexity-consciousness" and "union differentiates." "In any domain," he says, "whether it be the cells of a body, the members of a society or the elements of a spiritual synthesis – *union differentiates.*"[18] From subatomic particles to global consciousness, individual elements unite in a center to center union which releases creative energy leading to more complex units. The greater complexity leads to increased interiority, which makes possible more intimate creative union. In this process the elements do not lose their identity but rather have it intensified by union. "Following the confluent orbits of their centres, the grains of consciousness do not tend to lose their

---

responsibility to the global community of the earth, a responsibility that is both individual and collective." See Wayne Teasdale, *The Mystic Heart: Discovering a Universal Spirituality in the World's Religions* (Novato, CA: New World Library, 1999), p. 27.

[17] CE, p. 130 -- X, p. 150.

[18] PM, p. 262 -- I, p. 291.

outlines and blend, but, on the contrary, to accentuate the depth and incommunicability of their *egos*. The more 'other' they become in conjunction, the more they find themselves as 'self'."[19] As these differentiated unions become more complex, interiority is increased and energy is released towards the formation of a more complex and interiorized consciousness. "Regarded along its axis of complexity," Teilhard states, "the universe is, both on the whole and at each of its points, in a continual tension of organic doubling-back upon itself, and thus of interiorization."[20] At this point in history, the forces of planetization are bringing about an unprecedented complexification of what Teilhard terms the noosphere, or sphere of consciousness, through the convergence of cultures and religions. Teilhard himself saw the convergence of world religions as a phase of the complexification of the noosphere.[21]

Although he was much interested in Eastern religions[22] for their cosmic universalism as well as in humanist pantheisms for their devotion to the universal progress of humankind, Teilhard saw also their limitations. It is in Christianity that he found the universal Christ who integrates the divine and the human. He wrote: "The universal Christ, as I understood the name, is a synthesis of Christ and the universe. He is not a new godhead – but an inevitable deployment of the mystery in which Christianity is summed up, the mystery of the Incarnation."[23] Religions, especially Christianity should radiate love, hope, and peace through the lives of the believers in their journey inward, outward, onward, and upward to Omega Christ.

---

[19] PM, p. 262 -- I, p. 291.
[20] PM, p. 302 -- I, p. 335.
[21] Ewert H. Cousins, "Teilhard de Chardin and the Religious Phenomenon," International Symposium on the Occasion of the Birth of Teilhard de Chardin, United Nations Educational, Scientific and Cultural Organization, Paris, France, 16-18 September 1981.
[22] Teilhard was more familiar with Eastern religions than he was with Islam because he spent about 23 years of his life in China (1923-1946). No wonder we find in his essay "How I Believe" that was written in Peking on 28 October 1934, the following footnote: "Islam, in spite of the number of its adherents and its continual progress (in the less evolved strata of mankind, we may note) is not examined here, because to my mind (at least in its original form) it contributes no special solution to the modern religious problem. It seems to me to represent a residual Judaism, with no individual character of its own: and it can develop only by becoming either humanist or Christian." (CE, p. 121 -- X, p 142). Obviously, Teilhard would have written a special essay on Islam if he was writing today and not in 1934 from Peking.
[23] CE, p. 126 -- X, p. 146.

With the encounter of religions on the spiritual, intellectual, institutional, and practical levels, a new form of consciousness ought to occur. In Teilhard's theory of convergence of all things – religions included – the lines of revelation and evolution meet in Christ. The divine, the human, and the material world are realized in the Incarnation. Teilhard may not have been involved extensively in direct dialogue with the leaders of other religions to create the complexified religious consciousness he talked about, but he certainly discerned the dynamics of its emergence, pointed to the goal, and mapped the journey toward it. He would say, for example:

> We need a new theology... and a new approach to perfection, which must gradually be worked out in our houses of study and retreat houses, in order to meet the new needs and aspirations... But what we need perhaps even more... is for a new and higher form of worship to be gradually disclosed by Christian thought and prayer, adapted to the needs of all of tomorrow's believers without exception.[24]

In this context and if, as Teilhard thinks, history is the history of evolution and progress toward unity, ecumenism is going to be an important chapter in this history. However, this "ecumenism" should be understood as a global and cosmic one, and not as the word is understood today limited to the ecumenism of the Christian Churches. It is the unification of everything with everything; even matter is no longer to be seen as something different from spirit, for the world is "the divine milieu."

With great interest and confidence, Teilhard stated: "At this moment[25] a form of ecumenism is trying to assert itself: it is inevitably tied up with the psychic maturing of the earth, and therefore it will certainly come."[26] Then he talked about the

> (summit-ecumenism) 1, between Christians, concerned to bring out an ultra-orthodox and ultra-human Christianity, on a truly 'cosmic' scale.
>
> [and the] (basal-ecumenism) 2, between men in general, concerned to define and extend the foundations of a common human 'faith' in the future of mankind.[27]

---

[24] SC, p. 220 -- IX, p. 289.
[25] Teilhard wrote his essay "Ecumenism" on 15 December 1946, (See SC, pp. 197-98 -- IX, pp. 251-54).
[26] SC, p. 197 -- IX, p. 253.
[27] SC, p. 198 -- IX, p. 254.

Then, he immediately added:

> Combined, these two efforts would automatically lead us to the ecumenism we are waiting for; because faith in mankind, if carried as far as it can be taken, cannot, it would seem, be satisfied without a fully explicit Christ.[28]

We must keep in mind, as Teilhard believed, that we are responsible for what we make of this world and it is this Christ he talked about – the incarnated God – who will tell us what "type" of God we want to adore and what "type" of humanity we really want to see realized. The Incarnation of that Christ, therefore, is not only the event that was recorded in that particular day of history. It is also the continuous event that makes the history of humankind. This is certainly the most fundamental transformation there is, and those who resist it must be included in the list of the enemies of world peace and blessings.

---

[28] SC, p. 198 -- IX, p. 254.

CHAPTER TWENTY-THREE

TOWARD A THEOLOGICAL AND TELEOLOGICAL ECOLOGY

At the time when Teilhard de Chardin was writing, there was little attention, if any, to the environment issue, mainly because of the split in understanding reality. The spirit and all that was related to it was one thing, and the matter and all that was related to it was another thing. Not for Teilhard, though. Teilhard saw that "There is neither spirit nor matter in the world: the 'stuff of the universe' is *spirit-matter*."[1] He had the passionate desire to heal the tragic split that existed between religion and science, the within and the without, faith in God and faith in the world, love of God and love of the world, the sacred and the profane, and the work for heaven and the work for the earth; gone is the traditional dualism and all its implications. His enthusiasm and breath-taking vision led him to sometimes magnify a certain part of this vision in order to make a point on how important this, is, or how wrong the other side is. For example, he wrote:

> If, as the result of some interior revolution, I were to lose in succession my faith in Christ, my faith in a personal God, and my faith in spirit, I feel that I should continue *to believe* invincibly *in the world*. The world (its value, its infallibility and its goodness) – that, when all is said and done, is the first, the last, and the only thing in which I believe. It is by this faith that I

---

[1] HE, pp. 57-58 -- VI, p. 74. Mary Evelyn Tucker wrote: « One of Teilhard's greatest contributions to modern religious thought is his conception of reality as composed of both spirit and matter.... The epochal change is from the divine as transcendent to the world to the divine in the world – from a perspective which saw spirit and matter as always separate to one that sees their destinies intertwined in evolution; from a perspective that saw the Logos as given from without to one which begins to discover an inner ordering logos at the heart of all matter." (*The Ecological Spirituality of Teilhard*, Teilhard Studies number 13, Spring 1985, pp. 6, 10).

live. And it is to this faith, I feel, that at the moment of death, rising above all doubts, I shall surrender myself.[2]

Taken out of context, such a language smells of heretical beliefs and idolatrous convictions. Not for Teilhard, though. Teilhard sees Christ completely immersed and involved in the world, and the world completely evolving toward the Christ Omega. Then this evolving universe from Alpha to Omega becomes another way for explaining his vision of the same cosmic Christ. Why is it so? Because Teilhard took the doctrine of the Incarnation so seriously that he was not afraid to believe in its infinite conclusions. For in the man Jesus of Nazareth, God and humanity have become one. Jesus clearly affirmed it by saying, "The Father and I are one."[3] This could be interpreted in a larger sense to mean that Jesus was speaking not only of himself as a unique individual but of himself as permeating the humanity that became the fleshy manifestation of God. This opens the door to an understanding of Christ and Christianity of a forward-looking reality with all its challenges that lie ahead more than a backward-looking reality that calls to rigidity and conformity.

This is the Incarnation where God and humanity meet in a "hypostatic union,"[4] and this is where theology and ecology meet in an undivided union. No wonder, then, if caring for the earth is imperative, not only for practical reasons as global warming, clean air, and preservation of species, but also, and above all, for theological and teleological reasons that converge on the "greater Christ."

This is also what Teilhard tried to describe and convey through his writings. With his theological, philosophical, scriptural, spiritual, and scientific background, he saw the deep interior unity, complexity, diversity, and evolving consciousness of the whole universe, and he also saw God as still actively involved in the act of creating and guiding all humanity forward and upward toward himself. Teilhard's idea of evolution from matter to spirit to full unity with Omega God gives hope for the future by opening the door to infinite possibilities. His idea of

---

[2] CE, p. 99 -- X, p. 120.
[3] John 10:30.
[4] "Hypostatic union (from the Greek: ὑπόστασις *hypóstasis*, 'sediment, foundation, substance, subsistence') is a technical term in *Christian theology* employed in mainstream *Christology* to describe the union of Christ's humanity and divinity in one *hypostasis*, or individual existence. The *First Council of Ephesus* in 431 AD recognized this doctrine and affirmed its importance, stating that the humanity and divinity of Christ are made one according to nature and hypostasis in the *Logos*." See: https://en.wikipedia.org/wiki/Hypostatic_union

creation is a creation-in-progress rather that a creation completed and now static. God therefore must be, according to Teilhard, continuously and lovingly involved with ongoing creation and humanity from the beginning to the end – the Omega Point that is the eternal Christ of divine revelation in whom and to whom all evolution is moving. Teilhard uses the terminology of the Book of Revelation where it says, "'I am the Alpha and the Omega,' says the Lord God, who is and who was and who is to me, the Almighty,"[5] while, at the same time, he had in mind St. Paul's line, "In him we live and move and have our being."[6] Then, if God is eternally present and fully engaged in the world – in the "innerness" and the "outerness" of all things – we are called to action in all the dimensions of human action and according to each one's unique gifts and qualities while knowing and maintaining that "There are varieties of gifts, but the same Spirit."[7]

A vision like this must have major implications in theology-ecology understanding. Indeed, when Christ is at the center and apex of the evolving universe by being the cosmic Christ, then every human being in whom he resides and continues his evolving action becomes a cosmic and divine person as well, and must act guided by the energy of the Spirit.[8] This means ecology (human and environmental) is practical theology, and practical theology is ecology.[9]

Let us face it. We do have an ecological crisis. There is no way to fix it unless we allow theology to permeate our life. Llewellyn Vaughan-Lee summarized it well when he said: "If we are to restore the balance in our

---

[5] Revelation 1:8.
[6] Acts 17:28.
[7] 1 Corinthians 12:4.
[8] André Dupleix says: "For Teilhard, the 'transparency' of the world is definitely realized through evolution's constant movement, like a brilliance that stretches to invade everywhere in a continuous creation: 'Faith,' he says, 'is the practical conviction that the Universe, in the hands of the Creator, continues to be the clay which he molds to his liking in numerous possibilities. There are no rigid determinants of matter... but the supple combinations of the Holy Spirit which give consistency to the universe." See André Dupleix, *15 days of Prayer with Pierre Teilhard de Chardin*, trans. by Victoria Hébert and Denis Sabourin (Liguori, Missouri: Liguori Publications, 1999), p. 5.
[9] Many spiritual leaders are now leading in this spiritual ecology endeavor. Among many others, let us mention Pope Benedict XVI, Pope Francis, the "Green Patriarch," Bartholomew 1, the Ecumenical Patriarch of the Easter Orthodox Church, the engaged Buddhist teacher Thich Nhat Hanh, the Franciscan priest Richard Rohr, the Passionist priest Thomas Berry, the Sufi mystic Llewellyn Vaughan-lee....

world, we need to go beneath the surface to heal the split between spirit and matter and help to bring the sacred back into life."[10] This is exactly what Teilhard did throughout his writings, especially in his book *The Divine Milieu* – a title that says it all. The care for the soul is a part of the care of the universe. Embracing the whole is what is needed. Disconnection leads to crises. We seem to be educated to see the parts rather than the whole, and trained to think and act from the angle of separation, division, and segregation. Reality is a living whole and it required a shift into a holistic consciousness because everything is interdependent, interconnected, and interacting. The idea of someone or something being separate from their environment does not exist. What exists is interrelationship, interaction, and cooperation.

Teilhard based his entire vision on the Point Omega, and he described in great detail how "'the stuff of the universe'… *spirit-matter*"[11] is continuously evolving toward that Point,[12] and he saw that the great convergence and synthesis will be greater and greater when the process is nearer and nearer to that summit. In the Preface to his book *The Phenomenon of Man*, Teilhard wrote: "Like the meridians as they approach the poles, science, philosophy and religion are bound to converge as they draw nearer to the whole,"[13] and all particles and situations of life, and from any angle they come from, ought to converge at the summit.

Teilhard is putting an end to the spiritual-material dualism that was, because of its belief that the material side of life has little sacred value, one of the most important causes of the earth ecological crisis. He saw the sacramental and theological view of the creation. On this he was closer to the way of thinking of the Eastern Fathers of the Church than to the Western Fathers. Stephen Lawrence Hastings, Ph.D., explained this point very well in his doctoral dissertation. In the Abstract of this dissertation we read:

> This dissertation looks at Maximus the Confessor (c.580-662 CE), Nicholas of Cusa (1401-1464 CE), and Teilhard de Chardin (1881-1955 CE). Teilhard attests to an experience of natural sacrament in perceiving an

---

[10] Quoted in "About Spiritual Ecology," http://spiritualecology.org/about-spiritual-ecology
[11] HE, pp. 57-58 -- VI, p. 74.
[12] In the last page of Teilhard's diary, we read the important words of his vision: "Cosmogenesis – biogenesis – noogenesis – Christogenesis" (HM, p. 104 -- XIII, p. 119).
[13] PM, p. 30 -- I, p. 22.

increasingly transfigured creation, meaning the glory of God is ever more perceptible as a timely conscious insight into creation and as an emergent aspect of cosmogenesis and evolution moving toward Christ-Omega, the end and fulfillment of all creation. The teachings of Maximus readily support this sacramental view of creation by affirming a universal, ontological, and "real" presence of the Logos of God. A theological insight of Nicholas's doctrine of learned ignorance is that the Christian God always incarnates, transfigures, fulfills, and exceeds the entire cosmos. Together the teachings of Maximus and Nicholas support Teilhard's call for a theology of a Creator God robust enough to encompass the most expansive and complicated propositions about creation made by science, while remaining as close as the real presence of Christ in the Eucharist.[14]

In a remarkable text called "The Mass on the World,"[15] Teilhard suggests seeing not only the union between God and the universe, but also the prolongations of the continuous Incarnation in the world of matter. He wrote in a form of a poetic prayer:

> For me, my God, all joy and all achievement, the very purpose of my being and all my love of life, all depend on this one basic vision of the union between yourself and the universe. Let others, fulfilling a function more august than mine, proclaim your splendours as pure Spirit; as for me, dominated as I am by vocation which springs from the inmost fibres of my being, I have no desire, I have no ability, to proclaim anything except the innumerable prolongations of your incarnate Being in the world of matter; I can preach only the mystery of your flesh, you the Soul shining forth through all that surrounds us.[16]

Teilhard would also pray: "Lord, lock me up in the deepest depths of your heart; and then, holding me there, burn me, purify me, set me on fire, sublimate me, till I become utterly what you would have me be...."[17]

We still are talking about ecology. In order to care for this ecology, is there a better way than being what God wants us to be?

Indeed, when one goes back to the roots[18] of himself or herself and finds his or her fundamental purpose in life and does it, he or she cannot

---

[14] Stephen Lawrence Hastings, *Whole-Earth Consciousness in Maximus the Confessor, Nicholas of Cusa, and Teilhard de Chardin: Seeds for a 21st Century Sacramental Creation Spirituality and Ecological Ethics*, Boston University, 2015. See http://search.proquest.com/docview/1685958997
[15] HU, pp. 17-37 -- XIII, pp. 139-156.
[16] HU, pp. 36-37 – XIII, pp. 155-6.
[17] HU, p. 32 -- XIII, p. 152.

but take care of himself or herself, of others, of his or her environment, of the earth, and of all things all the way to the cosmic Christ. This can be done only by the energies of love that is the essence of evolution and of transformation. "The day will come when," Teilhard wrote, "after mastering the ether, the winds, the waves, the tides, gravitation, we shall harness for God the energies of love. And, on that day, for the second time in the history of the world, man will have discovered fire."[19] This is not only the journey to God but also the journey in God since "God is love,"[20] as St. John said.

Teilhard saw that, in order to get to that better place called the Omega Point, love must be the driving force and fire of our human and cosmic evolution. Along the way, he anticipated many of our civilizational and ecological concerns. Anthony M. Stevens-Arroyo rightly clarified this point by saying:

> The easiest point of entry of de Chardin's thought to civilizational theory today is in terms of the environment. Teilhard anticipated many of the environmentalist concerns of today because of his conception of the pyramid of life. We are, of course, familiar with related notions like "the food chain." If humanity pollutes and corrupts the planet so as to destroy the links of animals and nature and human beings, then humanity attacks itself. River water, for example, is not just "river water" but an organic connection in the food chain that is both controlled and used by humanity, but whose destruction would be a form of species suicide. Its tides connect it organically to cities alongside its banks, while also framing the commerce and migration of peoples and ideas for the planet.... Teilhard challenges the Hobbesian theories that defined civilization as a conquest over the forces of nature. The brute confidence that reason and human engineering can overcome all natural barriers is often cited as the positive legacy of the Enlightenment and the modern era. In de Chardin, that

---

[18] Going back to the roots reminds us of the poem of Sufi mystic Jalal ad-Din Muhammad Rumi (1207-1273):
> "Although you appear in earthly form
> Your essence is pure Consciousness.
> You are the fearless guardian
> of Divine Light.
> So come, return to the root of the root
> of your own soul."

See https://katerobertson.wordpress.com/2010/11/12/the-root-of-the-root-of-your-soul/

[19] TF, pp. 86-87 -- XI, p. 92.

[20] 1 John 4:16.

confidence in human experience is not focused on overcoming nature, but rather by aligning one's consciousness in concert with natural forces.[21]

Our consciousness is not supposed to be the controller but the responsible steward of the planet and of all other life forms. This requires us to make dramatic transformations in our patterns of production, consumption, and the way we do business. We should be the Spirit's unfolding manifestation of love, goodness, and caring. We should be able to lead with us others, and all that is, to our Creator. Here Pope Francis meets, and concurs with, Teilhard in a big way. He wrote in his encyclical letter *Laudato Si' On Care for Our Common Home*:

> The ultimate destiny of the universe is in the fullness of God, which has already been attained by the risen Christ, the measure of the maturity of all things. Here we can add yet another argument for rejecting every tyrannical and irresponsible domination of human beings over other creatures. The ultimate purpose of other creatures is not to be found in us. Rather, all creatures are moving forward with us and through us toward a common point of arrival, which is God, in that transcendent fullness where the risen Christ embraces and illumines all things. Human beings, endowed with intelligence and love, and drawn by the fullness of Christ, are called to lead all creatures back to their Creator.[22]

Since, "reality is charged with a divine Presence," as Teilhard said, and "the World, filled with God, no longer appears to our opened eyes as

---

[21] Anthony M. Stevens-Arroyo, "*Fire and Force: Civilization as Noosphere in the Works of Teilhard de Chardin.*" See http://www.readperiodicals.com/201204/2691947051.html

[22] Pope Francis, *Laudato Si' On Care for Our Common Home*, #83. See http://w2.vatican.va/content/francesco/en/encyclicals/documents/papa-francesco_20150524_enciclica-laudato-si.html -- In this context, Jean-Marc Moschetta wrote: "Dans le contexte de l'urgence écologique qui est celui de l'encyclique *Laudato Si'*, la pensée de Teilhard fonde véritablement l'argument théologique d'une 'écologie intégrale' en liant la dimension créatrice de Dieu et sa dimension rédemptrice. Selon Moltmann, 'Dieu ne serait pas le créateur de toutes choses s'il ne voulait pas la rédemption de toutes choses'. On ne peut pas dire que Dieu a créé les mondes et qu'il se contenterait de sauver la seule espèce humaine. Cette vision intégrative du salut est celle qui sous-tend l'encyclique *Laudato Si'* et elle se déploie dans le sillage de la christologie cosmique de Teilhard qui souligne si bien le caractère unifiant du processus convergent de l'histoire. » See Jean-Marc Moschetta, « Le Christ cosmique chez Teilhard : Fondement d'une 'écologie intégrale' » in *Teilhard Aujourd'hui*, Paris, mars 2016, No 57, p. 68.

anything but a milieu and an object of universal communion,"[23] we learn to experience God at the heart of all that exists. We love this person, this tree, this thing, this event, this earth, and God at the same time. Everyone and everything become a cherished gift, and we see the gift and the Giver in the same look.

The greatest tragedy of modern times is that we have lost the sense of the sacred and the feeling that we are a part of the interconnected web of life. There will be a great feeling of reverence for, and oneness with, all that "is" if we re-learn to reconnect with the sacred as many of our ancestors did.[24] Outer actions such as ecological treaties for taking care of the soil, for example, are necessary steps toward a solution; they are not the solution. The solution is more than a soil solution; it is a soul solution. Soul and soil, as Teilhard's *"spirit-matter,"* are one reality. With this consciousness shift, we won't see the world as a place for economic growth and consumer desires, but a place of wonder and magic that needs all our attention and care.

The way we see the world dictates the way we treat all that is in it. Ecumenical Patriarch Bartholomew of Constantinople made it clear this way:

> We are treating our planet in an inhuman, godless manner precisely because we fail to see it as a gift inherited from above. Our original sin with regard to the natural environment lies in our refusal to accept the world as a sacrament of communion, as a way of sharing with God and neighbor on a global scale. It is our humble conviction that divine and human meet in the slightest detail contained in the seamless garment of God's creation, in the last speck of dust.[25]

---

[23] SC, p. 168 -- IX, p. 213.

[24] Bill Plotkin wrote: "western civilization has buried most traces of the mystical roots of maturity, yet this knowledge has been at the heart of every indigenous tradition known to us, past and present, including those from which our own societies have emerged. Our way into the future requires new cultural forms more than older ones, but there is at least one thread of the human story that I'm confident will continue, and this is the numinous or visionary calling at the core of the mature human heart.... The process of becoming fully human – developing as nature and soul would have it – entails a radical shift in worldview and values.... Too many of us lack intimacy with the natural world and with our souls, and consequently we are doing untold damage to both. (See Bill Plotkin, *"Creating Twenty-First Century Life-Enhancing Societies,"*
http://spiritualecology.org/article/creating-twenty-first-century-life-enhancing-societies).

[25] See https://www.patriarchate.org/bartholomew-quotes

A real awakening is needed in order to be able to change the way we think and act. We need the correct way of "seeing." "Seeing. We might say that the whole of life lies in that verb—if not ultimately, at least essentially,"[26] insisted Teilhard. Not the way of separation, fear, and anger. But the way of interconnectedness,[27] interaction, and communion. Then we could say with Teilhard: "I acclaim you, [matter], as the divine *milieu*, charged with creative power, as the ocean stirred by the Spirit, as the clay moulded and infused with life by the incarnate Word."[28]

---

[26] PM, p. 31 -- I, p. 25.
[27] Allerd Stikker wrote: "Our denial of the interconnectedness of everything in the cosmos, including Earth's ecosystems, and of the triply-integrated nature of the planer lies at the root of our ecological crisis. If we are to solve the problems facing us today, we must analyze in greater depth what is happening during the evolutionary process and what we can learn from it." See Allerd Stikker, *Teilhard, Evolution, and Ecology* (American Teilhard Association, "Teilhard Studies" Number 73, Fall 2016), p. 5.
[28] HU, p.70 -- XIII, p. 90.

CHAPTER TWENTY-FOUR

TOWARD A NEW TYPE OF LIFE

The hour has struck for a change in consciousness. Something different is beginning. Call it what you would like: a global and universal transformation, a radical and mystical transfiguration, a revolution – individual or collective.... For Teilhard de Chardin, "Mankind has just entered into what is probably the most extensive period of transformation it has known since its birth ... Something is happening in the general structure of Spirit: it is a new type of life that is beginning."[1] It is no longer a question of searching for answers only, but also a kind of mutation to another state of consciousness that allows more fundamental decisions to be made. "For anyone who sees the universe in the form of a laborious common ascent towards the greatest consciousness," wrote Teilhard, "life, far from seeming blind, harsh or contemptible, assumes a new seriousness, new responsibilities and new connections."[2]

In this altered state of consciousness, our ways of seeing, thinking, and acting become different. In the realm of "becoming," where "I" is lived "we-ly," many aspects of life will change – things that include: "*esse*" becomes "*unire*"; wisdom becomes flame; smoke becomes fire; walls become bridges; possessing becomes sharing; being indifferent becomes caring; resentment becomes forgiveness. In this same realm, the very ground of a battle becomes an oasis, shell-fires become greetings, empty talks become concrete actions, humanitarian aid becomes a planned prevention of disasters, "charities" become explorations and expansions,[3] exploitation becomes generosity, and fear of others becomes a constructive connection. On this level, Teilhard speaks of a "constant increase in

---

[1] SC, pp. 128-29 -- IX, pp. 169-70.
[2] VP, p. 159 -- III, p. 223.
[3] N. M. Wildiers says : « La charité chrétienne représente plus qu'une goutte de baume sur les souffrances du prochain. Elle est la grande force universelle qui nous seconde et nous pousse dans notre aspiration a réaliser complètement notre existence humaine. Elle constitue la véritable source d'énergie dont l'homme a besoin pour accomplir sa tâche jusqu'au bout. » See N.M. Wildiers, *Teilhard de Chardin* (Paris: Editions Universitaires, 1960, 'Classiques du XXe Siècle'), p. 118.

psyche throughout time,"[4] of "a new domain of psychical expansion,"[5] of "a laborious common ascent towards the greatest consciousness,"[6] and he explained this mutation through the general concepts of complexification, ecumenism, and cosmogenesis.

Complexification

Teilhard believes that there is a universal drift towards more and more complex states of arrangements. It is not the infinitely big and infinitely small of Pascal, it is now the infinitely complex. In fact, there is more complexity in the atom than in an electron. There is more complexity in the molecule than in an atom. There is more complexity in the cell than in the chemical nuclei. There is also more centering.

In this process, at a certain point, matter produces a sort of consciousness – a rudimentary "psychism" – and begins to give certain life with the genesis of species; a cerebral mutation, a kind of an explosion of consciousness, a psychogenesis. This is a critical point in the evolution.

Teilhard believes that complexity-consciousness reaches its highest levels in the nervous system. Here, reflection – a special sort of consciousness – appears. Human beings are the first animals to know that they know. Under the influence of these new powers of consciousness, the entire human phylum, after a long period of divergence, is going to start to converge. Henceforth, the tendency for rapprochement among the elements of each group, and among the different groups, is going to become more and more marked. This is a breakthrough that allows new patterns of arrangements to take place and develop and, as Teilhard writes, "The higher the degree of complexity in a living creature, the higher its consciousness; and vice versa."[7]

With this thinking layer that Teilhard describes as the "noosphere," socialization, totalization, and planetization are possible.[8] This point of co-

---

[4] CE, p. 107 – X, p. 127.
[5] PM, p. 253 -- I, p. 281.
[6] VP, p. 159 -- III, p. 223.
[7] FM, p. 116 -- V, p. 144.
[8] Louis M. Savary noted: "Among persons in the noosphere both types of complexity (increasing physical complexity as well as consciousness, including the increasing complexity of information and knowledge) operate in combination, thus creating ever more physical complexity and ever more demand for increased consciousness. The increased complexity generated in groups of animals and humans leads to what Teilhard calls 'socialization,' the gradual formation and evolution of larger and larger social units or wholes. Teilhard lived to see social

reflection/thinking together is what can be called today "global consciousness." Here the noosphere continues to develop and the human mind continues to grow collectively, by interpenetration and interdependence through the links of techno-economic inventions and through interconnections of every kind. In fact, what is called reality is so many times more complex today than it was ever before to the point that we sometimes find it very difficult, if not impossible, to understand. See, for example, how extremely complex our social and cultural ties have become; problems between the East and the West, the North and the South, the rich and the poor; problems between races, religions, institutions, nations, political systems; problems between generations, sexes, languages, ways of life, etc. All this validates Teilhard's conviction that humanity is at the threshold of a new step in consciousness, both at personal and at social levels. Both individual development and higher social integration are necessary for human survival. They are not mutually exclusive; they are interdependent. The responsibility for evolution, at this point in time, lies with humanity itself much more than with external factors.

Complexity is not confusion. It is a symphony. A single note is simple. It is not complicated. It has its meaning when it joins other notes. The higher the complexity, the more beautiful the symphony.

Convergence and collectivization

Teilhard thinks that we are now, in evolution, at a time when the forces of divergence are giving way to the forces of convergence. We are converging. When human beings appeared on earth, they were able to live in small groups separated from each other. But with the increase in population it became impossible to travel endlessly without meeting other groups, whether for matters of common interest, or for wars. Little by little, individuals gathered in groups, tribes, and nations, and they had to deal with isolation, separation, hostility, then tolerance and solidarity. However necessary divergence was in the past, we are now witnessing the new phase of the human development – the phenomenon of convergence.

---

complexity worldwide in the formation of the United Nations and the growth of the multi-national corporation, but not long enough—he died in 1955—to witness the emerging potential of the internet and of 21st century social media to interconnect, almost instantly, thousands and even millions of people." See Louis M. Savary, *Expanding Teilhard's 'Complexity-Consciousness' law* (American Teilhard Association, "Teilhard Studies" Number 68, Spring 2014), p. 4.

"The age of nations has passed,"[9] wrote Teilhard, and now "races, peoples, and nations consolidate one another and complete one another by mutual fecundation."[10] We no longer just coexist and live side by side, we are learning now to meet, share, exchange, and find ways to help each other. Everyone is unique and we need each other to discover this uniqueness, develop it, and share it. We are heading to the age of collectivization.

Teilhard uses the word "collectivization" to indicate that the different social groups that were in the past spread and disconnected, tend now more and more to form an integrated whole leading to a "common soul." Teilhard wrote: "Like any other union the collectivization of the earth, rightly conducted, should 'super-animate' us in a common soul."[11]

At the present time, a "dominant" culture is no longer considered dominant. In the age of collectivization,[12] each culture has its own contribution to the whole. Collectivization phenomena are becoming increasingly obvious. What local events do not have their repercussions all over the world? What questions or problems do not have international reactions, answers, and solutions? What a particular nation's concerns are not shared by other nations' concerns? Humanity is increasingly interdependent. Civil wars are more and more international wars, and their solutions, too, are more international than just local. We are now a world community. Touch a single leaf, as it has been said, and you touch the world. Teilhard believed that increasing collectivization,[13] socialization, and totalization mean increasing consciousness, and consequently increasing chances for peace. Our different languages, different systems of governing, different religious convictions, different ethnic groups, and the different things we see, read, and fill our brains with, are the environments that are as concrete as the foods we eat and the waters we drink. They are part of the whole we interact with, and they are, if controlled, effective tools for reaching a higher consciousness.

---

[9] HE, p. 37 -- VI, p. 46.
[10] PM, p. 242 -- I, p. 269.
[11] HE, p. 80 -- VI, p. 100.
[12] Sociologist Emile Durkheim (1858-1917), philosopher Louis Althusser (1918-1990), and psychotherapist Carl Jung (1875-1961) talked about "collective consciousness" and "collective unconscious" to explain how an autonomous individual comes to identify with a larger group.
[13] Olivier Rabut says: To Teilhard, it is the collective and objective aspect of temporal progress that is so important. There can no longer be any question of polishing up one's own soul into something beautiful and useless; but we still have to build up our souls, inserting them into the movement of history and the movement of mankind toward the total Christ." See Rabut, O.P., *Teilhard de Chardin: A Critical Study* (New York: Sheed and Ward Ltd, 1961), p. 197.

Ecumenism

If history, as Teilhard thinks, is the history of the evolution and progress towards unity, ecumenism is going to be an important chapter in this history, especially when ecumenism is understood as a global reality and not limited, as understood today, to the unification of the Christian Churches. Therefore, ecumenism should mean the unification of everything with everything. Even matter itself should no longer be seen as something different from spirit precisely because the world is "The Divine Milieu."

Ecumenism will occur. Teilhard wrote: "At this moment a form of ecumenism is trying to assert itself: it is inevitably tied up with the psychic maturing of the earth, and therefore it will certainly come."[14]

Teilhard sees two kinds of ecumenism. He explained:

> (summit-ecumenism) 1, between Christians, concerned to bring out an ultra-orthodox and ultra-human Christianity, on a truly "cosmic" scale.
>
> (basal-ecumenism) 2, between men in general, concerned to define and extend the foundations of a common human "faith" in the future of mankind.[15]

But what stops humanity from joining together in this ecumenism at this time of history? The reason is, according to Teilhard, we still lack a "clear perception" of God and the "type of humanity" we really want. The right time of maturity that will allow ecumenism to occur did not arrive yet.[16]

For Teilhard, then, ecumenism does not mean the unification of Christians only, but it is a general notion for the unification of humanity. This unification will succeed when we develop a common project for the future. We must strive to grow for, as Teilhard put it, "all striving makes for nearness, not only within a corporate body but heart to heart."[17]

One of the ways for growing is to share with others, participate in their own growth, and maintain a healthy interaction with them without having the feeling of losing our own individuality, or feeling the fear of fusion with them. By being closer to others, we will grow in maturity and this will allow us to no longer feel the need to look back to the past and

---

[14] SC, p. 197 -- IX, p. 253.
[15] SC, p. 198 -- IX, p. 254.
[16] See SC, p. 198 -- IX, p. 254.
[17] FM, p. 143 -- V, p. 174.

search some common ground upon which we can agree, which is a poor method that makes everyone involved poor in the long run. Ecumenism is not a compromise. Ecumenism is a project to carry out in the future which makes everyone involved richer and that is because each one becomes more personal and more oneself by taking advantage of the common good resulting from the unification. Moreover, this will make the union richer also, because of the fact of putting collectively all the riches acquired by the different members through the years or centuries of their own histories.

Indeed, to have the windows of one's house wide open to the winds coming from all the corners of the earth is something that can be healthy. One can learn from all religions, all civilizations, all different social systems and convictions, and all individual actions and behaviors; one can be enriched and transformed by the experiences of others without giving up one's own identity and one's own faith.

The idea of a return to some kind of original monism of the early humanity in order to find unity is no longer something that can be considered. Today, we must see things from a different angle. With our new ways of thinking, feeling, and being, we are headed towards experiencing new forms of community and unity that are at the same time more pluralistic and more one, more universal and more particular, more differentiated and more unified, more futuristic and more complex, and where separations and oppositions of the past tend to disappear.

Teilhard's approach to the general ecumenism can be considered an inspiring step forward towards world peace.

Cosmogenesis

What is wrong with the world? Why does humanity look as if it is validating the ancient proverb "*Homo homini Lupus est*" (Man is wolf to man) and later adopted by modern philosophers, especially Thomas Hobbs? Why do we seem to be living the Sartrian conviction that hell is other people, or the Heidegger's definition that the human being is "being-toward-death"? Why are we always in a state of ultimate frustration and always living in a state of meaninglessness and emptiness?

One reason could be because of the fact of our limitedness, imperfection, and unfinished growth and evolution. Another reason could be because of our clinging to our ego and our rejection of anyone that does not serve our interests. Another reason could be our refusal to join together to build the earth and structure a better humanity.[18] These reasons and many more are true. Teilhard offered another answer. He stated it like this:

> This, then, is *the word that gives freedom*: it is not enough for man to throw off his self-love and *live as a social being*. *He needs to live* with his whole heart in union with the totality of the world that carries him along, *cosmically*.[19]

Indeed, "I" is, in fact, "we." We can never disconnect ourselves from the whole, even though we sometimes think we can. When we believe we can, we create the conditions that make hell on earth instead of peace on earth.

Once we drop the false belief of disconnection, we will see messengers continuously linking and bonding everything to everything else. Let us look around and read existence itself. Birds singing, flowers blossoming, stars twinkling, human hearts loving, hands shaking… all these instances, and thousands more, are messages. Touch a single leaf of a single tree and you have thereby touched the farthest star. That is because we exist in a cosmic net where nothing is unrelated and where we form with the whole an organic unity. "We are not like flowers in a bunch," Teilhard said, "but the leaves and flowers of a great tree, on which each appears at its time and place, according to the demands of the All."[20]

The universe, with all our human activities ceaselessly evolving and growing, becomes, according to Teilhard, "no longer an *order* but a *process*. No longer a cosmos but a cosmogenesis."[21] It is only in a

---

[18] Benjamin T. Hourani came correctly to the following observation. He wrote: "A superficial reading of Teilhard might suggest that he is non-political. In the ordinary sense of politics this is generally true. In fact, however, he is deeply political and even revolutionary. His effort to create 'a new concept of human activity' turns upside-down many long-held beliefs. It aims at destroying the old synthesis which he believed was becoming deranged. His politics is based on his notion that man is 'evolution conscious of itself' with all the responsibility for action to be borne by man…. Teilhard… calls for a new global order. What he envisages is never spelled out as he limits himself only to developing a concept of human activity which allows further evolution toward human liberation and unanimity. However the general thrust of his thought is in the direction of *a confederal union which differentiates rather than an organic unity of merger in which all identities dissolve*." See Benjamin T. Hourani, "Teilhard's Political Ecumene Empire or Commonwealth" in Leo Zonneveld and Robert Muller, ed., *The Desire to Be Human*, "International Teilhard Compendium" Centenary volume (Netherlands: Mirananda Publishers b.v. Wassenaar, 1983), pp. 210, 219.

[19] WTW, p. 27 -- XII, p. 33.

[20] HE, p. 49 -- VI, p. 62.

[21] AE, p. 272 -- VII, p. 282.

"cosmogenesis of union," said also Teilhard, "in which everything, by structure, became inflexibly lovable and loving,"[22] that we feel that there is a meaning for our individual existence. Because the "individual" exists no more. *We* are in the *All*. We are healed by one another. We are healed by mystical love. We are in another state of consciousness. We are in the cosmogenesis process. Each and every one of us is supposed to be "God's gift to the world," as Louis M. Savary wrote:

> If we assume that each person is God's gift to the world and that Divine Spirit is at all times giving life and meaning to every element of the divine milieu, then we can presume that Creative Spirit has been working to provide the perfect environment, timing, and connections, so that each person can fulfill his or her unique role and purpose in building the Body of Christ (the evolving universe).[23]

This is also the mystical path that John A. Grim and Mary Evelyn Tucker talked about when they wrote:

> For Teilhard the mystical path leads to a sense of evolution in which individual personalization converges from the meridians of overwhelming plurality toward centration on a powerful intuition of the whole. This whole, for Teilhard, is the Divine Milieu within which we live, and breathe, and have our becoming.[24]

We know we have been made for more – infinitely more. We are talking about a project of "divinization" – a word that Teilhard used for the word "deification" that was used by the Greek Fathers many centuries before him. We are talking about a true cosmogenesis that becomes a true Christogenesis, that is, the formation of the Universal Christ.[25] In all this

---

[22] AE, p. 266 -- VII, p. 275.
[23] See Louis M. Savary, *Expanding Teilhard's 'Complexity-Consciousness' Law* (American Teilhard Association, "Teilhard Studies" Number 68, Spring 2014), pp. 14-15.
[24] See John A. Grim and Mary Evelyn Tucker, *Teilhard's Vision of Evolution* (American Teilhard Association, "Teilhard Studies" Number 50, Spring 2005), p. 14.
[25] The last lines of "The Mass on the World" that Teilhard wrote in 1923 end with this prayer: "For me, my God, all joy and all achievement, the very purpose of my being and all my love of life, all depend on this one basic vision of the union between yourself and the universe. Let others, fulfilling a function more august than mine, proclaim your splendours as pure Spirit; as for me, dominated as I am by a vocation which springs from the inmost fibres of my being, I have no desire, I have no ability, to proclaim anything except the innumerable prolongations of your

continuous process, Teilhard helps us to identify the formidable, driving, and centrating energy—Omega[26]—with God who is the omnipotent, omnipresent, omniscient, the most transforming power, and whose true definition, according to saint John, is LOVE.[27] Through, in, and by this Love, peace becomes "possible," "certain," "inevitable," "indivisible," "dynamic," and "cosmic."[28]

---

incarnate Being in the world of matter; I can preach only the mystery of your flesh, you the Soul shining forth through all that surrounds us. It is to your body in this its fullest extension—that is, to the world become through your power and my faith the glorious living crucible in which everything melts away in order to be born anew; it is to this that I dedicate myself with all the resources which your creative magnetism has brought forth in me..." (HU, pp. 36-37 -- XIII, pp.155-156). To this prayer and many other prayers, Agustin Udias offers the following comment: "The text of his prayers clearly shows that his Christology was not only the result of theological reflection, but, above all, the fruit of a deep mystical experience. For him, neither can Christ be conceived separated from the universe nor can the universe be separated from Christ. Teilhard lived this presence of Christ in the world with an ardent passion and tried to share it with those with whom he came into contact despite all the misunderstanding and suspicion he encountered." See Agustin Udias, SJ, *Christogenesis: The Development of Teilhard's Cosmic Christology* (American Teilhard Association, "Teilhard Studies" Number 59, Fall 2009), p. 18.

[26] Teilhard clearly identified this evolutionary force by saying: "Christ-Omega: the Christ... who animates and gathers up all the biological and spiritual energies developed by the universe. Finally, then, Christ the evolver." (SC, p. 167 -- IX, p. 212).

[27] See 1 John 4:16.

[28] Please see chapter "Is Peace Possible?"

Conclusion

The Peace Revolution

The question that Teilhard de Chardin asked in his essay, "The Rise of the Other,"[1] written in 1942, should not surprise anyone who is aware of the ideas of "the greatest prophet of this age,"[2] as he was called. The question was: "If we are to be able to love one another must we not first *effect a change of plane?*"[3] Then he answered throughout his writings that "A new way of seeing, combined with a new way of acting – that is what we need,"[4] "… struck at its source, the conflict will die of its own accord, never to break out again,"[5] and "We are standing, at the present moment, not only at a change of century and civilization, but a *change of epoch.*"[6]

In order to reach this new way of seeing and acting that allows peace to prevail on earth, a revolution in human consciousness must occur. Such a revolution is far from being a bloody revolution – a bloody revolution seems often concerned with changing regimes and leaderships more than with working for the very causes the revolutionaries usually pretend to want to achieve. Teilhard's convictions are much deeper than that, and far beyond this kind of circumstantial reasoning.

The revolution that Teilhard is talking about is the most radical and everlasting revolution there is; it is the revolution in which everyone is a winner because everyone has learned to love.[7] There are no limitation or conditions to this, because it has the spark of the Divine and the Absolute.

---

[1] AE, pp. 59-75 -- VII, pp. 65-81.
[2] Joseph Needham, FRS, FBA, Director of the East Asian History of Science Library, Cambridge, President, Teilhard Centre for the Future of Man, London, in Foreword for Ursula King, *Toward a New Mysticism: Teilhard de Chardin and Eastern Religions,* (New York: Seabury Press, 1980), p. 7.
[3] AE, p. 74 -- VII, p. 81.
[4] AE, p. 295 -- VII, p. 308.
[5] AE, p. 20 -- VII, p. 26.
[6] VP, p. 75 -- III, p. 107.
[7] Teilhard de Chardin wrote: "Indeed, at the rate that consciousness and its ambitions are increasing, the world will explode if it does not learn to love" (VP, p. 214 -- VII, p. 300).

Welcome to the peace revolution -- the revolution in the making.

Come and join this revolutionary moment in the history of humanity, and help make peace a way of life that is not only possible, but also necessary, urgent, inevitable, indivisible, and cosmic. Let us make it a collaborative effort; I will do my part, you will do your part, and everyone will do his or her part. How? By individually and collectively adding, each and every day, one extra step in being more loving to each other, more understanding, and more human. Let us make a "human front"[8] whose aim is to change our culture in the most profound and radical way.

Imagine a world where:

* A higher consciousness – individually and collectively – is the common ground for understanding others and dealing with them.
* Individuals complete and enrich each other; "No Man Is an Island."[9] The individual is part of a larger whole. Everyone needs and wants to belong to a community. Wholeness is at the heart of life. Wholeness is healthy and life giving and, in its very core, it is the experience of oneness. We were born and we will remain relational. The "I" and the "Thou" exist and find a healthy way to interact with each other, and if not, they are inevitably going to perish together.
* Nations help each other to grow and develop in all aspects of life -- spiritually, culturally, economically, and structurally.
* A "human front"[10] is formed to confront the common dangers that the human race may face, and for the progress in all fields of knowledge and technology that benefit everyone and without excluding anyone.
* Civil discourses and respectful dialogues in each community and each nation, seeking always common ground and consensus on controversial issues, are the everyday practices.
* A sincere acceptance of the diversity of opinions and people, of the reality of "Union differentiates,"[11] and of the understanding that it is because we are different that we can form the unity that does not necessarily mean uniformity, is adopted.
* Human rights are interpreted correctly, honored, and developed.

---

[8] SC, p. 145 -- IX, p. 185.
[9] This is a poem written by John Donne. This is also a title of a book written by Thomas Merton.
[10] SC, p. 145 -- IX, p. 185.
[11] Please see chapter "Union Differentiates" of this book.

- * The "not-yet" future that is always at the horizon of the visions of individuals and of the world, is constantly approached by allowing them to become "more."[12]
- * Religions are meant to help live a good, fulfilled, and divine life. They are not meant, by any means, to discriminate and/or "kill" people physically, intellectually, or even spiritually.
- * A promotion of a culture of peace replaces a culture of violence, making sure that a special and prominent place is reserved, in our different studies, for a curriculum specializing in peace studies.
- * Movies, songs, games, television, books, newspapers, and magazines portray methods for peaceful resolution conflicts.
- * We realize that an authentic "inner ecology" is even more urgent than an outer ecology. Getting rid of all kinds of prejudices, fears, greed, and false "gods," can be, on the surface, a hurtful practice, but it is, at its very core and purpose, a healing one. A "moral surgery," such as this, is like a physical surgery; it hurts, but it heals.
- * Taking advantage of the "noosphere"[13] reality, promoted by technology and the media that help develop a collective consciousness, fosters and advances the cause of peace instead of promoting reasons for war.
- * All our leaders learn to work for the common good, always putting the interests of others before their own interests, and seeking always what is right, even if it was unpopular, over what is wrong, even if it was approved and celebrated by a majority.
- * We realize that we, all of us as the human race, are one humanity in one universe, and together we form one front for "building the earth."[14]
- * We know that, since we live in a "divine milieu,"[15] we should act as true members of that collective entity where we belong. "[We] can be saved," wrote Teilhard, "only by becoming one with the universe."[16]

---

[12] VP, p. 72 -- III, p. 103.
[13] Please see chapter "The Cyberpeace Way" of this book.
[14] See *Building the Earth* by Teilhard de Chardin (Wilkes-Barre, Pa.: Dimension Books, Inc., 1965).
[15] Please see chapter "The Divine Milieu: Our Home" of this book.
[16] CE, p. 128 -- X, pp. 148-149. Ilia Delio offered here the following interesting comment: "Teilhard de Chardin believed that 'we can be saved only by becoming one with the universe' [CE, p.128]. The problem, as he saw it, is the inability to resolve the conflict between the traditional God of revelation and the "new" God

* We are aware of the divine project: God created us to be co-creators. Therefore we have the mission to be builders not destructors. We are called to make a positive difference in the world. We are called to do whatever we can that will increase the consciousness of and in society, take care of others and their environments, and being the peace that is extended to others and to the whole creation.
* The whole universe is converging on the ultimate "Omega Point"[17] where it is supposed to be totally centered and unified. It is toward that ultimate point of unity that the whole creation – now "new heavens and a new earth, where righteousness is at home"[18] – is moving. With Christ a new stage of evolution took place and the birth of a new humanity occurred. "The whole creation and humanity," explained Bede Griffiths, "is created precisely for this unity in God through Christ."[19]
* A loving heart embraces everyone as a divine gift.
* There are existential understanding and realization that "The physical structure of the universe is love,"[20] that "Love is the most universal, the most tremendous and the most mysterious of the cosmic forces,"[21] that "The most telling and profound way of describing the evolution of the universe would undoubtedly be to trace the evolution of love,"[22] that "Love one another or you perish,"[23] and that "'Love one another'… the most powerful, and in

---

of evolution or to see salvation as becoming one with the universe. N. Max Wildiers writes, 'The conflict we are suffering today does indeed consist in the conflict between a religion of transcendence and a secularized world, between the 'God of the Above' and the 'God of the Ahead,' between a 'religion of heaven' and a 'religion of the earth'' ["Foreword," in CE, p.10]. Teilhard's solution to the problem of the God-world conflict is to rid ourselves of the old God of the starry heavens and embrace the God of evolution. Only in this way, he indicates, is God truly revealed in the world, which is a 'divine milieu.' To reject evolution is, in a sense, to reject God because God is the power of evolution, Omega, who is within and ahead." (Ilia Delio, OSF, *Making All Things New: Catholicity, Cosmology, Consciousness* (Maryknoll, N. Y.: Orbis Books, 2015), p. 93.

[17] Please see chapter "The Future Has a Goal" of this book.
[18] 2 Peter 3:13.
[19] Bede Griffiths, *A New Vision of Reality: Western Science, Eastern Mysticism and Christian Faith* (Springfield, IL: Templegate Publishers, 1989, 1990), p.110.
[20] HE, p. 72 -- VI, p. 90.
[21] HE, p. 32 -- VI, p. 40.
[22] HE, p. 33 -- VI, p. 41.
[23] HE, p. 153 -- VI, p. 189.

fact the *only* imaginable, principle of the earth's future equilibrium ... the only true peace."[24]
* History is no longer a history of wars and conquerors and criminals. History is the history of love. History is "Christogenesis."[25] "Christ is all and in all."[26]

Is this a utopian dream or what?

Dr. J. Needham correctly wrote: "I should say without any hesitation that Father Teilhard was called to be the greatest prophet of this age. That will become more and more clear, I believe, as time goes on."[27] Therefore what has been said is not a fiction story or just a series of good wishes. Not for a mystic. Especially, not for Teilhard. This is a real realm of becoming. The mystic sees the invisible. The mystic sees things happening, centuries before they occur. Teilhard, the mystic, is the radical realist.

"Love one another or you perish"[28] and "'Love one another'... the only true peace."[29] This is the ideal. This ideal is not a kind of utopian, chimerical, and unreachable goal. It is rather the most realistic solution for our never-ending crises and almost ceaseless wars.[30] It is so, precisely because "The physical structure of the universe is love"[31] and because love is the very definition of God – "God is love."[32] History has proven, time and time again, that what was and is really utopian, chimerical, and unrealistic, was and is to find solutions for wars outside the very realm of love. Whatever solution we came up with throughout the centuries may have worked for a while, or did not work at all—how many treaties were violated and short lived! How many wars were declared in the name of peace and "to just have peace!" We, therefore, have every reason to believe that it may not work in the future either. Only a true and genuine love will work. There is no bigger revolution than the revolution of love.

---

[24] AE, p. 20 -- VII, p. 26.
[25] HM, p. 90 -- XIII, p. 104.
[26] Colossians 3:11.
[27] Joseph Needham, FRS, FBA, Director of the East Asian History of Science Library, Cambridge, President, Teilhard Centre for the Future of Man, London, in Foreword for Ursula King, *Toward a New Mysticism: Teilhard de Chardin and Eastern Religions,* (New York: Seabury Press, 1980), p. 7.
[28] HE, p. 153 -- VI, p. 189.
[29] AE, p. 20 -- VII, p. 26.
[30] Some people dare to say that the number of years, in the recorded human history, in which no countries, cities or tribes were at war cannot be more than 300 years.
[31] HE, p. 72 -- VI, p. 90.
[32] 1 John 4:16.

There is no bigger security than the security of love.[33] There is no bigger peace than the peace of love. Could and should we perhaps say that peace is security's love, or even better, love's security? This is the kind of peace that goes to, and with, the very core of our being where God dwells.

"Love one another ... the most powerful, and in fact the *only* imaginable, principle of the earth's future equilibrium ... the only true peace."[34]

---

[33] "Nothing can bring a real sense of security into the home except true love." This suggestion written by Billy Graham can be extended to groups and nations as well.
[34] AE, p. 20 -- VII, p. 26.

CHRONOLOGY OF PIERRE TEILHARD DE CHARDIN'S LIFE

1881	Pierre Teilhard de Chardin is born on May 1 in Sarcenat, France. He was the fourth child of eleven brothers and sisters.
1892-1897	He is a student at the Jesuit Collège de Notre-Dame de Mongré.
1897	He receives a baccalauréat de philosophie.
1898	He receives a baccalauréat de mathématiques.
1899	On March 20, he enters the Jesuit noviciate at Aix-en-Provence.
1901	On March 25, he pronouces his first vows at Laval.
1902	He receives his licence ès lettres.
1902-1905	He studies philosophy at la maison Saint-Louis (Jersey).
1905-1908	He is appointed professor of chemistry and physics at le college secondaire Jésuite de la Sainte-Famille, in Cairo. He makes several scientific excursions.
1908-1912	He studies theology at "Ore Place" (Hastings, Sussex, England).
1911	On August 24, he is ordained a priest.
1912	He starts working with the celebrated paleontologist, Marcellin Boule, in Paris.

1913	He makes a scientific excursion to Spain with l'abbé Breuil.
1914	He is mobilized to the 13th section of infirmary of the army.
1915-1917	He is a stretcher-bearer. He receives the military medal and the Legion of Honor.
1918	He pronounces his solemn vows at Sainte-Foy-lès-Lyon.
1919	He is demobilized.
1919-1920	He receives his certificates in geology, botany, and zoology.
1922	He defends his doctoral dissertation ès sciences, and is appointed to a teaching position in Geology at L'Institut Catholique de Paris.
1923	He travels to China.
1924	He returns to France. He loses his teaching position at L'Institut Catholique de Paris.
1925	Beginning of an exile that lasted about 20 years.
1926	Departure to China.
1927-1928	Stay in France.
1929-1933	He takes several trips and scientific expeditions to Central Asia, U.S.A., Hawaii, Japan, The Gobi Desert, and London. In February 1932, his father dies. In September 1932, he returns to France for four months.
1933	He travels to China and the U.S.A.
1934-1936	He travels to the Tibetan border. He returns to France. He travels again to India, the Red Sea, Cashmir, and Bandung. In February 1936, his mother dies, and in August, his sister Marguerite-Marie dies.

1937-1939	He takes trips to U.S.A., France, China, Burma, Java, and Vancouver.
1939-1946	He has a long stay in China because of World War II.
1940	He co-founds, with Father Pierre Leroy, the Geo-biologic Institute of Peking.
1943	He creates, with Father Pierre Leroy, the Geo-biology magazine, *Geobiologia*.
1946	He returns to France.
1947	He is called to Rome and is refused a position at Le College de France. On June 1, he has a heart attack.
1948	He travels to the U.S.A., then returns to France.
1949	He has pleurisy. He travels to Rome.
1950	He is elected a member of L'Institut de France (Académie des sciences).
1951	He takes a trip to South Africa, then he returns to the U.S.A. where he continues to work with the Wenner Foundation in New York.
1952-1953	He takes trips to southern U.S.A. and to South Africa.
1954	He returns to France for two months. This was his last trip to his homeland.
1955	On April 10, Easter Sunday in New York, Teilhard dies suddenly at the age of 74. He is buried in the Jesuit Noviciate Cemetery, some forty miles away from New York City.

BIBLIOGRAPHY

I- Works by Pierre Teilhard De Chardin

Beside Teilhard's correspondence that has been published by different publishers, his main works have been published by Editions du Seuil, Paris, in a series of thirteen volumes entitled "ŒUVRES DE PIERRE TEILHARD DE CHARDIN."

A- *Œuvres de Pierre Teilhard de Chardin, Editions du Seuil, Paris*

I - *Le Phénomène Humain*. 1955. Eng. trans. *The Phenomenon of Man* by Bernard Wall. New York: Harper & Row, 1959. Also *The Human Phenomenon*. Trans. by Sarah Appleton-Weber. Sussex Academic Press, 2003.

II - *L'Apparition de l'Homme*. 1956. Eng. trans. *The Appearance of Man* by J.M. Cohen. New York: Harper & Row, 1965.

III - *La Vision du Passé*. 1957. Eng. trans. *The Vision of the Past* by J.M. Cohen. New York: Harper & Row, 1966.

IV - *Le Milieu Divin*. 1957. Eng. trans. *The Divine Milieu*. New York: Harper & Row, 1960. Revised Harper Torchbook edition published 1968 by Harper & Row, Publishers.

V - *L'Avenir de l'Homme*, 1959. Eng. trans. *The Future of Man* by Norman Denny. New York: Harper & Row, 1964.

VI - *L'Energie Humaine*, 1962. Eng. trans. *Human Energy* by J.M. Cohen. New York and London: Harcourt Brace Jovanovich, 1969.

VII - *L'Activation de l'Energie*. 1963. Eng. trans. *Activation of Energy* by René Hague. New York and London: Harcourt Brace Jovanovich, 1970.

VIII - *La Place de l'Homme dans la Nature: Le Groupe Zoologique Humain*. 1977. (Editions Albin Michel, 1956). Eng. trans. *Man's Place in Nature* by René Hague. New York: Harper & Row, 1966.

IX - *Science et Christ*. 1965. Eng. trans. *Science and Christ* by René Hague. New York: Harper & Row, 1968.

X - *Comment Je Crois*. 1969. Eng. trans. *Christianity and Evolution* by René Hague. New York and London: Harcourt Brace Jovanovich, 1971.

XI - *Les Directions de l'Avenir*. 1973. Eng. trans. *Towards the Future* by René Hague. New York and London: Harcourt Brace Jovanovich, 1975.

XII - *Ecrits du Temps de la Guerre*. 1976. (Also by Editions Bernard Grasset, 1965.) Eng. trans. *Writings in Time of War* by René Hague. London and New York: Collins and Harper & Row, 1968.

XIII - *Le Cœur de la Matière*. 1976. Eng. trans. *The Heart of Matter* by René Hague. New York and London: Harcourt Brace Jovanovich, 1978. (It also contains 5 essays that first appeared in the French edition of *Ecrits du Temps de la Guerre.)*

B- Letters

Lettres de Voyage (1923-1955), Paris: Bernard Grasset, 1956. Eng. trans. *Letters from a Traveller*. London and New York: Harper Torchbooks, Collins and Harper & Row, 1962.

Genèse d'une Pensée (Lettres, 1914-1919), Paris: Bernard Grasset Editeur, 1961. Eng. Trans. *The Making of a Mind. Letters from a Soldier-Priest (1914-1919)* by René Hague. New York: Harper & Row, 1965.

Lettres d'Egypte (1905-1908). France: Editions Aubier-Montaigne, 1965.

Lettres à Léontine Zanta. Bruges, Belgique: Desclée de Brouwer, 1965. Eng. trans. *Letters to Leontine Zanta* by Bernard Wall. New York: Harper & Row, 1969.

Lettres d'Hastings et de Paris (1908-1914), Aubier-Montaigne, 1965.

Blondel et Teilhard de Chardin. Correspondance commentée par H. de Lubac. Paris: Beauchesne, 1965. Eng. trans. *Pierre Teilhard de Chardin, Maurice Blondel: Correspondence* by William Whitman. New York: Herder and Herder, 1967.

Accomplir l'Homme: Lettres Inédites (1926-1952), Paris: Editions Bernard Grasset, 1968. Eng. trans. *Letters to two Friends (1926-1952).* New York: The New American Library, 1968.

Dans le Sillage des Siranthropes. Lettres Inédites de Pierre Teilhard de Chardin et J. Gunnar Anderson présentées par Pierre Leroy (1919-1934). Fayard, 1971.

Lettres Intimes à Auguste Valensin, Bruno de Solages, Henri de Lubac, André Ravier (1919-1955). Paris: Editions Aubier-Montaigne, 1974.

Lettres Familières de Pierre Teilhard de Chardin Mon Ami (1948-1955), présentées par Pierre Leroy. France: Editions du Centurion, 1976.

Lettres à Jeanne Mortier. Paris: Editions du Seuil, 1984.

Lettres Inédites. Lettres à l'Abbé Gaudefroy et à l'Abbé Breuil. Monaco: Editions du Rocher, Jean-Paul Bertrand, Editeur, 1988.

The Letters of Teilhard de Chardin & Lucile Swan. Edited by Thomas M. King, S.J., and Mary Wood Gilbert. Washington, D.C.: Georgetown University Press, 1993.

C- Other Works and Selected Writings

Etre Plus. (Directives extraites des écrits publiés ou inédits du père, de sa correspondance et de ses notes). Paris: Editions du Seuil, 1968.

Hymne de l'Univers. Paris: Editions du Seuil, 1961. English trans. *Hymn of the Universe* by Gerald Vann, O.P. London and New York: Collins and Harper & Row, 1965.

Let Me Explain. Texts selected and arranged by Jean-Pierre Demoulin. Trans. by René Hague and others. New York: Harper & Row, Publishers, 1970. *Je m'explique.* Paris: Editions du Seuil, 1966.

Pierre Teilhard de Chardin: Journal. (26 août 1915 – 4 janvier 1919). Text integral publié par Nicole et Karl Schmitz-Moormann. France: Librairie Arthème Fayard, 1975.

Pierre Teilhard de Chardin. Writings Selected with an Introduction by Ursula King. Maryknoll, N.Y: Orbis Books, "Modern Spiritual Masters Series", 1999.

Teilhard de Chardin : Reconciliation in Christ. Selected Spiritual Writings introduced and edited by Jean Maalouf. Hyde Park, N.Y.: New City Press, 2002.

D- *Chronology of Teilhard de Chardin's Works*

(Note: Limited only to the 13 volumes of the "OEUVRES" and the *Hymn de l'Univers*, published by Editions du Seuil. Roman numbers indicate the volume of the "OEUVRES" where the essay can be found, and capital letters indicate the title of the book in its English translation.)

1913   La préhistoire et ses Progrès, II – The Progress of Preshistory, AM.

1916   La Vie cosmique, XII – Cosmic Life, WTW.
La Maîtrise du Monde et le Règne de Dieu, XII – Mastery of the World and the Kingdom of God, WTW.
Le Christ dans la Matière. Trois Histoires comme Benson, XII – Christ in the World of Matter. Three stories in the Style of Benson, HU.

1917   La Lutte contre la Multitude. Interprétation possible de la figure du Monde, XII – The Struggle against the Multitude. A Possible Interpretation of the Form of the World, WTW.
Le Milieu mystique, XII – The Mystical Milieu, WTW.
La Nostalgie du Front, XII – Nostalgia of the Front, HM.
L'Union créatrice, XII – Creative Union, WTW.

1918   L'Ame du Monde, XII – The Soul of the World, WTW. La Grande Monade (Manuscrit trouvé dans une tranchée), XII – The Great Monad (A Manuscript Found in a Trench), HM.
L'Eternel Féminin, XII – The Eternal Feminine, WTW.
Mon Univers, XII – My Universe, HM.

Le Prêtre, XII – The Priest, WTW.
La Foi qui opère, XII – Operative Faith, WTW.
Forma Christi, XII – Forma Christi, WTW.
Note sur "L'Elément Universel" du Monde, XII – Note on the 'Universal Element' of the World, WTW.

1919 Sur la notion de Transformation créatrice, X – On the Notion of Creative Transformation, CE.
Note sur l'union physique entre l'Humanité du Christ et les fidèles au cours de la sanctification, X – Note on the Physical Union between the Humanity of Christ and the Faithful in the Course of Their Sanctification, CE.
Note pour servir à l'Evangelisation des Temps nouveaux, XII – Note on the Presentation of the Gospel in a New Age, HM.
Terre Promise, XII – The Promised Land, WTW.
L'Elément universel, XII – The Universal Element, WTW.
Les Noms de la Matière, XII – The Names of Matter, HM.
La Puissance spirituelle de la Matière, XII – The Spiritual Power of Matter, HU.

1920 Note sur l'essence du Transformisme, XIII – Note on the Essence of Transformism, HM.
Note sur le Christ-universel, IX – Note on the Universal Christ, SC.
Note sur les Modes de l'Action Divine dans l'Univers, X – Note on the Modes of Divine Action in the Universe, CE.
Chute, Rédemption et Géocentrie, X – Fall, Redemption, and Geocentrism, CE.
Note sur le Progrès, V – A Note on Progress, FM.

1921 Sur mon attitude vis-à-vis de l'Eglise officielle, XIII – On My Attitude to the Official Church, HM.
Science et Christ (ou Analyse et Synthèse). Remarques sur la manière dont l'étude scientifique de la Matière peut et doit servir à remonter jusqu'au Centre Divin, IX – Science and Christ or Analysis and Synthesis. Remarks on the way in which the scientific study of matter can and must help to lead us up to the divine centre, SC.
Les Hommes Fossiles. A propos d'un livre récent, II – Fossil Men. Reflections on a Recent Book, AM.

Comment se pose aujourd'hui la question du transformisme, III – How the Transformist Question Presents Itself Today, VP
La Face de la Terre, III – The Face of the Earth, VP.

1922 Note sur quelques représentations historiques possibles du péché originel, X – Note on Some Possible Historical Representations of Origianal Sin, CE.

1923 La Messe sur le Monde, XIII – The Mass on the World, HM and HU.
Panthéisme et Christianisme, X – Pantheism and Christianity, CE.
La paléontologie et l'Apparition de l'Homme, II – Paleontology and the Appearance of Man, AM.
La Loi d'irréversibilité en évolution, III – On the Law of Irreversibility in Evolution, VP.

1924 Mon Univers, IX – My Universe, SC.
Texte sur la fin du monde, V – The End of the World, FM.

1925 L'Histoire naturelle du Monde. Réflexions sur la valeur et l'avenir de la systématique, III – The Natural History of the World. Reflexions on the Value and Future of Systematics, VP.
Le Paradoxe transformiste. A propos de la dernière critique du transformisme par M. Vialleton, III –The Transformist Paradox. On the Latest Criticism by M. Vialleton, VP.
L'Hominisation. Introduction à une étude scientifique du Phénomène humain, III – Hominization. Introduction to a Scientific Study of the Phenomenon of Man, VP.

1926 Sur l'Apparence nécessairement discontinue de toute série évolutive, III – On the Necessarily Discontinuous Appearance of Every Evolutionary Series, VP.
Les Fondements et le Fond de l'idée d'évolution, III – The Basis and Foundations of the Idea of Evolution, VP.

1926-27 (révisé en 1932) Le Milieu Divin, IV (en entier) – The Divine Milieu, DM.

1928	Les Mouvements de la Vie, III – The Movements of Life, VP. Allocution pour le mariage d'Odette Bacot et Jean Teilhard d'Evry, XIII – At the Wedding of Odette Bacot and Jean Teilhard d'Evry, HM. Le Phénomène humain, IX – The Phenomenon of Man, SC.
1929	Le Sens humain, XI – The Sense of Man, TF.
1930	Que faut-il penser du Transformisme? III – What Should We Think of Transformism? VP. Une importante découverte de paléontologie humaine: Le Sinanthropus Pekinensis, II – Sinanthropus Pekinensis. An Important Discovery in Human Palaeontology, AM. Le Phénomène humain, III – The Phenomenon of Man, VP.
1931	L'Esprit de la Terre, VI – The Spirit of the Earth, HE.
1932	La Place de l'Homme dans la Nature, III – Man's Place in Nature, VP. La Route de l'ouest. Vers une mystique nouvelle, XI – The Road of the West: To a New Mysticism, TF.
1933	La Signification de la Valeur contructrice de la Souffrance, VI – The Significance and Positive Value of Suffering, HE. Le Christianisme dans le Monde, IX – Christianity in the World, SC. L'Incroyance moderne. Cause profonde et Remède, IX -- Modern Unbelief. Its Underlying Cause and Remedy, SC. Christologie et Evolution, X – Christology and Evolution, CE.
1934	L'Evolution de la Chasteté, XI – The Evolution of Chastity, TF. Les Fouilles préhistoriques de Peking, II – The Prehistoric Excavations of Peking, AM. Comment je crois, X – How I Believe, CE.
1935	La Faune pléistocène et l'Ancienneté de l'Homme en Amerique du Nord, II – The Pleistocene Fauna and the Age of Man in North America, AM. Allocution pour le mariage d'Eliane Basse et d'Hervé de la Goublaye de Menorval, XIII – At the Wedding of M. and Mme de la Goublaye de Ménorval, HM. La Découverte du Passé, III – The Discovery of the Past, VP.

1936 Esquisse d'un Univers personnel, VI – Sketch of a Personalistic Universe, HE.
Quelques réflexions sur la conversion du Monde. A l'Usage d'un Prince de l'Eglise, IX – Some Reflexions on the Conversion of the World, SC.
Sauvons l'Humanité. Réflexion sur la crise présente, IX – The Salvation of Mankind. Thoughts on the Present Crisis, SC.

1937 Le Phénomène spirituel, VI – The Phenonmenon of Spirituality, HE.
La Découverte du Sinanthrope, II – The Discovery of inanthropus, AM.
L'Energie Humaine, VI -- Human Energy, HE.

1938 Hérédité sociale et éducation. Notes sur la valeur humano-chrétienne de l'enseignement, V – Social Heredity and Progress. Notes on the Human-Christian Value of Education, FM.

1938-1940 (Remanié et complété en 1947 et 1948) Le Phénomène Humain, I (en entier) – The Phenomenon of Man, PM.

1939 La Grande Option, V – The Grand Option, FM.
Comment comprendre et utiliser l'Art dans la ligne de l'Energie humaine, XI – The Function of Art as an Expression of Human Energy, TF.
La Mystique de la Science, VI – The Mystic of Science, HE.
Quelques vues générales sur l'essence du christianisme, X – Some General Views on the Essence of Christianity, CE.
Les Unités humaines naturelles. Essai d'une Biologie et d'une Morale des races, III – The Natural Units of Humanity. An Attempt to outline a Racial Biology and Morality, VP.
L'Heure de choisir. Un sens possible de la guerre, VII – The Moment of Choice. A Possible Interpretation of War, AE.

1940 La Parole attendue, XI – The Awaited Word, TF.

1941 Réflexions sur le Progrès, V – Some Reflections on Progress, FM.
L'Atomisme de l'Esprit. Un essai pour comprendre la structure de l'étoffe de l'Univers, VII – The Atomism of Spirit. An Attempt to Understand the Structure of the Stuff of the Universe, AE.

1942 Note sur la notion de Perfection chrétienne, XI – A Note on the Concept of Christian Perfection, TF.
La Montée de l'Autre, VII – The Rise of the Other, AE.
L'Esprit nouveau. I. Le Cône du Temps. II. La Transposition "Conique" de l'Action, V – The New Spirit, FM.
Universalisation et Union: Un effort pour voir clair, VII – Universalization and Union. An Attempt at Clarifications, AE.
Le Christ évoluteur ou un développement logique de la notion de Redemption. Réflexions sur la nature de "l'Action formelle" du Christ dans le Monde, X – Christ the Evolver, or a Logical Development of the Idea of Redemption, CE.
La Place de l'Homme dans l'Univers. Réflexions sur la complexité, III – Man's Place in the Universe. Reflexions on Complexity, VP.

1943 Super-Humanité, Super-Christ, Super-Charité. De Nouvelles dimensions pour l'Avenir, IX – Super-Humanity, Super Christ, Super-Charity. Some New Dimensions for the Future, SC.
La Question de l'Homme Fossile. Découvertes Récentes et Problèmes actuels, II – The Question of Fossil Man. Recent Discoveries and Present-Day Problems, AM.
Réflexions sur le Bonheur, XI – Reflections on Happiness, TF.

1944 Introduction à la Vie chrétienne. Introduction au Christianisme, X – Introduction to the Christian Life. Introduction to Christianity, CE.
La Centrologie. Essai d'une dialectique de l'Union, VII – Centrology. An Essay in a Dialectic of Union, AE.

1945 Vie et Planètes. Que se passe-t-il en ce moment sur la Terre? V – Life and the Planets. What is happening at this moment on Earth, FM.
La Morale peut-elle se passer de soubassements métaphysiques avoués ou inavoués? XI – Can Moral Science Dispense with a Metaphysical Foundation? TF.
L'Analyse de la Vie, VII – The Analysis of Life, AE.
Action et Activation, IX – Action and Activation, SC.
Christianisme et Evolution. Suggestions pour servir à une Théologie nouvelle, X – Christianity and Evolution: Suggestions for a New Theology, CE.

Un Grand événement qui se dessine: La Planétisation humaine, V – A Great Event Foreshadowed: The Planetisation of Mankind, FM.

1946 Catholicisme et Science, IX – Catholicism and Science, SC.
Quelques réflexions sur le retentissement spirituel de la bombe atomique, V – Some Reflections on the Spiritual Repercussions of the Atom Bomb, FM.
Sur les degrés de certitude scientifique de l'idée d'Evolution, IX – Degrees of Scientific Certainty in the Idea of Evolution, SC.
Esquisse d'une dialectique de l'Esprit, VII – Outline of a Dialectic of Spirit, AE.
Oecumenisme, IX – Ecumenism, SC.

1947 La Foi en la Paix, V – Faith in Peace, FM.
Une Interprétation biologique plausible de l'Histoie humaine. La Formation de la "Noosphère", V – The Formation of the Noosphere. A Plausible Biological Interpretation of Human History, FM.
Place de la technique dans une Biologie générale de l'Humanité, VII – The Place of Technology in a General Biology of Mankind, VII, AE.
La Foi en l'Homme, V – Faith in Man, FM.
L'Apport spirituel de l'Extrême-Orient. Quelques Réflexions personnelles, XI – The Spiritual Contribution of the Far East: Some Personal Reflections, TF.
Quelques Réflexions sur les Droits de l'Homme, V -- Some Reflections on the Rights of Man, FM.
Evolution zoologique et Invention, III – Zoological. Evolution and Invention, VP.
Sur la valeur religieuse de la Recherche, IX – The Religious Value of Research, SC.
Le Rebondissement humain de l'Evolution et ses Conséquences, V – The Human Rebound of Evolution and its Consequences, FM.
Lettre à Emmanuel Mounier, IX – Letter to Emmanuel Mounier, SC.
Réflexions sur le péché originel, X – Reflections on Original Sin, CE.
Agitation ou Genèse? Y a-t-il dans l'Univers un axe principal d'évolution? (Un effort pour voir clair), V — Turmoil or Genesis?

Is there in the Universe a Main Axis of Evolution? (An Attempt to see Clearly), FM.

1948　Trois Choses que je vois (ou: Une Weltanschauung en trois points, XI – Two Principles and a Corollary (or a Weltanschauung in Three Stages), TF. Ma position intellectuelle, XIII -- My Intellectual Position, HM.
Sur la nature du Phénomène social humain et sur ses relations cachées avec la Gravité, VII – On the Nature of the Phenomenon of Human Society, and Its Hidden Relationship with Gravity, AE.
Les Directions et les Conditions de l'Avenir, V – The Directions and Conditions of the Future, FM.
Note-mémento sur la structure biologique de l'Humanité, IX – Note on the Biological Structure of Mankind, SC.
Comment je vois, XI – My Fundamental Vision, TF.
Titres et Travaux de Pierre Teilhard de Chardin, XIII – Qualifications, Career, Field-Work and Writings of Pierre Teilhard de Chardin, HM.
Observations sur l'Enseignement de la Préhistoire, XIII -- Note on the Teaching of Prehistory, HM.
A la Base de Mon Attitude (incipit), XIII – The Basis of My Attitude, HM. Remarque essentielle à propos du "Phénomène Humain", XIII – My 'Phenomenon of Man': An Essential Observation, HM.
Quelques Remarques sur la place et la part du Mal dans un Monde en évolution. Appendice de "Le Phénomène Humain", I – Appendix: Some Remarks on the Place and Part of Evil in a World in Evolution, PM.
Allocution pour le Mariage de Christine Dresch et Claude-Marie Haardt, XIII – At the Wedding of Christine Dresch and Claude-Marie Haardt, HM.

1949　Les Conditions psychologiques de l'Unification humaine, VII – The Psychological Conditions of the Unification of Man, AE.
Un Phénomène de contre-évolution en Biologie humaine ou la peur de l'existence, VII – A Phenomenon of Counter-Evolution in Human Biology or the Existential Fear, AE.
L'Essence de l'Idée de Démocratie. Approche biologique du problème, V – The Essence of the Democratic Idea. A Biological Approach to the Problem, FM.

Une Nouvelle Question de Galilée: oui ou non l'Humanité se meut-elle biologiquement sur elle-même? V – Does Mankind Move Biologically upon itself? Galileo's Question Re-Stated, FM. Le Sens de l'espèce chez l'Homme, VII – The Sense of the Species in Man, AE.
La Place de l'homme dans la Nature. Le groupe zoologique Humain, VIII (en entier) – Man's Place in Nature. The Human Zoological Group.
Le Coeur du problème, V – The Heart of the Problem, FM.
La Vision du Passé. Ce qu'elle apporte à la Science et ce qu'elle lui ôte, III – The Vision of the Past. What It Brings to and Takes away from Science, VP.

1950   Sur l'existence probable, en avant de nous, d'un "Ultra-Humain" (Réflexions d'un biologiste), V – On the Probable Existence ahead of Us of an 'Ultra-Human' (Reflections of a Biologist), FM.
L'Energie spirituelle de la Souffrance, VII –The Spiritual Energy of Suffering, AE. Comment concevoir et espérer que se réalise sur Terre l'unanimisation humaine? V – How May We Conceive and Hope That Human Unanimisation Will Be Realised on Earth? FM.
Quest-ce que la Vie? IX – What Is Life? SC.
Du Préhumain à l'Ultra-Humain ou "Les Phases d'une planète vivante", V – From the Pre-Human to the Ultra-Human: The Phases of a Living Planet, FM.
Le Phénomène chrétien, X – The Christian Phenomenon, CE.
Evolution de l'idée d'évolution, III – Evolution of the Idea of Evolution, VP.
Les Australopithèques et le Chaînon manquant ou "Missing Link" de l'évolution, II – The Australopithecines and the 'Missing Link' in Evolution, AM.
L'Evolution de la responsabilité dans le Monde, VII – The Evolution of the Responsibility in the World, AE.
La Carrière Scientifique du P. Teilhard de Chardin, XIII – The Scientific Career of Pierre Teilhard de Chardin, HM.
Pour y voir clair. Réflexions sur deux formes inverses d'esprit. VII– A Clarification. Reflections on Two Converse Forms of Spirit, AE.
Le Coeur de la Matière, XIII – The Heart of Matter, HM.

Monogénisme et Monophylétisme. Une distinction essentielle à faire, X – Monogenism and Monophyletism: An Essential Distinction, CE.
Le Goût de vivre, VII – The Zest for Living, AE.

1951 La Structure phylétique du Groupe humain, II – The Phyletic Structure of the Human Group, AM.
Un Seuil mental sous nos pas: du Cosmos à la Cosmogénèse, VII – A Mental Threshold across Our Path: From Cosmos to Cosmogenesis, AE.
Réflexions sur la probabilité scientifique et les conséquences religieuses d'un Ultra-Humain, VII -- Reflections on the Scientific Probability and the Religious Consequences of an Ultra-Human, AE.
Note sur la réalité actuelle et la signification évolutive d'une Orthogénèse humaine, III – Note on the Present Reality and Evolutionary Significance of a Human Orthogenesis, VP.
La Biologie, poussée à fond, peut-elle nous conduire à émerger dans le Transcendant? IX – Can Biology, Taken to its Extreme Limit, Enable Us to Emerge into the Transcendent, SC.
La Convergence de l'Univers, VII – The Convergence of the Universe, AE. Quelques Remarques "Pour y voir clair" sur l'essence du sentiment mystique, XI – Some Notes on the Mystical Sense: An Attempt at Clarification, TF.
Notes de Préhistoire Sud-Africaine, II – Notes on South African Prehistory, AM.
Transformation et Prolongements en l'Homme du Mécanisme de l'Evolution, VII – The Transformation and Continuation in Man of the Mechanism of Evolution, AE.
Un Problème Majeur pour l'Anthropologie: Y a-t-il, oui ou non, chez l'Homme, prolongation et transformation du processus biologique de l'Evolution? VII – A Major Problem for Anthropology: Is there or is there not, in Man, a Continuation and Transformation of the Biological Process of Evolution? AE.

1952 Australopithèques, Pithécanthropes et Structure phylétiquedes Hominiens, II – Australopithecines, Pithecanthropians and the Phyletic Structure of the Hominians, AM.
Observations sur les Australopithécinés, II – Observations on the Australopithecines, AM. La Réflexion de l'Energie, VII – The Reflection of Energy, AE.

Ce que le monde attend en ce moment de l'Eglise de Dieu: Une généralisation et un approfondissement du sens de la Croix, X – What the World Is Looking for from the Church of God at This Moment: A Generalizing and a Deepening of the Meaning of the Cross, CE.
Hominisation et Spéciation, III – Hominization and Speciation, VP.
La Fin de l'Espèce, V – The End of the Species, FM.

1953　Réflexions sur la compression humaine, VII – Reflections on the Compression of Mankind, AE.
En Regardant un cyclotron. Réflexions sur le reploiement sur soi de l'Energie humaine, VII –Reflections on the Folding-Back upon Itself of Human Energy, AE.
Contingence de l'Univers et goût humain de survivre, ou comment repenser, en conformité avec les Lois de l'Energétique, la notion chrétienne de création? X – The Contingency of the Universe and Man's Zest for Survival, or How Can One Rethink the Christian Notion of Creation to Conform with the Laws of Energetics? CE.
L'Energie d'Evolution, VII – The Energy of Evolution, AE.
Une Suite au Probléme des origines humaines. La Multiplicité des mondes habités, X – A Sequel to the Problem of Human Origins: The Plurality of Inhabited Worlds, CE.
L'Etoffe de l'Univers, VII – The Stuff of the Universe, AE.
Mes Litanies, X – My Litany, CE.
Le Dieu de l'Evolution, X – The God of Evolution, CE.
Sur la probabilité d'une bifurcation précoce du Phylum humain au voisinage immédiat de ses origines, II – On the Probability of an Early Bifurcation of the Human Phylum in the Immediate Neighbourhood of the Origins, AM.
L'Activation de l'Energie humaine, VII – The Activation of Human Energy, AE.

1954　Un Sommaire de ma perspective "Phénoménologique" du monde, XI – A Summary of My 'Phenomenological' View of the World, TF. Les Singularités de l'Espèce Humaine, suivi d'un Apendice: Remarques complémentaires sur la Nature du Point Oméga ou de la Singularité du phénomène chrétien, II – The Singularities of the Human Species. Appendix: Complementary Remarks on the

Nature of the Point Omega, or the Unique Nature of the Christian Phenomenon, AM.

Les Recherches pour la découverte des origines humaines en Afrique au sud du Sahara, II – The Search for the Discovery of Human Origins South of the Sahara, AM.

Le Phénomène Humain (Comment, au-delà d'une "Anthropologie" philosophico-juridicao-litteraire, établir une Science de l'Homme, C'est-à-dire une Anthropodynamique et une Anthropogénése?), XIII – The Phenonmenon of Man. (How Can One Go beyond a Philosophico-Juridico-Literary 'Anthropology' and Establish a True Science of Man: An Anthropodynamics and an Anthropogenesis?), HM.

L'Afrique et les origines humaines, II – Africa and Human Origins, AM.

1955   Une Défense de l'Orthogénèse à propos des figures de spéciation, III – A Defense of Orthogenesis in the Matter of Patterns of Speciation, VP.

Barrière de la Mort et Co-Reflexion, ou de l'Eveil imminent de la conscience humaine au sens de son irréversion, VII – The Death-Barrier and Co-Reflection, or the Imminent Awakening of Human Consciousness to the Sense of Its Irreversibility, AE.

Le Christique, XIII – The Christic, HM.

Recherche, Travail et Adoration, IX – Research, Work, and Worship, SC.

Dernière page du journal de Pierre Teilhard de Chardin, V – Last Page of the Journal of Pierre Teilhard de Chardin. FM.

E- Index of Writings

(Note : Limited to the thirteen volumes entitled "ŒUVRES DE PIERRE TEILHARD DE CHARDIN." published by Editions du Seuil, Paris.)

A

Action et Activation (9 août 1945), IX, 221-233.
Activation (L') de l'Energie humaine (6 décembre 1953), VII, 409-416.
Afrique (L') et les Origines humaines (septembre 1954), II, 277-291.
Agitation ou Genèse ? y a-t-il dans l'Univers un axe principal d'Evolution?
    (Un effort pour voir clair) (20 décembre 1947), V, 275-289.
A la base de mon attitude (incipit) (7 octobre 1948), XIII, 179-182.

Allocution pour le mariage d'Eliane Basse et d'Hervé de la Goublaye de Ménorval, (15 juin 1935), XIII, 165-170.
Allocution pour le mariage d'Odette Bacot et de Jean Teilhard d'Evry (14 juin 1928), XIII, 157-163.
Allocution pour le mariage de Christine Dresch et Claude-Marie Haardt (21 décembre 1948) XIII, 187-190.
Ame (L') du Monde (Epiphanie = 6 janvier 1918), XII, 243-259. Analyse (L') de la Vie (10 juin 1945), VII, 137-146.
Analyse et Synthèse, cf. Science et Christ..., IX, 47-62.
Apport (L') spirituel de l'Extrême-Orient. Quelques réflexions personnelles (19 février 1947), XI, 147-160.
Atomisme (L') de l'esprit. Un essai pour comprendre la structure de l'étoffe de l'Univers (13 septembre 1941), VII, 29-63.
Australopithèques, Pithécanthropes et Structure phylétique des Hominiens (21 janvier 1952), II, 245-248.
Australopithèques (Les) et le Chaînon manquant ou "Missing Link" de l'évolution (juin 1950), II, 177-183.

B

Barrière de la mort et co-réflexion, ou De l'éveil imminent de la conscience humaine au sens de son irréversion (1er janvier 1955), VII, 419-429.
Biologie (La), poussée à fond, peut-elle nous conduire à émerger dans le Transcendant? (probablement mai 1951, sûrement avant le 24 mai), IX, 279-280.
Bulletin scientifique. La Face de la Terre (5-20 décembre 1921), III, 43-67.

C

Carrière (La) scientifique du P. Teilhard de Chardin (juillet 1950), XIII, 191-196.
Catholicisme et Science, (août 1946), IX, 237-241.
Centrologie (La). Essai d'une dialectique de l'union (13 décembre 1944), VII, 105-134.
Ce que le Monde attend en *ce* moment de l'Eglise de Dieu : Une généralisation et un approfondissement du sens de la Croix (14 septembre 1952), X, 251-262.
Christ (Le) dans la Matière. Trois Histoires comme Benson (14 octobre 1916), XII, 107-127.

Christ (Le) évoluteur ou un développement logique de la notion de Rédemption. Réflexions sur la nature de l'"action formelle" du Christ dans le Monde (8 octobre 1942), X, 161-176.

Christianisme et Evolution. Suggestions pour servir à une théologie nouvelle (11 novembre 1945), X, 201-216.

Christianisme (Le) dans le Monde (mai 1933), IX, 131-147.

Christique (Le) (mars 1955), XIII, 93-117.

Christologie et Evolution (Noël = 25 décembre 1933), X, 93-114. Chute, Rédemption et Géocentrie (20 juillet 1920), X, 47-58.

Coeur (Le) de la Matière (15 août-30 octobre 1950), XIII, 19-91 (avec en Appendice : Le Tableau (14 octobre 1916) et La Puissance spirituelle de la Matière (8 août 1919).

Coeur (Le) du problème (8 septembre 1949), V, 339-349.

Comment comprendre et utiliser l'art dans la ligne de l'énergie humaine (13 mars 1939), XI, 93-97.

Comment concevoir et espérer que se réalise sur terre l'unanimisation humaine ? (18 janvier 1950), V, 367-374.

Comment je crois (28 octobre 1934), X, 115-152.

Comment je vois (12 août 1948) : Appendice I. Note au Phénomène humain. Sur certaines analogies ou relations cachées entre gravité et conscience. - 2. Note au Phénomène chrétien. Sur la nature "biaxe" de l'Incarnation. - 3. Note à la Métaphysique. Sur la notion d'"entités couplées" (26 août 1948), XI, 177-223.

Comment se pose aujourd'hui la question du Transformisme (5-20 juin 1921), III, 17-40.

Conditions (Les) psychologiques de l'Unification humaine (6 janvier 1949), VII, 177-185.

Contingence de l'Univers et Goût humain de survivre, ou Comment repenser, en conformité avec les lois de l'Energétique, la notion chrétienne de Création ? (1er mai 1953), X, 263-272.

Convergence (La) de l'Univers (23 juillet 1951), VII, 295-309.

D

Découverte (La) du passé (15 septembre 1935), III, 259-269.

Découverte (La) du Sinanthrope (5 juillet 1937), II, 121-131. Défense (Une) de l'Orthogénèse à propos des figures de spéciation (janvier 1955), III, 383-391.

Dernière page du Journal de Pierre Teilhard de Chardin, V, 404-405.

Dieu (Le) de l'Evolution (Christ-Roi = 25 octobre 1953), X, 283-292.
Directions (Les) et les Conditions de l'Avenir (30 juin 1948), V, 293-305.
Du préhumain à l'ultra-humain ou "Les Phases d'une planète vivante" (27 avril 1950), V, 377-385.

E

Elément (L') universel (21 février 1919), XII, 429-445.
Energie (L') d'Evolution (24 mai 1953), VII, 38i-393.
Energie (L') humaine (6 août-8 septembre 1937) avec Appendice, le Principe de la conservation du personnel (20 octobre 1937),VI,143-198. Energie (L') spirituelle de la souffrance (8 janvier 1950), VII, 255-257.
En quoi consiste le corps humain ?, (août 1919), IX, 33-35.
En regardant un cyclotron, réflexions sur le reploiement sur soi de l'énergie humaine (avril 1953), VII, 367-377.
Esprit (L') de la Terre (9 mars 1931), VI, 25-57.
Esprit (L') nouveau. I. Le Cône du Temps. II. La Transposition "conique" de l'Action (13 février 1942), V, 109-126.
Esquisse d'un Univers personnel. A personalistic Universe (4 mai 1936) VI, 149-158.
Esquisse d'une dialectique de l'Esprit (25 novembre 1946), VII, 149-158.
Essence (L') de l'idée de démocratie. Approche biologique du problème. Pour L'U.N.E.S.C.O., en réponse à une enquête (2 février 1949), V, 309-315.
Eternel (L') Féminin (19-25 mars 1918), XII, 279-291.
Etoffe (L') de l'Univers (14 juillet 1953), VII, 397-406.
Evolution de l'idée d'évolution (juin-juillet 1950), III, 347-349.
Evolution (L') de la chasteté (février 1934), XI, 65-92.
Evolution (L') de la responsabilité dans le Monde (5 juin 1950), VII, 219-221.
Evolution zoologique et Invention (avril 1947), III, 329-331.

F

Face (La) de la Terre (5-20 décembre 1921), III, 43-67.
Faune (La) pléistocène et l'Ancienneté de l'Homme en Amérique du Nord (1935), II, 113-118.
Fin (La) de l'Espèce (9 décembre 1952), V, 389-395.
Foi (La) en l'Homme (février 1947), V, 235-243.

Foi (La) en la Paix (janvier 1947), V, 191-197.
Foi (La) qui opère (28 septembre 1918), XII, 335-361.
Fondements (Les) et le Fond de l'idée d'évolution (Ascension = 14 mai 1926), III, 165-197.
Forma Christi (13 et non 22 décembre 1918), XII, 363-386.
Fouilles (Les) préhistoriques de Peking (20 mars 1934), II, 99- 110.

G

Goût (Le) de vivre (novembre 1950), VII, 239-251.
Grand (Un) Evénement qui se dessine : La Planétisation humaine (25 décembre 1945), V, 159-175.
Grande (La) Monade (manuscrit trouvé dans une tranchée) (15 janvier 1918), XII, 261-278.
Grande (La) Option (3 mars 1939), V, 57-81.
Groupe (Le) zoologique humain. Structure et Directions évolutives (4 août 1949). La Place de l'Homme dans la Nature. Le Groupe zoologique humain, VIII (en entier).

H

Hérédité sociale et Education. Notes sur la valeur humano-chrétienne de l'enseignement (1938, paru dans *Etudes* en avril 1945), V, 41-53.
Heure (L') de choisir. Un sens possible de la guerre (Noël = 25 décembre 1939), VII, 19-26.
Histoire (L') naturelle du Monde. Réflexions sur la valeur et l'avenir de la Systématique (janvier 1925), III, 145-157.
Hominisation et Spéciation (novembre-décembre 1952), III, 365-379.
 Hominisation (L'). Introduction à une étude scientifique du Phénomène humain (6 mai 1925), III, 77-111.
Hommes (Les) fossiles. A propos d'un livre récent (20 mars 1921), II, 41-50.

I

Incroyance (L') moderne. Cause profonde et remède (25 octobre 1933), IX, 149-153.
Interprétation (Une) biologique plausible de l'Histoire humaine. La Formation de la "Noosphère" (janvier 1947), V, 201-231.
Introduction à la Vie chrétienne. Introduction au Christianisme (29 juin 1944), X, 177-200.

L

Lettre à Emmanuel Mounier (2 novembre 1947), IX, 291-293.
Loi (La) d'irréversibilité en Evolution (21 mars 1923), III, 73-74.
Lutte (La) contre la multitude. Interprétation possible de la figure du Monde (26 février-22 mars 1917), XII, 129-152.

M

Maîtrise (La) du Monde et le Règne de Dieu (20 septembre 1916), XII, 83-105.
Ma Position intellectuelle (avril 1948), XIII, 171-174.
Mes Litanies (vers octobre 1953 ?), X, 293-294.
Messe (La) sur le Monde (1923), XIII, 139-156.
Milieu (Le) divin (novembre 1926-mars 1927, révisé en 1932), IV (en entier).
Milieu (Le) mystique (13 août 1917), XII, 153-192.
Monogénisme et Monophylétisme. Une distinction essentielle à faire (août 1950), X, 245-250.
Montée (La) de l'Autre (20 janvier 1947), VII, 67-81.
Mon Univers (14 avril 1918), XII, 293-307.
Mon Univers (25 mars 1924), IX, 65-114.
Morale (La) peut-elle se passer de soubassements métaphysiques avoués ou inavoués ? (23 avril 1945), XI, 141-146.
Mouvements (Les) de la Vie (avril 1928), III, 201-210
Mystique (La) de la Science (20 mars 1939), VI, 203-223.

N

Noms (Les) de la Matière (Pâques = 20 avril 1919), XII, 447-464.
Nostalgie (La) du Front (septembre 1917), XII, 225-241.
Note-Memento sur la Structure biologique de l'Humanité (3 août 1948), IX, 267-271.
Note pour servir à l'Evangélisation des Temps nouveaux (Epiphanie, 1919), XII, 395-414.
Note sur "l'Elément universel" du Monde (22 décembre 1918), XII, 387-393.
Note sur l'essence du Transformisme (1920), XIII, 123-131.
Note sur l'union physique entre l'Humanité du Christ et les fidèles, au cours de la sanctification (1919 ou janvier 1920 ?), X, 19-26.
Note sur la notion de Perfection chrétienne (1942), XI, 111-117.

Note sur la réalité actuelle et la signification évolutive d'une Orthogénèse humaine (5 mai 1951), III, 353-362.
Note sur le Christ-universel (janvier 1920), IX, 39-44.
Note sur le Progrès (10 août 1920), V, 23-37.
Note sur les modes de l'action divine dans l'Univers (janvier 1920), X, 33-46
Note sur quelques représentations historiques possibles du péché originel (15 avril 1922 ou très peu avant), X, 59-70.
Note de Préhistoire Sud-Africaine (1951 vers novembre), II, 237-242.
Nouvelle (Une) question de Galilée : oui ou non l'Humanité se meut-elle biologiquement sur elle-même ? (4 mai 1949), V, 319-386.

O

Observations sur l'Enseignement de la Préhistoire (23 septembre 1948), XIII, 175-178.
Observations sur les Australopithécinés (mars 1952), II, 251-256.
Oecuménisme (15 décembre 1946), IX, 253-254.

P

Paléontologie (La) et l'Apparition de l'Homme (mars-avril 1923), X, 71-92.
Paradoxe (Le) transformiste. A propos de la dernière critique du Transformisme par M. Vialleton (janvier 1925), III, 115-142.
Parole (La) attendue (31 octobre 1940), XI, 99-109.
Phénomène (Le) chrétien (10 mai 1950), X, 231-244.
Phénomène (Le) humain (septembre 1928), IX, 117-128.
Phénomène (Le) humain (novembre 1930), III, 227-243.
Phénomène (Le) humain (juin 1938-juin 1940), l'avertissement est de mars 1947, le résumé ou post-face,'l'Essence du Phénomène humain'date peut-être de mars 1947 ; l'appendice "Quelque[s] Remarques sur la place et la part du Mal dans un Monde en évolution"est du 28 octobre 1948), I (en entier).
Phénomène (Le) humain (Comment, au-delà d'une "Anthropologie" philoso-phico-juridico-littéraire, établir une Science de l'Homme, c'est-à-dire une Anthropogénèse et une Anthropodynamique ?) (avant juin 1954), XIII, 197-200.
Phénomène (Le) spirituel (mars 1937), VI, 117-139.
Phénomène (Un) de contre-évolution en Biologie humaine ou la Peur de l'Existence (26 janvier 1949), VII, 189-202.

Place de la Technique dans une Biologie générale de l'Humanité (16 janvier 1947), VII, 161-169.
Place (La) de l'Homme dans l'Univers. Réflexions sur la Complexité (15 novembre 1942), III, 305-326.
Place (La) de l'Homme dans la Nature (1932),. III, 247-256.
Planétisation (La) humaine, cf. Un Grand Evénement qui se dessine : La Planétisation humaine, V, 159-175.
Pour y voir clair. Réflexions sur deux formes inverses d'esprit (25 juillet 1950), VII, 225-236.
Préhistoire (La) et ses Progrès (5 janvier 1913), II, 28-38.
Prêtre (Le) (8 juillet 1918), XII, 309-333.
Problème (Un) majeur pour l'Anthropologie : Y a-t-il, oui ou non, chez l'Homme, prolongation et transformation du processus biologique de l'Evolution ? (30 décembre 1951), VII, 327-332.
Puissance (La) spirituelle de la Matière (8 août 1919), XII, 465-479.

Q

Qu'est-ce que la Vie ? (2 mars 1950), IX, 275-276.
Que faut-il penser du Transformisme ? (janvier 1930), III, 213-223.
Quelques Réflexions sur la conversion du Monde. A l'usage d'un Prince de l'Eglise (9 octobre 1936), IX, 157-166.
Quelques Réflexions sur le retentissement spirituel de la bombe atomique (septembre 1946), V, 179-187.
Quelques Réflexions sur les Droits de l'Homme (22 mars 1947), V, 247-249.
Quelques Remarques "Pour y voir clair" sur l'essence mystique (hiver 1951), XI, 225-229.
Quelques vues générales sur l'essence du Christianisme (mai 1939), X, 153-160.
Question (La) de l'Homme fossile. Découvertes récentes et Problèmes actuels (15 septembre 1943), II, 135-174.

R

Rebondissement (Le) humain de l'Evolution et ses Conséquences (23 septembre 1947), V, 253-271.
Recherche, Travail et Adoration (mars 1955), IX, 283-289.
Recherches (Les) pour la découverte des origines humaines en Afrique au Sud du Sahara (juin 1954), II, 265-273.
Réflexion (La) de l'Energie (27 avril 1952), VII, 335-353.

Réflexions sur la Compression humaine (18 janvier 1953), VII, 357-363.
Réflexions sur la probabilité scientifique et les conséquences religieuses d'un Ultra-Humain (Pâques 25 mars 1951), VII, 281-291.
Réflexions sur le Bonheur (28 décembre 1943), XI, 119-140.
Réflexions sur le Péché originel (15 novembre 1947), X, 217-230.
Réflexions sur le Progrès. I. L'Avenir de l'Homme vu par un paléontologiste (22 février 1941). II. Sur les bases possibles d'un Credo humain commun (30 mars 1941), V, 85-106.
Remarque essentielle à propos du "Phénomène humain" (17 octobre 1948), XIII, 183-186.
Route (La) de l'Ouest. Vers une Mystique nouvelle (8 septembre 1932), XI, 45-64.

S

Sauvons l'Humanité. Réflexions sur la Crise présente (11 novembre 1936), IX, 169-191.
Science et Christ (ou Analyse et Synthèse). Remarques sur la manière dont l'Étude scientifique de la matière peut et doit servir à remonter jusqu'au Centre Divin (27 février 1921), IX, 47-62.
Sens (Le) de l'Espèce chez l'Homme (31 mai 1949), VII, 205-210.
Sens (Le) humain (février-mars 1929), XI, 19-44.
Seuil (Un) mental sous nos pas : du Cosmos à la Cosmogénèse (15 mars 1951 et non 1961), VII, 261-277.
Signification (La) et la Valeur constructrice de la Souffrance (1er avril 1933), VI, 61-66.
Singularités (Les) de l'Espèce humaine, suivi d'un. Appendice, Remarques complémentaires sur la nature du point Oméga ou de la singularité du Phénomène chrétien (25 mars 1954), II, 295-374.
Sommaire (Un) de ma perspective "phénoménologique" du Monde (14 janvier 1954), XI, 231-236.
Structure (La) phylétique du Groupe humain (février 1951), II, 187-234.
Suite (Une) au problème des origines humaines. La Multiplicité des mondes habités (5 juin 1953), X, 273-282.
Super-Humanité, Super-Christ, Super-Charité. De nouvelles dimensions pour l'Avenir (août 1943), IX, 191-218.
Sur l'apparence nécessairement discontinue de toute série évolutive (17 mars 1926), III, 161-162.
Sur l'existence probable, en avant de nous, d'un "Ultra-Humain" (Réflexions d'un biologiste) (6 janvier 1950), V, 353-364.

Sur la nature du Phénomène social humain et sur *ses* relations cachées avec la gravité (23 avril 1948), VII, 173-174.
Sur la notion de Transformation créatrice (1919 ou début de 1920 ?), X, 27-32.
Sur la probabilité d'une bifurcation précoce du Phylum humain au voisinage immédiat de ses origines (23 novembre 1953), II, 259-261.
Sur la valeur religieuse de la Recherche (20 août 1947), IX, 257-263.
Sur les degrés de certitude scientifique de l'idée d'évolution (15-20 novembre 1946), IX, 245-249.
Sur mon attitude vis-à-vis de l'Eglise officielle (5 janvier 1921), XIII, 133-137.

T

Terre Promise (février 1919), XII, 415-428.
Titres et travaux de Pierre Teilhard de Chardin (septembre 1948), XIII, 201-221.
Transformation et Prolongements en l'Homme du mécanisme de l'évolution (19 novembre 1951), VII, 313-323.
Trois Choses que je vois ou : Une Weltanschauung en trois points (février 1948), XI, 161-175.

U

Union (L') créatrice (novembre 1917), XII, 193-224.
Unités (Les) humaines naturelles. Essai d'une Biologie et d'une Morale des races (5 juillet 1939), III, 273-301.
Universalisation et Union : Un effort pour voir clair (20 mars 1942), VII, 85-101.

V

Vie (La) cosmique (24 avril 1916) avec un bref Nota daté du 17 mai 1961, XII, 17-82.
Vie et Planètes. Que se passe-t-il en ce moment sur la Terre ? (10 mars 1945), V, 129-156.
Vision (La) du Passé, ce qu'elle apporte à la Science et ce qu'elle lui ôte (17-22 octobre 1949), III, 335-343.

II- Works on the Thought of Teilhard de Chardin

Archevêque, Paul L'. *Teilhard de Chardin : Nouvel Index Analytique.* Québec, Canada: Les Presses de l'Université Laval, 1972.
Association des Amis de Pierre Teilhard de Chardin. *La Convergence Spirituelle de l'Humanité : Un Œcumenisme éargi avec Pierre Teilhard de Chardin.* Saint-Etienne, France : Aubin Editeur, 1998.
Barthélemy-Madaule, Madeleine. *La Personne et le Drame Humain chez Teilhard de Chardin.* Paris : Editions du Seuil, 1967.
—. *Bergson et Teilhard de Chardin.* Paris : Editions du Seuil, 1966.
Baudry, Gérard-Henry. *Ce que croyait Teilhard.* France : Mame, 1971.
Bergeron, Sœur Ina, and Anne-Marie Ernst. *Le Christ Universel et l'Evolution.* Paris : Les Editions du Cerf, 1986.
Bravo, Francisco. *La Vision de l'Histoire chez Teilhard de Chardin.* Paris : Cerf, 1970.
Braybrooke, N., ed. *Teilhard de Chardin. Pilgrim of the Future.* New York: Seabury, 1964. London, 1966.
Bruteau, Beatrice. *Evolution Toward Divinity: Teilhard de Chardin and the Hindu Traditions.* Wheaton, Ill: The Theosophical Publishing House, 1974.
Cahiers du Rocher (les), diriges par Pierre Sipriot. *Pierre Teilhard de Chardin : Naissance et Avenir de l'Homme.* France: Editions du Rocher, Jean-Paul Bertrand, Editeur, 1987.
Chauchard, Paul. *Teilhard de Chardin on Love and Suffering.* Trans. by Marie Chêne. Glen Rock, New Jersey: Deus Books-Paulist Press, 1966.
Cochrance Arthur C. *The Mystery of Peace.* Elgin, IL: Brethren Press, 1986.
Collopy, Michael, and Jason Gardner, ed., *Architects of Peace: Visions of Hope in Words and Images.* Novato, CA: New World Library, 2000.
Corbishley, Thomas. *The Spirituality of Teilhard de Chardin.* Paramus, N.J., and New York: Paulist Press, 1971.
Cousins, Ewert H., ed. *Process Theology.* New York: Newman Press, 1971.
Cousins, Ewert H., ed. *Hope and the Future of Man.* Philadelphia: Fortress Press, 1973.
Cuénot, Claude. *Pierre Teilhard de Chardin. Les Grandes Etapes de Son Evolution.* Plon, 1958, Le Rocher, 1986.

—. *Teilhard de Chardin*. Editions du Seuil, "Ecrivains de Toujours," 1962.

—. *Nouveau Lexique Teilhard de Chardin*. Paris: Editions du Seuil, 1968.

Dodson, Edward O. *The Teilhardian Synthesis, Lamarckism, and Orthogenesis*. American Teilhard Association for the Future of Man, Inc., "Teilhard Studies" Number 29, Summer 1993.

Delio, Ilia OSF. *The Unbearable Wholeness of Being: God, Evolution, and the Power of Love*. Maryknoll, N.Y.: Orbis Books, 2013.

—. *Christ in Evolution*. Maryknoll, NY: Orbis Books, 2008.

—. ed. *From Teilhard to Omega: Co-creating an Unfinished Universe*. Maryknoll, N.Y.: Orbis Books, 2015.

—. *Making All Things New: Catholicity, Cosmology, Consciousness*. Maryknoll, N.Y.: Orbis Books, 2015.

Duffy, Kathleen, SSJ. *Teilhard's Mysticism: Seeing the Inner Face of Evolution*. Maryknoll, NY: Orbis Books, 2014.

—. ed. *Rediscovering Teilhard's Fire*. Philadelphia: St. Joseph's University Press, 2010.

Dupleix, André. *15 days of Prayer with Pierre Teilhard de Chardin,* trans. by Victoria Hébert and Denis Sabourin. Liguori, Missouri: Liguori Publications, 1999.

Fabel, Arthur. *Teilhard 2000: The Vision of a Cosmic Genesis at the Millennium*. American Teilhard Association for the Future of Man, Inc., "Teilhard Studies" Number 36, Spring 1998.

Fabel, A., and D. St. John, eds. *Teilhard in the 21st Century: The Emerging Spirit of Earth*. Maryknoll, NY: Orbis Books, 2003.

Faricy, Robert L, S.J. *Teilhard de Chardin's Theology of the Christian in the World*. New York: Sheed and Ward, 1967.

—. *The Spirituality of Teilhard de Chardin*. Minneapolis, Minnesota: Winston Press – Collins Publishers, 1981.

Grim John A., and Mary Evelyn Tucker. *Teilhard's Vision of Evolution*. American Teilhard Association for the Future of Man, Inc., "Teilhard Studies" Number 50, Spring 2005.

Grau, Joseph A. *Morality and the Human Future in the Thought of Teilhard de Chardin*. Cranbury, N.J. and London: Associated University Press, 1976.

—. *The Creative Union of Person and Community: A Geo-Humanist Ethic*. American Teilhard Association for the Future of Man, Inc., "Teilhard Studies" Number 22, Fall/Winter 1989.

Gray, Donald P. *The One and the Many: Teilhard de Chardin's Vision of Unity*. New York: Herder and Herder, 1969.

Grumett, D. *Teilhard de Chardin: Theology, Humanity and Cosmos.* Leuven (Louvain) and Dudley, MA: Peeters, 2005.

Hart, Brother Patrick, ed., *The Literary Essays of Thomas Merton.* New York: New Directions Publishing Corporation, 1981.

Hefner, Philip. *The Promise of Teilhard: The Meaning of the Twentieth Century in Christian Perpective.* Philadelphie and New York: J.B. Lippincott Co., 1970.

Heller, Michael. *Teilhard's Vision of the World and Modern Cosmology.* American Teilhard Association for the Future of Man, Inc., "Teilhard Studies" Number 58, Spring 2009.

Jiroušova, Frantiská. *Teilhard de Chardin's Theory of Spiritual Evolution.* American Teilhard Association for the Future of Man, Inc., "Teilhard Studies" Number 70, Spring 2015.

King, Thomas M., S.J. *Teilhard de Chardin.* Wilmington, Delaware: Michael Glazier, Inc., 'The Way f the Christian Mystics,' 1988.

—. *Teilhard's Mass: Approaches to "the Mass on the World."* New York/Mahwah, N.J: Paulist Press, 2005.

—. *Teilhard's Mysticism of Knowing.* New York, N.Y.: The Seabury Press, 1981.

King, Thomas M., and James F. Salmon, S.J., ed. *Teilhard and the Unity of Knowledge*, 'The Georgetown University Centennial Symposium.' New York/Ramsey: NJ.: Paulist Press, 1983.

King, Ursula. *Spirit of Fire: The Life and Vision of Teilhard de Chardin.* Maryknoll, N.Y.: Orbis Books, 1996, 1998.

—. *Toward a New Mysticism: Teilhard de Chardin and Eastern Religions.* New York: Seabury Press, 1980.

—. *Teilhard de Chardin and Eastern Religions: Spirituality and Mysticism in an Evolutionary World.* Mahwah, N.J.: Paulist Press, 2011.

—. *The Spirit of One Earth: Reflections on Teilhard de Chardin and Global Spirituality.* New York, N.Y.: Paragon House, 1989.

—. *Christ in All Things: Exploring Spirituality with Teilhard de Chardin.* Maryknoll, NY: Orbis Books, 1997.

Kraft, R. Wayne. *Love as Energy.* American Teilhard Association for the Future of Man, Inc., "Teilhard Studies" Number 19, Spring/Summer 1988.

Krieg, Robert A. *Romano Guardini: Spiritual Writings.* Maryknoll, N.Y.: Orbis Books, "Modern Spiritual Masters Series," 2005.

Leon-Dufour, Michel. *Teilhard de Chardin et le Problème de l'Avenir Humain.* Paris : Editions « Albert Blanchard, » 1983.

Lepp, Ignace. *Teilhard et la Foi des Hommes.* Paris : Editions Universitaires, 1963.

Ligneul, André. *Teilhard and Personalism*, trans. by Paul Joseph Oligny, O,F.M. and Michael D. Meilach, O.F.M. Glen Rock, N.J., New York, N.Y: Paulist Press Deus Books, 1968.

Lubac, Henri de, S.J. *The Religion of Teilhard de Chardin*. Trans. by René Hague. Garden City, N.Y: Image Books, a Division of Doubleday & Company, Inc., 1968.

—. *Teilhard de Chardin: The Man and His Meaning*. Trans. by René Hague. New York: Burns & Oates Ltd., 1965.

—. *The Faith of Teilhard de Chardin*. London: Burns & Oates, 1965.

—. *Teilhard et Notre Temps*. France: Aubier, "Foi Vivante," 1971.

Lukas, Mary, and Ellen Lukas, *Teilhard: The Man, The Priest, The Scientist*. Garden City, NY: Doubleday and Company, Inc., 1977.

Lyons, J.A. *The Cosmic Christ in Origen and Teilhard de Chardin*. New York: Oxford University Press, 1982.

Maalouf, Jean. *Le mystère du mal dans l'œuvre de Teilhard de Chardin*, « Thèses/Cerf », Les Editions du Cerf, 1986.

—. *The Divine Milieu: A Spiritual Classic for Today and Tomorrow*. American Teilhard Association for the Future of Man, Inc., "Teilhard Studies" Number 38, Autumn 1999.

—. Teilhard and the Feminine. American Teilhard Association for the Future of Man, Inc., "Teilhard Studies" Number 47, Autumn 2003.

—. ed. *Teilhard de Chardin: Reconciliation in Christ*. Hyde Park, N.Y.: New City Press, "Selected Spiritual Writings," 2002.

—. « Introduction à la théologie de l'histoire chez Teilhard de Chardin » in *La Terre Est Mon Pays* by Bernard Pierrat, Jean Maalouf, Jean-Paul Sorg, Christiane Roederer. France : Aubin Editeur, Collection : Objectif Demain, 2008.

—. « Teilhard de Chardin et le mystère du mal. Evolutionisme ? Stoïcisme ? Christocentrisme ? » in *Revue des Sciences Philosophiques et Théologiques,* Tome 65, No 2. Paris : Librairie Philosophique J. Vrin, 1981.

—. *If We Just See What They See: Peace According to Albert Einstein, Thomas Merton, Pope John XXIII, Thick Nhat Hanh, Mahatma Gandhi, Teilhard de Chardin, Mother Teresa of Calcutta.* Bloomington, Indiana: AuthorHouse, 2007.

Maloney, George A. S.J. *The Cosmic Christ: From Paul to Teilhard*. New York: Sheed and Ward, Inc., 1968.

—. *Mysticism and the New Age*. New York: Alba House, 1991.

Martin, Sister Maria Gratia, I.H.M. *The Spirituality of Teilhard de Chardin*. New York, NY: Newman Press, 1968.
Marving, Kessler, S.J. and Bernard Brown, S.J. *Dimensions of the Future: The Spirituality of Teilhard de Chardin*. Washington: Corpus Books, 1968.
Mathieu, Pierre-Louis. *La Pensée Politique et Economique de Teilhard de Chardin*. Paris : Editions du Seuil, 1969.
McGurn, Sister Margaret, I.H.M. *Global Spirituality : Planetary Consciousness in the Thought of Teilhard de Chardin and Robert Muller*. Ardsley-on-Hudson, N.Y.: World Happiness and Cooperation, 1981.
McMenamin, Mark S. S. Evolution of the Noösphere. American Teilhard Association for the Future of Man, Inc., "Teilhard Studies" Number 42, Spring 2001.
Mermod, Denis. *La Morale chez Teilhard de Chardin*. Paris: Editions Universitaires, 1967.
Meynard, Th., ed. *Teilhard and the Future of Humanity*. New York: Fordham University Press, 2006.
Mondras, Ronald. *Ignatian Humanism: A Dynamic Spirituality for the 21st Century*. Chicago: LoyolaPress, 2004.
Mooney, Christopher F., S.J. *The Making of Man: Essays in the Christian Spirit*. New York, N.Y.: Paulist Press, 1971.
—. *Teilhard de Chardin and the Mystery of Christ*. Garden City: N.Y.: Doubleday and Co., Inc., Image Books, 1968.
—. *Cybernation, Responsibility and Providential Design*. American Teilhard Association for the Future of Man, Inc., "Teilhard Studies" Number 24, Summer 1991.
Moschetta, Jean Marc « Le Christ cosmique chez Teilhard : Fondement d'une 'écologie intégrale' in *Teilhard Aujourd'hui : Vers une écologie intégrale, l'apport de Pierre Teilhard de Chardin* (Saint-Léger Editions, mars 2016).
O'Manique, J. *Energy in Evolution: Teilhard's Physics of the Future*. London: Garnstone, 1969.
Onimus, Jean. *Pierre Teilhard de Chardin ou la Foi au Monde*. Paris : Librairie Plon, « La Recherche de l'Absolu », 1963.
Ordonnaud, Georges. *La Construction de la Terre: (Participation de l'humanité actuelle à un "front général d'avancée humaine")*. Lyon, France (publisher N/A), 1981.
Ouince, René d'. *Un Prophète en Procès : Teilhard de Chardin dans l'Eglise de son Temps* (t. 1), *Teilhard de Chardin et l'Anenir de la Pensée Chrétienne* (t. 2). Paris : Aubier-Montaigne, 1970.

Rabut, Olivier, O.P. *Teilhard de Chardin: A Critical Study*. New York: Sheed and Ward Ltd., 1961.
Ratzinger, Joseph Cardinal [Pope Benedict XVI]. *The Spirit of the Liturgy*. san Francisco: Ignatius Press. 2000.
Rideau, Emile. S.J. *Teilhard Oui ou Non*. Paris : Librairie Fayard, 'Jalons,'1967.
—. *La Pensée du Père Teilhad de Chardin* Paris: Editions du Seuil, 1965.
Salmon, James, SJ, and John Farina, ed. *The Legacy of Pierre Teilhard de Chardin*. New York/Mahwah, NJ: Paulist Press, 2011.
Savary, Louis M. *Teilhard de Chardin The Divine Milieu Explained: A Spirituality for the 21st Century*. Mahwah, New Jersey: Paulist Press, 2007.
—. *The New Spiritual Exercises: In the Spirit of Pierre Teilhard de Chardin*. New York/Mahwah, NJ: Paulist Press, 2010.
—. *Expanding Teilhard's "Complexity-Consciousness" Law*. American Teilhard Association for the Future of Man, Inc., "Teilhard Studies" Number 68, Spring 2014.
Skehan, James W., SJ. *Praying with Teilhard de Chardin*. Winona, MN: Saint Mary's Press, 'Companions for the Journey,' 2001.
Smith, Wolfgang. *Teilhardism and the New Religion: A Thorough Analysis of the Teachings of Pierre Teilhard de Chardin*. Rockford, Illinois: Tan Books and Publishers, Inc., 1988.
Smulders, Pierre. *La Vision de Teilhard de Chardin: Essai de Réflections Théologiques*. Paris: Desclée de Brouwer, 1965.
Stikker, Allerd. *Teilhard, Evolution, and Ecology*. American Teilhard Association for the Future of Man, Inc., "Teilhard Studies" Number 73, Fall 2016.
Teasdale, Wayne. *The Mystic Heart: Discovering a Universal Spirituality in the World's Religion*. Novato, CA: New World Library, 1999.
Trinité, Philippe de la, O.C.D. *Pour ou Contre Teilhard de Chardin Penseur Religieux*. Saint-Céneré, Fraance: Edition Saint-Michel, 1970.
Udias, Agustin, SJ. *Christogenesis: The Development of Teilhard's Cosmic Christology*. American Teilhard Association for the Future of Man, Inc., "Teilhard Studies" Number 59, Fall 2009.
Wildiers, N.M. *Teilhard de Chardin*. Paris: Editions Universitaires, 'Classiques du XXe Siècle,' 1960.
—. *An Introduction to Teilhard de Chardin*. Trans. by Hubert Hoskins. London: Collins, Fontana Books, 1968.
Zaehner, R. C. *Evolution in Religion: A Study in Sri Aurobindo and Pierre Teilhard de Chardin*. Oxford: Clarendon Press, 1971.

Zonneveld, Leo and Robert Muller, ed. *The Desire to Be Human*, "International Teilhard Compendium" Centenary volume. Netherlands: Mirananda Publishers b.v. Wassenaar, 1983.

—. *Humanity's Quest for Unity*. A United Nations Teilhard Colloquium. Netherlands: Mirananda, 1985.

III - For Further Reading

Alt, Franz. *Peace Is Possible: The Politics of the Sermon on the Mount.* Trans. by Joachim Neugroschel. New York: Schocken Books, 1985.

Armstrong, Karen. *A History of God: The 4000-Year Quest of Judaism, Christianity and Islam.* New York: Alfred A. Knopf, 1994.

—. *The Great Transformation: The Beginning of Our Religious Traditions.* New York: Alfred A. Knopf, 2006.

Bachelard, Gaston. *La Psychanalyse du Feu.* France : Editions Gallimard, 1949, 1989.

Balthasar, Hans Urs Von. *Théologie de l'Histoire.* Paris: Le Signe/Fayard, 1970.

—. Liturgie Cosmique : Maxime le Confesseur. Paris: Aubier/Editions Montaigne, 1947.

Barbour, Ian G. *When Science Meets Religion.* HarperSanFrancisco, A Division of HarperCollinsPublishers, 2000.

Bayard, Jean-Pierre. *La Symbolique du Feu.* Guy Trédaniel Editeur, Editions de la Maisnie, 1986.

Bergson, Henri. *Creative Evolution.* Lanham, MD: University Press of America, reprint, 1983.

Borysenko, Joan, Ph.D. *Fire in the Soul: A New Psychology of Spiritual Optimism.* New York, N.Y.: Warner Books, Inc., 1993.

Bruteau, Beatrice. *Radical Optimism: Rooting Ourselves in Reality.* New York, NY: The Crossroad Publishing Company. 1993.

Buber, M. *Between Man and Man.* New York: Macmillan, 1965.

—. *I and Thou.* New York: Charles Scribner's Sons, 1958.

Capra, Fritjof. *The Turning Point: Science, Society and the Rising Culture.* New York: Simon and Schuster, 1982.

—. *The Tao of Physics: An Exploration of the Parallels Between Modern Physics and Eastern Mysticism.* Berkeley, CA: Shambhala, 1975.

Carles, Jules. *Le Transformisme.* Paris: Presses Universitaires de France, « Que Sais-Je ? » 1970.

Casey, Michael. *Fully, Fully Divine: An Interactive Christology*. Liguori, Missouri: Liguori/Triumph, An imprint of Liguori Publications, 2004.

Chauchard, Paul. *Physiologie de la Conscience*. France : Presses Universitaires de France, « Que Sais-Je ? »1948.

Cooney, William. *The Quest for Meaning: A Journey through Philosophy, the Arts, and Creative Genius*. Lanham, Maryland: University Press of America,® Inc., 2000.

Davies, Paul. *The Mind of God: The Scientific Basis for a Rational World*. New York, N.Y.: Simon & Schuster, 1992.

Dear, John. *The God of Peace: Toward a Theology of Nonviolence*. Maryknoll, N.Y.: Orbis Books, 1994.

Desa Wilfrid. *The Planetary Man*. New York: The Macmillan Company, 1961, 1972.

Donders, Joseph G. *The Global Believer*. Mystic, CT: Twenty-Third Publications, 1986.

Douglass, James W. *The Nonviolent Coming of God*. Maryknoll, N.Y: Orbis Books, 1991, 1998.

Dubay, Thomas, S.M. *Fire Within: St. Teresa of Avila, St. John of the Cross, and the Godpel—on Prayer*. San Francisco: Ignatius Press, 1989.

Duffy, Regis, O.F.M., and Angelus Gambatese, O.F.M., editors. *Made in God's Image: The Catholic Vision of Human Dignity*. New York/Mahawah, N.J.: Paulist Press, 1999.

Edwards, Denis. *Jesus and the Cosmos*. New York/Mahwah, N. J.: Paulist Press, 1991.

—. *The God of Evolution*. New York/Mahwah, N.J.: Paulist Press, 1999.

Einstein, Albert. *The World as I See It*. New York: Philosophical Library, 1949.

—. *Ideas and Opinions*. New York: Crown Publishers, Inc., 1954.

Elgin, Duane. *Promise Ahead: A Vision of Hope and Action for Humanity's Future*. New York, N.Y.: William Morrow, An Imprint of HarperCollins Publishers, 2000.

Eliade, Mircea. *The Sacred and The Profane: The Nature of Religion*. Trans. by Willard R. Trask. New York: Houghton Mifflin Harcourt Publishing Company, 1987.

Enomiya-Lassalle, Hugo. *Living in the New Consciousness*. Boston: Shambhala Publications, Inc., 1988.

Ferencz, Benjamin B., and Ken Keyes, Jr. *Planethood: The Key to Your Future.* Coos Bay, OR: Love Line Books, 1991.

Ferguson, John. *War and Peace in the World's Religions.* New York: Oxford University Press, 1978.

Fox, Matthew. *The Coming of the Cosmic Christ: The Healing of Mother Earth and the Birth of a Global Renaissance.* San Francisco: Harper & Row, Publishers, 1988.

Galilea, Segundo. *The Future of Our Past: The Spanish Mystics Speak to Contemporary Spirituality.* Notre Dame, Indiana: Ave Maria Press, 1985.

Gallie, W.B. *Philosophers of Peace and War.* New York: Cambridge University Press, 1979.

Gardet, Louis. *La Mystique.* Paris: Presses Universitaires de France, « Que Sais-Je ? »1970.

Girard, René. *Violence and the Sacred.* Trans. by Patrick Gregory. Baltimore, Maryland: Johns Hopkins University Press, 1979.

Graham, Billy. *World Aflame.* Garden City, N.Y.: Doubleday & Company, Inc., 1965.

Grant, W. Harold, Magdala Thompson, and Thomas E. Clarke. *From Image to Likeness: A Jungian Path in the Gospel Journey.* Mahwah, N.J.: Paulist Press, 1983.

Griffiths, Bede. *A New Vision of Reality: Western Science, Eastern Mysticism and Christian Faith.* Springfield, IL: Templegate Publishers, 1989, 1990.

—. *Return to the Center.* Springfield, Illinois: Templegate Publishers, 1977.

Guardini, Romano. *The End of the Modern World.* Wilmington, Delaware: ISI Books – Intercollegiate Studies Institute, 1998.

Hanh, Thick Nhat. *Love in Action: Writing on Nonviolent Social Change*, ed., by Arnold Kotler. Berkeley, CA: Parallax Press, 1993.

—. *Peace Is Every Step: The Path of Mindfulness in Everyday Life*, ed., by Arnold Kotler. New York: Bantam Books, 1991.

Happold, F.C. *Mysticism: A Study and an Anthology.* New York, N.Y.: Penguin Books Ltd, 1963, 1964, 1970.

Hart, Brother Patrick, ed., *The Literary Essays of Thomas Merton.* New York: New Directions Publishing Corporation, 1981.

Henderson, Charles P., Jr. *God and Science: The Death and Rebirth of Theism.* Atlanta, Georgia: John Knox Press, 1986.

Herrera, Robert A. *Lamps of Fire: Studies in Christian Mysticism.* Petersham, MA: St. Bede's Publications,1986.

Howard, Michael. *Studies in War and Peace*. New York: The Viking Press (reprint). 1970.
Johnston, William. *The Inner Eye of Love. Mysticism and Religion*. New York: Harper & Row, 1978.
—. *Mystical Theology: The Science of Love*. Maryknoll, N.Y.: Orbis Books, 1995.
—. *The Still Point*. New York: Fordham University Press, 1970.
Kant, Immanuel. *Perpetual Peace and Other Essays on Politics, History, and Morals*. Trans. with Intro. By Ted Humphrey. Indianapolis, IN: Hackett Publishing Company, Inc., 1983.
Keating, Thomas. *Intimacy with God*. New York: Crossroad. 1994.
—. *Invitation to Love: The Way of Christian Contemplation*. Rockport, MA: Element, 1992.
—. *Awakenings*. New York, N.Y.: The Crossroad Publishing Company, 1996.
Keyes, Ken, Jr. *Handbook to Higher Consciousness*. Coos Bay, Oregon: Living Love Publications, 1984.
Lossky, Vladimir. *In the Image and Likeness of God*. Ed. By John H. Erickson and Thomas E. Bird. Crestwood, N.Y.: St Vladimir's Seminary Press, 1985.
Maalouf, Jean. *Practicing the Presence of the Living God : A Retreat with Brother Lawrence of the Resurrection*. Washington, D.C.: ICS Publications, 2011.
—. *The Healing Power of Peace*. New London, CT: Twenty-Third Publications, A Division of Bayard, 2005.
—. *The Healing Power of Hope*. Toronto, Ontario, Canada: Novalis – Mystic, CT: Twenty-Third Publications, A Division of Bayard, 2004.
—. *The Healing Power of Purpose*. Toronto, Ontario, Canada: Novalis – Mystic, CT: Twenty-Third Publications, A Division of Bayard, 2003.
—. *The Healing Power of Truth*. Pasay City, Philippines: Paulines Publishing House, 2011.
—. *Christmas Shock: The Human Experience of God*. Xlibris Corporation, 2010.
—. *If We Just See What They See: Peace According to Albert Einstein, Thomas Merton, Pope John XXIII, Thich Nhat Hanh, Mahatma Gandhi, Teilhard de Chardin, Mother Teresa of Calcutta*. Bloomington, IN: AuthorHouse, 2007.
—. *Where Has God Gone? Religion – The Most Powerful Instrument for Growth or Destruction*. Xlibris Corporation, 2015.

—. *Making All Things New: The Promise of Christmas.* Xlibris Corporation, 2011.

—. *Change Your World: Awakening to the Power of Truth – Beauty – Simplicity – Change.* Xlibris Corporation, 2013.

Mantzaridis, Georgios I. *The Deification of Man: St Gregory Palamas and the Orthodox Tradition.* Trans. by Liadain Sherrard. Crestwood, N.Y.: St Vladimir's Seminary Press, 1984.

Marrou, Henri-Irénée. *Théologie de l'Histoire.* Paris: Editions du Seuil, 1968.

Maloney, George A., S.J. *Man, the Divine Icon: The Patristic Doctrine of Man Made according to the Image of God.* Pecos, New Mexico: Dove Publications, 1973.

—. Invaded by God: Mysticism and the Indwelling Trinity. Denville, N.J.: Dimension Books, 1979.

Merton, Thomas. *Contemplation in a World of Action.* Garden City, NY: Image Books – A Division of Doubleday & Company, Inc., 1965.

—. *Love and Living,* Ed. by Naomi Burton Stone & Brother Patrick Hart. New York: A Harvest/HBJ Book, Harcourt Brace Jovanovich, Publishers, 1985.

—. *The New Man.* New York, N.Y.: The Noonday Press, a division of Farrar, Straus and Giroux, 1961.

—. *New Seeds of Contemplation.* New York, N.Y.: New Directions Books, 1961.

—. *The Nonviolent Alternative.* Ed. By "Gordon C. Zahn. Revised edition of Thomas Merton on Peace. New York: Ferrar-Straus-Giroux, 1980, 1986.

—. No Man Is an Island. New York: A Harvest/HBJ Book, Harcourt Brace Jovanovich, Publishers, 1955.

Moltmann, Jürgen. *Theology of Hope.* New York and Evanston: Harper & Row, Publishers, 1967.

Mounier, Emmanuel. *Personalism.* Notre Dame, Indiana: University of Notre Dame Press, trans. by Philip Mairet, first published in England by Routledge & Kegan Paul Ltd., 1952.

Mourgeon, Jacques. *Les Droits de l'Homme.* France : Presses Universitaires de France, « Que Sais-Je ? »1978.

Mouroux, Jean. *Sens Chrétien de l'Homme.* Paris: Editions Montaigne/Aubier, 1945.

Péguy, Charles. *The Portal of the Mystery of Hope*, trans. David Louis Schindler, Jr. Grand Rapids, Michigan: William B. Eerdmans Publishing Company, 1996.

Muller, Robert. *New Genesis. Shaping a Global Spirituality.* Garden City, N.Y.: Doubleday & Co., Inc., Images Books, 1984.

—. *Most of All They Taught Me Happiness.* New York: Doubleday & Company, Inc., 1978.

Nathan, Ott and Heinz Norden, ed. *Einstein on Peace.* New York: Simon and Schuster, 1960.

Nellas, Panayiotis. *Deification in Christ: The Nature of the Human Person.* Trans. by Norman Russell. Crestwood, N.Y.: St Vladimir's Seminary Press, 1997.

Newberg, Andrew, and Mark Robert Waldman. *How God Changes Your Brain.* New York, N.Y.: Ballantine Books, 2009.

Ornstein, Robert. *The Evolution of Consciousness.* New York, N.Y.: Prentice Hall, 1991.

Otto, Rudolf. *The Idea of the Holy: an Inquiry Into the Non-Rational Factor in the Idea, of the Divine and Its Relation to the Rational.* Trans. by John W. Harvey. New York: Oxford University Press, 1958.

Panikkar, Raimon. *Christophany: The Fullness of Man*, trans. by Alfred Dilascia. Maryknoll, N.Y.: Orbis Books, 2004.

Peck, M. Scott. *The Different Drum: Community Making and Peace.* New York: Simon and Schuster, 1987.

Polkinghorne, John. *Belief in God in an Age of Science.* New Haven and London: Yale University Press, 1998.

Rahner, Karl. *Spirit in the World.* New York, N.Y.: The continuum Publishing company, 1994.

—. *The Love of Jesus and the Love of Neighbor.* Trans. by Robert Barr. New York, N.Y.: The Crossroad Publishing company, 1983.

—. *The Spirit in the Church.* New York, N.Y.: A Crossroad Book/The Seabury Press, 1979.

—. *Prayers for a Lifetime.* Ed. by Albert Raffelt. New York, N.Y.: The Crossroad Publishing Company, 1995.

Rohr, Richard, with John Bookser Feister. *Jesus' Plan for a New World: The Sermon on the Moun*t. Cincinnati, Ohio: St. Anthony Messenger Press, 1996.

Rolheiser, Ronald. *The Holy Longing: The Search for a Christian Spirituality.* New York, N.Y.: Doubleday, a division of Random House, Inc., 1999.

—. *Sacred Fire*: *A Vision for a Deeper Human and Christian Maturity.* New York, N.Y.: Crown Publishing, a division of Random House, Inc., 2014.

Samson, P. R., and D. Pitt, eds. *The Biosphere and Noosphere Reader: Global Environment, Society and change.* London and New York: Routledge, 1999.

Schillebeeckx, E., O.P. *Christ the Sacrament of the Encounter with God.* New York: Sheed and Ward, 1963.

Stikker, A. *The Transformation Factor: Towards an Ecological Consciousness.* Rockport, MA: Element, 1992.

Sulivan, Jean. *Dieu au-delà de Dieu.* France: Editions Gallimard, 1968.

Sween, Duane, ed. *The Peace Catalog: A Guidebook to a Positive Future.* Seattle, Washington: Press for Peace, 1984.

Swimme, Brian. *The Hidden Heart of the Cosmos: Humanity and the New Story.* Maryknoll, N.Y.: Orbis Books, 1996.

Tart, Charles, ed. *Altered States of Consciousness.* Garden City, N.Y.: Doubleday Anchor Books, 1972.

Thils, Gustave. *Théologie des Réalités Terrestres. I Préludes. II Théologie de l'Histoire.* Belgique: Desclée de Brouwer, 1946, 1949.

Thunberg, Lars. *Man and the Cosmos: The Vision of St Maximus the Confessor.* Crestwood, N.Y.: St Vladimir's Seminary Press, 1985.

Topel, L. John, S.J. *The Way to Peace: Liberation through the Bible.* Maryknoll, N.Y.: Orbis Books, 1979, 1982.

UNESCO, *Paix sur la Terre: Anthologie de la Paix.* Paris: Unesco, 1980.

Vaillant, François. *La Non-Violence dans l'Evangile.* Paris: Les Editions Ouvrières, 1991.

Van Fleet, James K. *Hidden Power: How to Unleash the Power of Your Subconscious Mind.* Paramus, New Jersey: Prentice Hall, 1987.

Whitson, R. E. *The Coming Convergence of World Religions.* New York: Newman Press, 1971. Revised edition, Lima, OH: Wyndham Hall Press, 1992.

Willkie, Wendell L. *One World.* New York: Simon and Schuster, 1943.

Zorgbibe, Charles. *La Paix.* Paris: Presses Universitaires de France, "Que Sais-Je", 1984.

ACKNOWLEDGMENTS

Excerpts from ACTIVATION OF ENERGY by Pierre Teilhard de Chardin, translated from the French by Rene Hague. Copyright © 1969 by Editions du Seuil. English Translation Copyright © 1970 by William Collins Sons & Company Limited and Houghton Mifflin Harcourt Publishing Company. Reprinted by permission of Houghton Mifflin Harcourt Publishing Company. All rights reserved.

Excerpts from THE HEART OF MATTER by Pierre Teilhard de Chardin, translated from the French by Rene Hague. Copyright © 1976 by Editions du Seuil. English Translation Copyright © 1978 by William Collins Sons & Company Limited and Houghton Mifflin Harcourt Publishing Company. Reprinted by permission of Houghton Mifflin Harcourt Publishing Company. All rights reserved.

Excerpts from TOWARD THE FUTURE by Pierre Teilhard de Chardin, translated from the French by Rene Hague. Copyright © 1973 by Editions du Seuil. English Translation Copyright © 1975 by William Collins Sons & Co. Ltd. and Houghton Mifflin Harcourt Publishing Company. Reprinted by permission of Houghton Mifflin Harcourt Publishing Company. All rights reserved.

Excerpts from CHRISTIANITY AND EVOLUTION by Pierre Teilhard de Chardin, translated from the French by Rene Hague. Copyright © 1969 by Editions du Seuil. English Translation Copyright © 1971 by William Collins Sons & Company Limited and Houghton Mifflin Harcourt Publishing Company. Reprinted by permission of Houghton Mifflin Harcourt Publishing Company. All rights reserved.

Excerpts from LE CŒUR DE LA MATIERE by Pierre Teilhard de Chardin, © Editions du Seuil, 1976. Eng. trans. *The Heart of Matter* by René Hague. New York and London: Harcourt Brace Jovanovich, 1978. (It also contains 5 essays that first appeared in the French edition of *Ecrits du Temps de la Guerre*.)

Excerpts from LES DIRECTIONS DE L'AVENIR by Pierre Teilhard de Chardin, © Editions du Seuil, 1973. Eng. trans. *Towards the Future* by René Hague. New York and London: Harcourt Brace Jovanovich, 1975.

Excerpts from COMMENT JE CROIS by Pierre Teilhard de Chardin, © Editions du Seuil, 1969. Eng. trans. *Christianity and Evolution* by René Hague. New York and London: Harcourt Brace Jovanovich, 1971.

Excerpts from SCIENCE ET CHRIST by Pierre Teilhard de Chardin, © Editions du Seuil, 1965. Eng. trans. *Science and Christ* by René Hague. New York: Harper & Row, 1968.

Excerpts from L'ACTIVATION DE L'ENERGIE by Pierre Teilhard de Chardin, © Editions du Seuil, 1963. Eng. trans. *Activation of Energy* by René Hague. New York and London: Harcourt Brace Jovanovich, 1970.

Excerpts from L'ENERGIE HUMAINE by Pierre Teilhard de Chardin, © Editions du Seuil, 1962. Eng. trans. *Human Energy* by J.M. Cohen. New York and London: Harcourt Brace Jovanovich, 1969.

Excerpts from LA VISION DU PASSE by Pierre Teilhard de Chardin, © Editions du Seuil, 1957. Eng. trans. *The Vision of the Past* by J.M. Cohen. New York: Harper & Row, 1966.

Excerpts from "Teilhard de Chardin and the Religious Phenomenon" by Ewert H. Cousins. International Symposium on the Occasion of the Birth of Teilhard de Chardin, © UNESCO - United Nations Educational, Scientific and Cultural Organization, Paris, France, 16-18 September 1981.

Excerpts from "The Earth Charter" © Earth Charter International – Earth Charter Initiative. http://earthcharter.org/discover/the-earth-charter/

Excerpts from "Teilhard's Political Ecumene Empire or Commonwealth" by Benjamin T. Hourani in Leo Zonneveld en Robert Muller (eds.) *The Desire to be Human,* a global reconnaissance in human perspectives in the age of transformation written in honour of Pierre Teilhard de Chardin. International Teilhard Compendium. Centenary Volume. Mirananda Publishers, Wassenaar, ©1983. By kind permission of Gerolf T'Hooft, Milinda Uitgevers, Waarbeke, Belgium, acting on behalf of Mirananda Publishers.

Excerpts from "Interdisciplinary Integration and Dualism in Society" by Allerd Stikker in Leo Zonneveld en Robert Muller (eds.) *The Desire to be Human,* a global reconnaissance in human perspectives in the age of transformation written in honour of Pierre Teilhard de Chardin. International Teilhard Compendium. Centenary Volume. Mirananda Publishers, Wassenaar, ©1983. By kind permission of Gerolf T'Hooft, Milinda Uitgevers, Waarbeke, Belgium, acting on behalf of Mirananda Publishers.

Excerpts from "Teilhardian Thought as a Methodology for Discernment of Socio-Cultural Options in an Evolutionary World" by J. De Marneffe, s.j. in Leo Zonneveld en Robert Muller (eds.) *The Desire to be Human,* a global reconnaissance in human perspectives in the age of transformation written in honour of Pierre Teilhard de Chardin. International Teilhard Compendium. Centenary Volume. Mirananda Publishers, Wassenaar, ©1983. By kind permission of Gerolf T'Hooft, Milinda Uitgevers, Waarbeke, Belgium, acting on behalf of Mirananda Publishers.

INDEX

(This index refers only to the main text and not the notes)

above, 4, 33, 55, 64, 69, 75, 79, 100, 114, 117, 133, 136, 141, 172, 198, 199, 200, 202, 207, 215, 221

Absolute, 32, 35, 37, 63, 76, 125, 139, 149, 180, 180, 232

action, 21, 25, 27, 31, 33, 34, 47, 48, 70, 72, 77, 78, 90, 97, 123, 169, 172, 176, 177, 178, 180, 207, 216

activities, 25, 27, 41, 45, 46, 56, 68, 74, 95, 107, 109, 164, 165, 178, 180,, 189, 196, 229

ahead, 4, 21, 52, 76, 113, 117, 124, 129,136,137,152, 162, 170, 180, 200, 201,215

alpha, 71, 172, 201, 215, 216

axis, 71, 192, 211

become, 3, 4, 5, 15, 18, 19, 23, 27, 32, 33, 34, 36, 41, 50, 53, 54, 56, 58, 61, 76, 86, 90, 91, 103, 104, 105, 108, 115, 123, 126, 129, 133, 151, 177, 198, 201, 211, 215, 223, 231, 234, 236

cause, 16, 25, 96, 103, 108, 121, 140, 141, 151, 169, 173, 189, 191, 198, 203, 204, 206, 232, 234

center, 17, 36, 41, 51, 52, 61, 63, 64, 71, 76, 89, 91, 103, 105, 111, 163, 183, 210, 216

change, 2, 3, 5, 12, 16, 31, 33, 44, 46, 56, 60, 81, 87, 89, 91, 95, 96, 110, 114, 150, 164, 166, 173, 200, 222, 223, 232

choice, 1, 2, 17, 33, 43, 46, 77, 123, 144, 149

Christ, 4, 41, 43, 44, 47, 48, 50, 52, 53, 54, 55, 56, 58, 60, 61, 62, 64, 65, 67, 68, 70, 71, 86, 90, 111, 112, 123, 124, 125, 126, 151, 152, 168, 176, 177, 178, 180, 183, 206, 208, 211, 213, 215, 216, 220

Christianity, 42, 44, 46, 60, 68, 70, 140, 176, 209, 211, 212, 216, 227

Christic, 64, 72, 123, 146

Christogenesis, 63, 71, 72, 125, 146, 230, 234

civilization, 3, 5, 11, 66, 88, 96, 108, 113, 163, 165, 167, 184, 187, 196, 219, 228, 232

communion, 47, 65, 67, 71, 74, 78, 85, 127, 221, 222

complexity, 95, 105, 106, 123, 129, 164, 169, 173, 178, 202, 210, 211, 215, 224, 225

consciousness, 3, 5, 19, 31, 32, 36, 41, 47, 52, 62, 76, 77, 85, 87, 89, 90, 91, 92, 93, 96, 97, 103, 104, 105, 106, 108, 109, 110, 113, 114, 115, 117, 118, 126, 129, 146, 151, 155, 160, 161, 162, 163, 165, 166, 169, 171, 176, 180, 197, 199, 210, 212, 220, 223, 224, 226

convergence, 11, 13, 26, 63, 66, 71, 76, 80, 95, 96, 105, 123, 127, 142, 146, 147, 169, 191, 192, 197, 209, 210, 211, 212, 217, 225

cosmic, 9, 11, 13, 20, 49, 52, 56, 61, 64, 67, 71, 93, 121, 169,,180, 212, 219, 227, 229, 231, 233, 235
cosmogenesis, 71, 125, 139, 146, 169, 218, 224, 228, 229,, 230
creation, 17, 41, 46, 49, 52, 53, 54, 55, 56, 57, 60, 70, 71,85, 86, 91, 93, 106, 109, 111, 112, 116, 117, 124, 135, 154, 155, 173, 176, 177, 178, 183, 200, 216, 217, 218, 235
crisis, 3, 13, 145, 216, 217
culture, 5, 15, 17, 18, 19, 43, 94, 98, 115, 116, 122, 139, 140, 143, 144, 146, 149, 163, 165, 192, 196, 211, 226, 233, 234

dialogue, 28, 144, 209, 212, 233
diaphany, 63, 75, 98, 168, 208
dichotomy, 42, 43, 45, 46, 68, 77
differentiation, 95, 96, 102, 131
divergence, 105, 106, 210, 224, 225
divine, 43, 45, 54, 61, 63, 65, 70, 71, 77, 112, 124, 136, 148, 178, 207, 212, 216, 217, 220, 221, 222, 227, 230, 232
divinization, 53, 54, 68, 72, 90, 98, 230
dualism, 25, 42, 60, 68, 71, 132, 133, 134, 138, 214, 217
dynamic, 12, 13, 25, 63, 64, 67, 69, 76, 94, 108, 133, 150, 152, 171, 197, 206, 210, 212, 231

earth, 2, 3, 4, 5, 10, 11, 12, 14, 16, 24, 41, 46, 47, 48, 49, 54, 57, 58, 62, 66, 67, 70, 73, 74, 75, 77, 85, 86, 87, 89,92, 96, 97, 99, 100, 101, 107, 109, 113, 115, 122, 123, 126, 127, 129, 130, 131, 132, 134, 142, 143, 144, 145, 146, 148, 154, 126, 171, 172, 173, 208, 229
ecumenism, 94, 187, 189, 212, 213, 224, 227

effort, 4, 12, 32, 52, 95, 131, 161, 180, 182, 183, 189, 198, 199, 207, 208, 213, 233
element, 63, 64, 70, 79, 96, 99, 102, 103, 104, 105, 132, 135, 142, 145, 169, 210, 224, 230
energy, 2, 12, 21, 23, 25, 26, 28, 33, 37, 41, 45, 64, 72, 76, 77, 103, 127, 128, 130, 145, 146, 148, 168, 169, 170, 172, 173, 174, 175, 177, 207, 210, 211, 216, 231
evil, 11, 16, 42, 57, 77, 116, 147, 184, 191, 203, 204
evolution, 5, 18, 19, 23, 28, 52, 61, 62, 64, 66, 70, 71, 74, 75, 76, 77, 79, 91, 94, 98, 105, 109, 110, 111, 112, 116, 117, 128, 136, 142, 145, 149, 169, 170, 173, 192, 210, 212, 219, 225, 228, 235

fire, 2, 6, 27, 33, 159, 167, 168, 170, 172, 173, 174, 218, 219, 223,
freedom, 13, 14, 48, 115, 142, 144, 154, 171, 209, 229
front, 1, 3, 34, 36, 92, 97, 106, 108, 144, 187, 207,233, 234
fulfillment, 25, 47, 48, 66, 104, 123, 124, 134, 179, 183, 206, 208, 209, 218
fusion, 79, 95, 103
future, 4, 5, 9, 10, 16, 17, 25, 27, 30, 41, 66, 78, 93, 107, 112, 115, 122, 126, 130, 131, 142, 143, 146, 152, 153, 154, 169, 208, 210, 215, 228, 234, 236, 237

grace, 43, 47, 48, 55, 56, 126, 127
growth, 11, 13, 15, 18, 28, 43, 45, 60, 62, 64, 66, 75, 90, 104, 107, 11, 171, 182, 184, 185, 191, 201, 202, 203, 210, 221, 227, 228

heart, 1, 2, 4, 12, 13, 19, 24, 25, 32, 33, 34, 35, 36, 46, 47, 59, 64, 81, 85, 86, 87, 92, 102, 106, 109, 117, 127, 138, 141, 142, 144, 146, 150, 154, 16, 164, 165, 168, 169, 171, 173, 200, 218, 227, 229, 233, 235

history, 2, 5, 9, 17, 30, 33, 41, 47, 53, 55, 66, 78, 79, 86, 104, 106, 109, 113, 115, 121, 122, 123, 124, 126, 130, 141, 154, 165, 173, 178, 196, 201, 204, 212, 213, 227

hope, 4, 10, 14, 26, 98, 100, 111, 112, 122, 124, 125, 128, 129, 143, 144, 145, 146, 147, 148, 149, 150, 151, 152, 153, 154, 155, 167, 176, 180, 200, 201, 211, 215

humanity, 1, 4, 5, 9, 10, 11, 18, 20, 25, 27, 33, 41, 49, 51, 52, 56, 60, 77, 79, 94, 96, 97, 106, 111, 112, 114, 123, 127, 130, 139, 155, 173, 185, 188, 191, 209, 215, 225, 227, 228, 234, 235

immanence, 75, 116, 148, 207

Incarnation, 41, 43, 44, 45, 47, 49, 50, 51, 53, 56, 57, 59, 60, 61, 68, 70, 71, 90, 112, 176, 177, 178, 201, 211, 212, 213, 215

life, 1, 3, 4, 5, 6, 10, 11, 12, 14, 17, 19, 21, 25, 26, 27, 31, 32, 37, 42, 45, 46, 48, 58, 60, 64, 65, 69, 74, 76, 87, 89, 91, 111, 117, 122, 127, 134, 143, 144, 152, 155, 161, 174, 178, 182, 199, 217, 222, 223, 233

matter, 1, 10, 12, 13, 19, 20, 27, 32, 37, 42, 45, 47, 48, 51, 55, 56, 57, 58, 61, 63, 65, 68, 69, 73, 77, 134, 135, 141, 164, 176, 177, 207, 214, 217, 218, 222, 224, 225, 227

milieu, 63, 66, 67, 70, 72, 75, 106, 110, 112, 133, 172, 177, 178, 207, 212, 221, 222, 227, 230, 234

mysticism, 65, 68, 69, 72, 75, 76, 77, 79, 136, 164, 182, 184

nature, 1, 12, 19, 41, 48, 52, 53, 56, 61, 72, 90, 105, 106, 112, 140, 141, 143, 144, 151, 205, 219, 220

noosphere, 103, 109, 110, 112, 113, 114, 115, 116, 117, 123, 135, 154, 165, 190, 198, 208, 211, 224, 225, 234

Omega, 51, 62, 64, 66, 71, 76, 111, 113, 121, 123, 124, 125, 127, 135, 148, 149, 155, 172, 176, 178, 197, 201, 206, 207, 211, 215, 216, 218, 219, 231, 235

origin, 50, 51, 55, 172

Parousia, 66, 88, 153

past, 10, 16, 17, 18, 27, 60, 105, 107, 121, 124, 130, 164, 208, 225, 226, 227, 228

person, 11, 16, 31, 36, 46, 51, 53, 58, 123, 130, 131, 133, 134, 136, 196, 230

personalization, 4, 78, 79, 96, 129, 130, 131, 132, 133, 137, 139, 146, 197, 230

phenomenon, 10, 105, 113, 149, 150, 160, 161, 174, 187, 198, 210, 217, 225

philosophy, 36, 58, 78, 79, 80, 85, 86, 98, 134, 159, 171, 217

process, 5, 13, 28, 47, 51, 55, 56, 63, 64, 68, 70, 71, 72, 79, 90, 95, 102, 105, 116, 146, 154, 172, 184, 210, 229, 230, 231

progress, 3, 4, 13, 16, 19, 61, 65, 68, 72, 112, 115, 131, 132, 136, 145, 147, 149, 151, 155, 162,

169, 171, 180, 182, 197, 198, 199, 202, 212, 216, 227, 233
purpose, 3, 22, 33, 50, 51, 53, 71, 92, 98, 113, 116, 117, 121, 122, 127, 149, 173, 197, 204, 210, 218, 220, 230, 234

reality, 1, 12, 26, 28, 29, 32, 35, 36, 42, 43, 47, 58, 60, 65, 70, 72, 73, 78, 90, 107, 110, 123, 134, 147, 150, 155, 159, 165, 186, 215, 233, 234
reconciliation, 2, 26, 36, 42, 79, 80, 91, 102, 126, 127, 153, 154, 164, 180, 187, 196
reflection, 87, 137, 145, 159, 224, 225
religion, 1, 14, 15, 18, 19, 33, 42, 70, 74, 76, 78, 79, 86, 87, 90, 91, 94, 98, 116, 139, 140, 141, 144, 146, 176, 187, 196, 206, 204, 205, 206, 207, 208, 209, 210, 211, 212, 214, 217, 225, 228, 234
research, 93, 106, 182, 189, 198, 203, 204
responsibiliry, 17, 31, 61, 64, 77, 86, 87, 127, 136, 143, 191, 196, 204, 209, 210, 229
road, 4, 116, 129, 162, 168, 171, 201

salvation, 49, 50, 57, 60, 66, 123, 145, 147, 154 sanctity, 61
science, 3, 24, 74, 75, 76, 78, 79, 80, 110, 116, 117, 123, 139, 144, 146, 162, 164, 170, 174, 198, 208, 214, 217, 218
see, 1, 2, 4, 5, 9, 10, 13, 19, 20, 23, 29, 33, 34, 35, 37, 44, 53, 57, 63, 65, 70, 77, 85, 88, 91, 96, 100, 106, 125, 159, 160, 161, 162, 163, 164, 165, 166, 198, 200, 205, 209,221
soul, 3, 12, 19, 25, 30, 33, 34, 35, 36, 46, 53, 56, 59, 60, 69, 81, 86, 96, 97, 141, 145, 159, 160, 163, 164, 180, 182, 183, 205, 217, 218, 221, 226
spirit, 19, 25, 42, 45, 46, 47, 53, 54, 68, 73, 77, 78, 126, 129, 143, 176, 198, 214, 216, 217, 221, 230
spirituality, 35, 46, 47, 48, 63, 68, 69, 70, 71, 73, 75, 77, 85, 89, 119, 182, 190, 209
survival, 25, 78, 98, 111, 114, 117, 147, 155, 173, 199, 225
synthesis, 27, 74, 75, 78, 80, 86, 88, 98, 99, 102, 108, 131, 169, 188, 210, 211, 217

theology, 33, 50, 53, 58, 124, 134, 212, 215, 216, 218
transcendence, 75, 148, 235
transformation, 4, 5, 13, 33, 54, 66, 72, 77, 87, 89, 98, 106, 124, 125, 126, 127, 133, 146, 149, 182, 184, 213, 219, 223

union, 11, 13, 16, 25, 26, 32, 52, 54, 67, 79, 80, 88, 95, 100, 102, 103, 104, 105, 123, 129, 130, 131, 133, 134, 135, 144, 161, 168, 171, 176, 182, 192, 198, 200, 202, 204, 210, 215, 218, 229, 233
unity, 12, 16, 20, 34, 35, 36, 48, 60, 66, 67, 68, 74, 75, 79, 93, 94, 95, 96, 99, 103, 110, 112, 129, 162, 163, 165, 181, 182, 184, 215, 227, 228, 229, 235
universal, 5, 9, 10, 16, 35, 61, 65, 70, 96, 97, 108, 123, 132, 138, 140, 142, 143, 146, 148, 160, 169, 196, 197, 211, 228, 230, 235
universe, 4, 10, 11, 13, 23, 26, 33, 34, 36, 47, 50, 51, 56, 62, 63, 67, 69, 71, 72, 92, 110, 112, 117, 123, 131, 135, 142, 146, 148, 162, 169, 173, 176, 201,

206, 207, 211, 215, 217, 220, 234, 235

value, 2, 3, 14, 19, 25, 34, 36, 61, 65, 77, 87, 89, 90, 98, 144, 147, 148, 159, 172, 180, 181, 183, 195, 207, 214, 217
vision, 5, 10, 11, 25, 26, 60, 66, 67, 72, 92, 95, 97, 101, 109, 124, 126, 143, 144, 160, 161, 162, 164, 166, 173, 176, 178, 180, 182, 192, 195, 197, 214, 215, 216, 217, 218, 234

whole, 4, 5, 9, 10, 11, 12, 13, 23, 33, 35, 41, 46, 48, 52, 55, 56, 60, 67, 68, 70, 71, 72, 74, 77, 79, 80, 86, 94, 99, 101, 105, 107, 108, 111, 125, 126, 130, 131, 135, 143, 144, 147, 152, 153, 159, 161, 162, 163, 176, 178, 183, 198, 201, 204, 208, 211, 215, 217, 222, 226, 229, 230, 233, 235

within, 3, 4, 19, 20, 25, 31, 33, 34, 35, 44, 45, 55, 63, 65, 66, 67, 71, 75, 76, 79, 81, 85, 89, 106, 107, 123, 132, 134, 139, 151, 152, 167, 171, 175, 177, 182, 207, 215, 227, 230
work, 2, 4, 9, 12, 13, 27, 31, 32, 41, 46, 48, 59, 62, 64, 65, 66, 68, 70, 71, 75, 86, 87, 88, 104, 105, 107, 112, 113, 121, 122, 129, 138, 153, 155, 161, 171, 173, 178, 179, 182, 183, 185, 188, 190, 191, 195, 197, 200, 210, 214, 234, 236
world, 1, 2, 4, 5, 12, 13, 15, 16, 17, 19, 20, 25, 27, 32, 36, 41, 42, 44, 45, 47, 48, 62, 65, 66, 67, 68, 71, 75, 76, 86, 90, 91, 107, 115, 116, 152, 153, 155, 167, 177, 180, 183, 188, 189, 204, 206, 214, 234, 235
worship, 19, 33, 183, 206, 212

ABOUT THE AUTHOR

Jean Maalouf, Ph.D., Ph.D., is the author of more than forty books and studies that include:

Le mystère du mal dans l'œuvre de Teilhard de Chardin (Cerf, 1986),

The Divine Milieu: A Spiritual Classic for Today and Tomorrow ("Teilhard Studies" Number 38, 1999),

Teilhard and the Feminine ("Teilhard Studies" Number 47, 2003),

Teilhard de Chardin: Reconciliation in Christ (New City Press, 2002),

«Introduction à la théologie de l'histoire chez Teilhard de Chardin » in *La Terre est mon pays* (Aubin Editeur, 2008),

«Teilhard de Chardin et le mystère du mal. Evolutionisme? Stoïcisme? Christocentrisme? » in *Revue des Sciences Philosophiques et Théologiques* (Tome 65, No 2, Vrin, 1981),

If We Just See What They See: Peace According to Albert Einstein, Thomas Merton, Pope John XXIII, Thich Nhat Hanh, Mahatma Gandhi, Teilhard de Chardin, Mother Teresa of Calcutta. (AuthorHouse, 2007).

Dr. Maalouf's books have been published in the United States of America, Canada, Colombia, France, India, Mexico, Spain, Philippines, Portugal, and UK. Also, he has written many articles on topics of religion, spirituality, mysticism (Eastern and Western), philosophy, psychology, and peace and social issues for journals and magazines such as *Catholic Digest, Celebration, National Herald* (New Delhi), *Peace Research Reviews* (Canada), *Praying, Revue des Sciences Philosophiques et*

Théologiques (Paris), *Spirit & Life, Spiritual Life, Teilhard Perspective.* He is a member of several professional associations that include American Academy of Religion, American Teilhard Association, Association des Amis de P. Teilhard de Chardin (Paris), The Authors Guild, Contemplative Outreach, Centering Prayer, National Writers Union, Fellowship of Catholic Scholars, Catholic Writers Guild, and The Society of Christian Philosophers.

The messages in Dr. Maalouf's writings seem deeply personal as if they were written just for the person who is reading them, and yet, they are timeless and universal. His works were hailed by critics with terms such as these: "Jean Maalouf brings his experience as doctor of philosophy and humanities to bear in works of spirituality. His focus is one of gentle revolution in human development," "Maalouf has written in the style of Meister Eckhart, John of the Cross, and St. Irenaeus," "Maalouf's gift for writing about the most sublime truths in the most simple language allows him… to touch and transform the hearts of believers and non-believers alike." He is blessed with the art of provoking thoughts that inspire new choices, influence decisions, and get the attention of both the religious and secular worlds, as well as the academic and the non-academic ones. In a culture that often relegates God to loftiness, he knows how to provide compelling images of God in unexpected places—in the most ordinary stuff of our daily lives. It is no wonder then, that he sees, because of the continuous Incarnation in everyday life, how one can transform his or her daily life through moments of grace in life.

ALSO BY DR. JEAN MAALOUF

Publications in English

Bold Prayers from the Heart
The Burning Flame of Love
Change Your World: Awakening to the Power of Truth – Beauty – Simplicity - Change
Christmas Shock: The Human Experience of God
The Divine Milieu: A Spiritual Classic for Today and Tomorrow (Essay)
Experiencing Jesus with Mother Teresa
Fully Alive: God's Prescription for a Happier and Healthier Life
Heal Your Life: awakening to the Power of Faith – Hope – Love - Prayer
The Healing Power of Beauty
The Healing Power of Change
The Healing Power of Faith
The Healing Power of Forgiveness
The Healing Power of Friendship
The Healing Power of Hope
The Healing Power of Joy
The Healing Power of Kindness
The Healing Power of Love
The Healing Power of Peace
The Healing Power of Prayer
The Healing Power of Purpose
The Healing Power of Simplicity
The Healing Power of Truth
I Can Tell God Anything: Living Prayer
If We Just See What They See: Peace According to Albert Einstein, Thomas Merton, Pope John XXIII, Thick Nhat Hanh, Mahatma Gandhi, Teilhard de Chardin, Mother Teresa of Calcutta
Intimacies: The Miracle of Love
I've Got One Life to Live: Radiant Health God's Way
Jesus Laughed and Other Reflections on Being Human
The Little Way: Fresh Air for the Soul — A Retreat with Saint Thérèse of Lisieux

Live a Life That Matters: Awakening to the Power of Purpose — Kindness — Forgiveness -- Friendship
Making All Things New
Mother Teresa: Essential Writings (Editor)
Pathways: Finding God in the Present Moment
Pope John XXIII: Essential Writings (Editor)
Practicing the Presence of the Living God: A Retreat with Brother Lawrence of the Resurrection
Praying with Mother Teresa
Teilhard and the Feminine (Essay)
Teilhard de Chardin: Reconciliation in Christ (Editor)
Touch a Single Leaf: Teilhard and Peace
Touchstones for Peace (Essay)
Transformation in Prayer: 99 Sayings by M. Basil Pennington (Editor)
Where Has God Gone?
Your New Adventure: Make the Most of the Rest of Your Life

Contributor to:
   Encyclopedia of Catholic Social Thought, Social Science, and Social Policy

Publications in French

Le Mystère du Mal dans L'Oeuvre de Teilhard de Chardin
Teilhard de Chardin et le mystère du mal. Evolutionisme? Stoïcisme? Christocentrisme? (Essay)
Le Réenchantement du Monde (Co-author)
La Terre Est Mon Pays (Co-author)

Publications in Spanish (Translated from English)

Dile a Dios Lo Que Sientes: Oración Desde La Vida
El Poder Sanador De La Alegría
El Poder Sanador De La Amistad
El Poder Sanador De La Bondad
El Poder Sanador De La Esperanza
El Poder Sanador De La Fe
El Poder Sanador De La Oración
El Poder Sanador Del Amor
El Poder Sanador De La Paz
El Poder Sanador Del Perdón

El Poder Sanador De Tener Un Propósito
Juan XXIII: Escritos Esenciales
Madre Teresa de Calcuta: Escritos Esenciales
Orando Con La Madre Teresa
Orando Con La Madre Teresa De Calcuta

Publications in Portuguese (Translated from English)

O Poder Da Cura Pela Alegria
O Poder Da Cura Pela Amizade
O Poder Da Cura Pela Paz
O Poder Da Cura Pelo Amor